Inquiry, Logic and International Politics

INQUIRY, LOGIC AND
INTERNATIONAL POLITICS

Benjamin A. Most
University of Iowa

Harvey Starr
Indiana University

UNIVERSITY OF SOUTH CAROLINA PRESS

Library of Congress Cataloging-in-Publication Data

Most, Benjamin A., d. 1986.
   Inquiry, logic and international politics.

   (Studies in international relations)
   Bibliography: p.
   Includes index.
   1. International relations—Research. I. Starr,
Harvey. II. Title. III. Series: Studies in inter-
national relations (Columbia, S.C.)
JX1291.M68 1989   327.1'01   88-33984
ISBN 0-87249-613-9
ISBN 0-87249-630-9 (pbk.)

"Time is too valuable, life too short, to waste my time on dead ends."

Benjamin A. Most (1986:14)

To the memory of BEN MOST
student and teacher, colleague and friend

Contents

Acknowledgments ix

1: Introduction:
Cumulation, Theory and the Logic of Inquiry **1**

2: Opportunity and Willingness:
A Pre-Theoretic Framework **23**

3: Basic Logic and Research Design:
Conceptualization, Case Selection, and the Form of
Relationships **47**

4: Conceptualizing War:
Attributes and Process **68**
Appendix to Chapter 4 **92**

5: Foreign Policy Substitutability and "Nice" Laws:
Integrating Process and Theory **97**
Appendixes to Chapter 5 **124**

6: The Logic of International Structure:
Power, War, and Micro-Macro Linkages **133**
Appendix to Chapter 6 **162**

7: Conclusion:
Closure, Cumulation, and International
Relations Theory **168**

Notes 191
References 213
Index 229

Figures

Figure 1.1. Depictions of the Research Process **15**
Figure 1.2. The Analysts' Cube **19**
Figure 2.1. Opportunity/Willingness and War **41**
Figure 3.1. Necessary and Sufficient Relationships between X and Y **50**
Figure 3.2. Elaboration of Necessary and Sufficient Relationships **62**
Figure 6.1. Post–World War II Dyads **139**
Figure 6.2. Imbalanced and Balanced Dyads: Selected Hypothetical Systems **143**
Figure 6.3. Proportion of Imbalanced Dyads: Selected Hypothetical Systems **144**

Tables

Table 3.1. Sampling Only Examples with the Occurrence of an Independent Variable **51**
Table 3.2. Sampling Only Examples with the Occurrence of a Dependent Variable **53**
Table 3.3. Consequences of Selective Sampling **54**
Table 3.4. Alternative Hypotheses and Consequences of Logic in Design **64**
Table 4.1. A Preliminary Illustration **70**
Table 4.2. A Simple Interaction Possibility **77**
Table 4.3. A More Complex Interaction Possibility **80–81**
Table 4.4. A Deterrence/Balance Illustration **86**
Table 5.1. Hypothetical Action-Reaction Process **105–106**
Table 6.1. Outline of Simulation Procedures **162–163**
Table 6.2. Simulation of Systems with 10 States and 5 Major Powers **164**
Table 6.3. Simulated Conflict Initiations: PR(W) = 0.02 **165**
Table 6.4. Simulated Conflict Initiations: PR(W) = 0.05 **166**
Table 6.5. Simulated Conflict Initiations: PR(W) = 0.02 and 0.05 **167**

ACKNOWLEDGMENTS

As this project has evolved over the years, numerous individuals and institutions have been instrumental in providing us support—both financial and intellectual. In regard to the former, much of our work has been facilitated by the National Science Foundation under grants SES 82-08779 and SES 82-08815. At various times the University of Iowa, Indiana University, and the Indiana Consortium for Security Studies each provided some form of support in our overall research and writing endeavors. Harvey Starr would also like to thank the Department of Political Science at Emory University (particularly Lee Epstein) for supporting a talk at that institution. The feedback and reaction were instrumental in the revision of a number of points.

In regard to those who have traveled with us on this rather long intellectual journey, one hardly knows where to begin. The ideas in this book slowly developed during the period over which we were investigating the diffusion of violent international conflict. In that sense we were influenced by those scholars working in the field, and who reacted to, and commented upon, our work.

As the ideas that form the core of this book developed we were also extremely fortunate to have been involved with a rather unique forum for interchange and creativity. For several years we participated in the Illinois-Indiana-Iowa Seminar on Complex Systems (or, the Triple I). Founded by Dina Zinnes at Illinois and Elinor Ostrom at Indiana, the Triple I was a continuing workshop at which the participants presented and critiqued the work of the other participants. With a common set of interests—the notion of complex systems, the processes through which they operated, and the search for commonalities across levels of analysis and substantive fields—the Triple I always provided lively discussion and generated new ways for us to look at our work. While other people would sit in at times, the core of the seminar, in addition to Most and Starr, included: (a) from Illinois, Dina Zinnes, Dick Merritt, Claudio

Cioffi-Revilla, Steve Seitz, Robert Muncaster; (b) from Indiana, Lin Ostrom, Vincent Ostrom, Roberta Herzberg, Roger Parks; and (c) from Iowa, Bob Boynton, and Barbara Hill.

All of the above provided a continuing sounding board for the analyses presented in this book. Other individuals at Iowa, with whom Ben Most also had a continuing dialogue over these issues are John Nelson and Dick Jankowski. At Indiana, Harvey Starr had a similar dialogue with Ted Carmines, Frank Hoole, and Mike McGinnis (who was brave enough to use an early draft in his graduate seminar).

While numerous colleagues in the field of international relations have influenced our thinking, two whose interest and ongoing reactions were especially important to our work were Randy Siverson and Bruce Bueno de Mesquita. A special tip of the hat to them! We must also thank the journals in which earlier versions of various chapters have appeared. Chapters 2 through 6 are revised versions of articles previously published in the *American Journal of Political Science, International Interactions, Journal of Conflict Resolution,* and *World Politics.* We need to acknowledge the comments of a number of anonymous journal referees, and the feedback we have received on the published articles.

And certainly, we must acknowledge the support, interest, and assistance that have been provided by the University of South Carolina and its Press—Chuck Kegley and Don Puchala, the series editors, and Ken Scott, Director at the Press. In addition, we need to thank the anonymous reviewers, as well as Mike Ward, who reviewed the manuscript un-anonymously. Ward not only provided very useful feedback, but unselfishly volunteered ideas and material used in revising the manuscript. Without the support and interest from the editors, the Press and the reviewers, this book would never have happened.

The easy part is completed. The tough part remains. This book is dedicated to the memory of Ben Most, who had so much more to give to the scholarly community—who had so much more to teach me—when he died on November 10, 1986. If "acknowledgment" means an "admission" as well as "an expression of thanks or appreciation" then I must admit that this clearly would have been a better book had Ben worked on it through its final stages. I want to thank Sandy, Matthew, and Megan Most for their support, and their faith that the book could be brought to fruition. With their help, and that of all those noted above, it has been. Thanks.

Inquiry, Logic and International Politics

1

INTRODUCTION:
Cumulation, Theory and the Logic of Inquiry

INTRODUCTION: AIMS AND GENERAL ISSUES

The aims of the following presentation are both quite modest and brash. Much of what we will say about logic, its place in the development of research design and its interaction with theory, data, and analysis, will not be surprising to students of logic or philosophy of science. By the time we reach the end of this discussion, however, we will have said some very brash things about the study of political science, international politics, and international conflict. Through the use of logic, simulation, and empirical data of various kinds, we will have reached conclusions regarding the search for generalizations, the place of general laws, the use of critical tests to judge between contending explanations, the use of micro-macro distinctions, the relationships between environmental or contextual structures and the choices and behavior of environed entities, and specific differences in perspective on systemic and decision-maker levels of analysis in the study of international politics.

In taking up these issues we venture into the emerging cottage industry that concerns the nature, scope, study, and progress of the field of international relations. Over the past decade much of the research and writing on the study of international politics, especially "scientific" or quantitative approaches, has tended to be introspective.[1] Looking back at the work that has been completed, scholars have concluded that much progress has been made in what Dina Zinnes (1976a) has called *"additive* cumulation." That is, analysts' descriptive sense of international relations and foreign policy phenomena has substantially expanded in quantity and quality. New data sets exist. Scholars cite one another. The understanding of a variety of analytical techniques has greatly improved. In terms of what Zinnes calls *"integrative* cumulation," however, the record is generally much less impressive. Scholars have asked "where have all the theories gone?" in the long road to theory in international relations research (e.g., Phillips, 1974).

Many argue that theoretical understanding has not been greatly advanced. The results do not seem to add up very readily; there is great difficulty in synthesizing seemingly disparate work. Researchers do not seem to be identifying solutions to the theoretical, methodological and policy problems that challenge them. The field seems incapable of bringing closure to important theoretical and empirical questions.

The value of such reviews is clear. The discussions yield important suggestions for recasting systematic and quantitative research on international politics. The first purpose of this book is to augment the "cumulation" literature by focusing on topics that are germane to most current researchers in international politics. We begin with two basic contentions. We argue that scholars need to recognize the existence of a *research triad* consisting of method, theory, and logic, and that *each* leg of this triad is critical for advancing our knowledge of international phenomena.[2] Second, we argue that analysts have not generally understood the nature of that triad and that they have therefore paid primary attention to standard methodological questions regarding the collection of data, their quality, and the choice of appropriate analytical techniques. Diagnoses of the failure to make much headway toward an integrative understanding of international relations and foreign policy phenomena have focused primarily on the quality of existing data sets, the need to develop new or "better" data, the utility of various statistical or mathematical procedures, and analysts' tendency to use an ad hoc hypothesis testing approach (regarding the latter, see Zinnes, 1976b).

While methodology texts and general discussions of research strategies—which discuss various aspects of data and design—may be found in abundance, few efforts are made to probe conceptual and epistemological research issues in the international relations field. While standard questions of method are important (as will be elaborated below), they have overshadowed both theoretical issues on one hand, and logical/epistemological concerns, on the other. Bruce Bueno de Mesquita (1985a:128, 130) summarizes this position when arguing: "To the extent that logical consistency is accepted as an elemental requirement of all research, *formal, explicit theorizing*

takes intellectual, if not temporal precedence over empiricism. . . .
Too often, however, our empirical predilections lead us to fail to explore the *logical* basis for the empirical expectations derived from competing hypotheses" (emphasis in original).[3]

We will demonstrate in the following chapters that a concern with the logical underpinnings of research leads inexorably to broader conceptual and theoretical concerns. Our focus is therefore on a *series* of theoretical, conceptual, logical and epistemological issues which, though quite simple and not unique to the study of international relations, are generally unrecognized and which impede the development of a base of verifiable and generalizable knowledge about the causes and consequences of international phenomena. We argue that an additional explanation of the failure to produce meaningful cumulation and results may be that international relations scholars have often failed to recognize those difficulties. Furthermore, in many cases analysts' theoretical arguments, concepts, research designs, statistical/mathematical procedures, and general understanding of the means and ultimate ends of the research enterprise in international relations are logically inconsistent.

Using War to Illustrate the Arguments

Often, scholars begin with questionable epistemological assumptions, utilize inappropriate techniques, and ultimately search for the wrong ends. This has occurred across all areas and subjects in the study of international relations. While our examples are drawn from international relations as a whole, and our conclusions are expanded to deal with the general foreign policy making process (see chapter 5 in particular), we draw primarily from the area of international conflict and war to illustrate our arguments.

There are a number of reasons for such a focus. The first, and simplest, is that this is the research area with which we are most familiar. In addition, international conflict and war have been, and continue to be, important and central concerns to the study of international relations; the decision process related to the use of force, or to go to war, is illustrative of the processes behind major foreign policy decisions. Using this approach, we are also more readily able to draw illustrations from our own research on the diffusion of violent conflict. We often make reference to our own work on the study of *diffusion* to indicate ways in which to avoid these logical traps—from conceptualization (Most and Starr, 1981), through research design, to analysis and interpretation (e.g., Most and Starr,

1980; Starr and Most 1983, 1985a).[4] We have, thus, developed our arguments most fully in regard to the conceptualization and study of "war," as presented in chapter 4.[5] However, we will also find that treatments of alliance, systemic polarity and war, dyadic power relationships and war, and many other substantive areas consist of results that fail to add up because of flaws in analysts' logic that have weakened both theory and research design.

Using this specific area of inquiry we can present our arguments without expanding the present volume into a comprehensive international relations theory textbook. By developing one ongoing example in depth, we hope to enhance the reader's comprehension of a series of rather complex arguments and analyses. This may be more easily done if the same concepts and foci are carried on from chapter to chapter.

One central concern in this volume is that research design may not be logically consistent with the empirical phenomena and related theory it is supposed to study. War is a useful example of a whole range of phenomena that are resultants of the interaction of states or other international actors. As we will show, many of the problems to be discussed arise from the failure to understand that many international phenomena are *interdependent outcomes* of the interaction of two or more actors. This failure is a central reason for our concern with the logic of research design.

As can be demonstrated through analytic tools such as game theory, many of the things we study in international relations occur only as the combined, interdependent choice of two or more actors. War may be the most clear-cut example of this pervasive phenomena. This characterization of war is systematically developed in chapters 3 and 4 (after the framework of "opportunity and willingness" is developed in chapter 2). However, this characteristic is certainly not limited to war, but is similar in the creation of alliances, the formation of IGOs (or in some models, the creation of international regimes), and the conclusion of treaties or agreements in any area. In chapter 5 our analyses are generalized to foreign policy, and we discuss alliance theory, general security theory, and broad questions of international cooperation.

One important part of the conceptualization of "process" we present derives from our concern with phenomena that are the product of state interaction. Here, process means the interdependent outcome of two or more actors choosing policy options from a menu of opportunities or possibilities that constrain their choice.

That is, process, in part, denotes a conscious process of choice in each of two or more actors, and that the international phenomena under study occurs only through the interaction of the results of such choice. As discussed in chapter 2, this view is quite different from deterministic theories of international relations which can be based on the structure of the international system, or, as discussed in chapter 4, on the characteristics of individual states.

Thus, war is being used to illustrate a broad range of international behavior. The arguments presented are not intended to be confined to war, and examples will be given to show how the arguments relate to other phenomena. International conflict and war, do, however, provide us with a manageable focus for the development of our overall presentation.

Logic and Inquiry

While questions of necessity and sufficiency are introduced and developed in depth in chapter 3, one simple result of that discussion can be noted here to illustrate our concern with the impact of logic. Many research projects are based on the form "if X, then Y." This form delineates *sufficiency*, that X always leads to Y. However, more often than not, the research is designed to analyze only those cases where Y actually occurs (collecting all examples of war, crisis, alliance, diplomatic exchange, etc.). When this is done, statistical analysis can reveal *only* that Y is always preceded by X (X does not always lead to Y). This latter form delineates a *necessary* relationship. Thus, the design does not match and cannot answer the question posed. One simple remedy is to collect data on cases where Y is not the result (-Y) as well, in order to test sufficiency (X always leads to Y, but Y is not always preceded by X). Bueno de Mesquita (e.g., 1981a, 1985a) is one of the few students of international politics who has explicitly taken the issue of necessity and sufficiency into account, and has produced appropriate research designs.[6]

In the following chapters we attempt to demonstrate—rather than simply assert—the existence, nature, and importance of the theoretical and epistemological questions with which we are concerned. In addition to indicating shortcomings as noted above, more positively, we indicate the implications of analysts' failure to recognize such concerns and develop a variety of potential solutions to each difficulty. The implications of those procedures for theory in international relations are outlined, often using illustrations drawn from our own work on international conflict. Inferences are drawn in regard to such topics as:

1. New conceptualizations of what it may mean to "explain" international relations and foreign policy phenomena[7].
2. A reanalysis of the ultimate end of research in international relations, focusing particularly on empirical generalizations, "true" or "nice" laws.
3. The conceptual and theoretical limitations of "middle-range" theory and the need for renewed efforts to construct "grand theory."
4. The utility of beginning, rather than concluding, with "stylized" facts and explanations.
5. The related issue of the problem of gaining closure on theoretical and empirical questions—designing research programs so that more promising avenues can be pursued, and less promising areas can be identified and bypassed.
6. The critical importance and (yet) subtle interplay between analysts' theoretical arguments and their research design; the holistic quality of the research triad of logic, theory, and method.
7. The weaknesses of static attribute analysis, and the need for more dynamic, process-oriented approaches to the study of international relations.
8. The crucial importance of a second triad—the ecological triad of Harold and Margaret Sprout composed of entity, environment, and the entity-environment relationship; the importance of micro-macro linkages, and micro-macro/process-structure linkages.

Several of the themes introduced above require further development, particularly as they help introduce the concepts of opportunity and willingness, which are presented in depth in chapter 2. These concepts, in turn, provide an anchor for the arguments to be presented in all of the following chapters.

CUMULATION

Discussions concerning the development of theory, or the general health of the study of international relations have focused on the notion of cumulation (see, for example, Rosenau, 1976a, part 2; Starr, 1974; Zinnes, 1980; Hopmann, Singer and Zinnes, 1981; Rus-

sett, 1983; Most and Starr, 1984; and Papadakis and Starr, 1987).
Many scholars speak of cumulation in the same terms that others
speak of progress. For example, Dryzek (1986:301, 302) defines progress as "an increasing ability to explain and connect complex phenomena," with science progressing through "accumulation."[8]
Boynton (1976:145) neatly sums up this conception of cumulation
by noting that it is "a frame of mind of the practitioners of the
field," that suggests "what is known now that was not known before and what can be done now that could not be done before."

Several commentators have distinguished between different types
of cumulation. The distinction between "narrow" views of cumulation that stress accumulations of data and findings and "broad"
conceptions that focus on theoretical development (Rosenau,
1976b:6), is most clearly drawn by Zinnes (1976a:162). Zinnes's terminology of "additive" and "integrative" cumulation rather than
narrow and broad, has become standard usage (corresponding also
to Ashley's [1976:152] notions of "expansive" and "selective" cumulation, respectively).

For Zinnes, additive cumulation occurs when "one study adds
some information to the existing literatures on the subject,"
through such activities as the citation of previous findings, using
previously collected data, secondary or reanalysis of existing data,
the incorporation of new cases or new variables into the analysis, or
expanding the application of models, indices or techniques to new
cases or research questions.

With integrative cumulation, the earlier studies are "crucial" to
the conceptual and theoretical components of the subsequent
study's research design. As Boynton (1976:146, 147) notes, "From
this perspective it is assumed that the present research could not
have been done except for the work that preceded it. . . . Cumulative thinking is a merging of past, present and future." For Zinnes,
integrative cumulation implies that a new study "ties together and
explains a set of research findings" (emphasis in original), thus going beyond earlier studies. While phrased differently, the broad or
integrative mode of cumulation, for Rosenau and Ashley, as well as
Alker's (1976:53) cumulation in "the strong sense," also implies a
theoretical guide to inquiry, performing "Lakatos-like positive and
negative heuristic functions" (Ashley, 1976:152). Lakatos (1970)
presents a strategy for the development and evaluation of a research
program based on such heuristics, driven by the progressive
problem-shift.

While both additive and integrative cumulation have an important role in the development of a discipline, additive cumulation is but one component of integrative cumulation. It is integrative cumulation, with its stress on theory, its development, evolution and change, that most clearly indicates "progress" or the "maturation" of a discipline. It is the perceived lack of integrative cumulation that has concerned international relations scholars, and that has prompted many of the reconceptualizations of the research process proposed in this book.

Several scholars (e.g., Siverson, 1976; Papadakis and Starr, 1985) have clearly divided the impediments to cumulation into two broad categories: the sociology and psychology of academia, and the theoretical/intellectual. The thrust of most critiques (e.g., Alker, 1976; Zinnes 1976a) deals with the latter, the discipline's inability to synthesize its islands of theory (see also Guetzkow, 1950), through the lack of attention to the broader *process* of theorizing. This process includes positive heuristics, problem evolution (if not a strict "problem-shift"), what Rosenau (1976b, 1980a, 1980b) calls "puzzles,"[9] or what Alker calls "metascientific orientations." These are the directions we hope to follow in the chapters to come. We agree with Zinnes that scholars have spent too much time in "the additive mentality"—overly preoccupied with data and data collection, statistical and programming methodological issues.

Integrative cumulation clearly implies the search for and development of coherent theory that goes beyond additive concerns and "ad hoc hypothesis testing" (see Zinnes, 1976b), to the generation of further theory. These terms could include criteria such as those presented by Lakatos (1978:32) in regard to theory falsification. A "better" theory has "excess empirical content," predicting "novel" facts as well as the "unrefuted content" of the previous theory. Better theory thus should push scholars beyond asking "what" questions, which tend to be univariate and descriptive. It should also push us beyond "why" questions into the "how" questions— questions of *process*. However, while some analysts have asked "how" questions, they have tended to presume the existence of a single puzzle, answer or process. Better theory needs to be more interactive and dialectical, with the interplay that permits the discovery of processes. In the following chapters we argue that most of the phenomena that we are interested in understanding are *outcomes of processes*. We demonstrate that it is not possible to recover such processes by focusing on the attributes of any single participant or on linear/additive combinations of all participants.

Integrative cumulation, thus, also implies that the *study* of international relations phenomena is as much a *process* as the phenomena itself. Thinking of the study of international political phenomena as a process, whether in terms of Lakatos's successive problem-shifts, Rosenau's evolution of puzzles, or Lave and March's (1975) steps for the development of disciplined speculation, aids in the search for better theory. Initially, we can illustrate the process as one which captures the theory/research feedback loop (which, indeed, may reflect mostly additive cumulation):

$$theory \rightarrow findings \rightarrow theory$$

A good deal of what we wish to argue in the following chapters is that this view is incomplete, and indeed may not be capable of moving beyond additive cumulation. The more useful feedback loop to develop includes the crucial linkages between theory and research design as well:

$$theory \rightarrow research\ design \rightarrow theory$$

and ultimately:

$$theory \rightarrow research\ design \rightarrow findings \rightarrow theory$$

We believe that the application of logic to theory and the theory-research design linkage will go far in meeting the problems that have limited integrative cumulation in the study of international politics. We argue that if one takes time with the logical structures of research design and theory, then the strategy for developing a "research program" will yield better results, and more quickly (see Most, 1986, as well as Cioffi's commentary on Lakatos, undated). We will continue to touch on issues central to current debates in the philosophy of science—cumulation necessarily includes elements of paradigm consensus and paradigm shift as considered by Kuhn (1962) and Lakatos (1978). However, philosophy of science is *not* the central focus of our analyses, and we will try not to become embroiled in the details of its debates.

Our primary focus is the relationships among the three components of the research triad—logic, theory, and methodology. Indeed, we wish to redefine thinking about the elements of the triad. Above we utilized the standard notion of feedback loops in the research process—useful in indicating that the elements have consequences for the whole process, a *process* that *continues* through modification, dialectic and similar dynamics.

To shift metaphors, rather than speaking of a feedback loop, we can think of the researcher (and the research community as a whole) as a *juggler.* The image is now one where each element of the triad needs to be held in the air at the same time in a complex set of inter-relationships, indicating that for the juggler to be successful, *all* the balls (elements of the triad) must be kept going simultaneously. If any fall the enterprise fails. In this sense no element is more important than any other. While the feedback loop image implies a beginning point for research (if not an end-point), the juggler image makes it clear that international relations scholars do not come to their research de novo. A considerable body of data, "facts," hypotheses, models, etc., does exist. If, however, the triad consists of logic as well as theory and methodology, lack of cumulative progress may be explained by the failure to keep the logic leg successfully in the air with the other two (or that many scholars juggle only two elements, and thus cannot "succeed").

Excerpts from Bueno de Mesquita's (1985a:134–35) conclusion clarify these points:

> Rather, the means for achieving scientific progress when training future researchers should include explicit theorizing, whether verbal or mathematical, grounded in axiomatic logic, from which hypotheses with empirical referents may be extracted. . . . Such research should be careful to note whether the relevant hypotheses stipulate necessary, sufficient, or necessary and sufficient, conditions for a given outcome to obtain. They should be careful to use criteria for evaluating the evidence that are consistent with the expectations implied by the differences between necessary, sufficient, or necessary and sufficient conditions.

THE RESEARCH TRIAD AND RESEARCH DESIGN

One aim of this book, then, is to emphasize the elements of logic, and their relationship to such general issues of epistemology as raised above and highlighted by Bueno de Mesquita. In addition, we wish to introduce here, and develop in later chapters, just how each leg of the research triad is crucial to research design as well.

It is obvious that the development of theory depends to a great extent on logic. As theory is conceived broadly to be internally consistent and nontautological, it requires logical analysis to delineate weaknesses in this area. As theory demonstrates the connection between concepts and the relationships between ideas, it also requires logical analysis. In summarizing Boynton's (1982a) discussion of the use of "formal languages" such as symbolic logic, Gillespie (1982:15–16) notes several ways in which formalization helps us theorize: (1) Formalization "provides a language for looking at a problem that will enable us to define what we are looking for and its elements." (2) "Formal languages can aid us in political inquiry [in] that they help us to specify relationships between ideas." (3) "Once we have linked together ideas, the formal language can help us to derive deductions from them; the formal language also forces us to specify relationships that the English language normally slides over very easily." (4) Formal languages "enable us to relate statements to one another." (5) "Finally, formal languages give us a way to make deductions from our ideas that we otherwise might not contemplate."

In sum, logic helps us to understand exactly what it is that we wish to understand and study, where it is we wish to go. It also has implications for *how* we will get there. Method, too, requires the application of logic. A methodology may be reliable, and even valid, but is the methodology actually addressing the questions that are being posed by the theory? actually addressing the puzzle under consideration? The juggler image indicates that logic, theory, and method are all necessary. Logic ties theory and methodology together, each of which informs and shapes the application of that logic.

Theory and analysis are ideally aimed at helping us make broader statements and deduce more general relationships, processes and dynamics. That is, theory and analysis are aimed at helping us make more informed comparative statements about what evidence, analyzed in terms of different theories/models, or developed using various types of research designs and approaches, constitutes an adequate basis for drawing such inferences. One conclusion we hope to demonstrate in this book is that no methodological way of proceeding is always appropriate; analysts and interpreters need to figure out what they want to study and select the methods which are appropriate to those ends. Theories and methods are essentially *tools,* and it seems irrelevant to debate whether or not tools are, in principle, good or bad. Rather it seems to us more sensible to be concerned with whether or not they are useful to whatever task it is at hand. One aim of this book is to aid international relations scholars in making such judgments.

While we will later address ourselves to the specific utility of various approaches, including the case study, a brief logical critique of the case study approach can be used to illustrate a number of the points concerning the role of logic in the research triad. Suppose we are concerned with defeat in war, and we have *one* case in which a defeat (Y) occurred. We study that case in great detail. We try to be as explicit and detailed as possible (to avoid problems of aggregation and lack of detail often associated with quantitative methodologies), and try to be careful about maintaining the temporal precedence of the factors that might have caused Y (so that we can talk in causal terms and not simply correlational ones). In the course of the analysis we observe that in this case the political leaders were unwilling to wage all-out-war. We eventually conclude that it was this factor (called X^1) that produced the defeat (Y). Lack of political will to fight all-out war was sufficient for defeat. One inference could be: If one fights a war, one ought to fight to win.

The reasoning is plausible. Unfortunately, the conclusion is not supported by the evidence. Working with one case and one case alone cannot show that any factor was either necessary or sufficient for the result. While a lack of will (X^1) may have characterized our case, a number of other potential explanatory factors may also have been present, e.g., a locally superior enemy, an ill-suited battlefield strategy, an ally of questionable military capability, and so on. Another analyst, for example, could look at the same case, observe that the losing state had difficulties in projecting its military capabilities to the distant site of the fighting (X^2), and conclude that it was loss-of-strength over distance that explains the defeat. Here, the inference could be: Never fight far from home, or improve the ability to project force.

This inference also seems plausible, and that is just the point. Any of a nearly endless list of factors could be cited as the source of defeat and would have the *same* logical status as explanation X^1 (lack of will). While a debate might ensue among proponents of the different arguments it would shed more heat than light. There is no way to demonstrate that any of the factors (or combination thereof) was *necessary or sufficient* for the defeat when we are working with only one case.

Given only one case, we have one occurrence each of X^1, X^2 and Y. Since we are not looking at any instances in which victories occurred (-Y), we cannot say that X^1 or X^2 always precede (i.e., are sufficient for) Y. That is, there could have been many instances where X^1 or X^2 occurred but *victories* (-Y) resulted, and the single case study approach would not show it. With only one instance of X^1, X^2 and Y, we have similar problems with necessary conditions. With only one case we cannot say that Y is always preceded by X^1 or X^2 (i.e., that X^1 or X^2 are necessary for Y). There might be many cases in which Y resulted even though X^1 or X^2 were absent. A single case study design would simply not be able to show that pattern— no matter what the question or the phenomenon under study, a *single* case study cannot say anything about necessity or sufficiency.

At present, this simple illustration should suffice to indicate how the application of logic relates both to general theoretical issues— what to look at for what reasons—as well as research design. It is logically impossible to identify cause and effect relationships and sort out general linkages from those that are simple happenstance unless one adopts an explicitly comparative and systematic approach. The question of how broadly comparative or general such an approach should be is introduced below and developed in later chapters. While there is no assurance that a comparative/systematic method definitely enables a researcher to identify cause and effect, it *is* clear that a single-case study method cannot suffice.

Mancur Olson (1982:12) has summed up the issue as follows. The logical difficulty delineated above helps

> to explain why the histories of each country and period are rewritten periodically and a different story told each time. Part of the explanation is that new sources are found, new interests emerge, and better analyses are developed; but partly, *when there is no limit to the length of an explanation and no rules* about which of the infinite number of outcomes is selected for explanation, *an enormous*—if not infinite—*number of plausible stories can be told, and it is mainly a matter of taste which of these explanations is preferred.* Scholar after scholar can then write plausible book after plausible book, but none need to be definitive and there is no accumulation of knowledge of causes and effects (emphasis added).

Another way to consider the holistic nature of the research triad is to look at various activities that are dealt with in discussions of the research design process. It is clear that scholars see this, as they should, as a cyclic process composed of feedback loops. In figure 1.1 we have reproduced Gurr's (1975:16) "map of the research process in politimetrics" and Raymond's (1974'5:42) "dynamic and circular" representation of scientific explanations. Each clearly indicates that theory and method are needed for the process of mutual development and expansion.

Gurr presents as good an outline of the *clusters of activities* that constitute the research/research design process as can be found in any number of useful treatments of research design. Following our juggler imagery, we prefer to use "clusters of activities" rather than Gurr's notion of "steps" or the notion of stages or phases in the research process. Our usage thus avoids the implication of some linear progression in the research process, but continues the notion that there are several activities that must take place coterminously to successfully bring the research design to fruition and for successful research and cumulation.

Gurr (1972:chap. 1) offers four elements in the development of research design. The first involves formulating the question, or "problemation." The second involves specification and operationalization, which we interpret somewhat more broadly than Gurr, beginning with the basic set of concepts involved in the study (Gurr begins with considering what type of "data matrix" the researcher will need, and how to go about filling it). The third involves data collection and processing, while the fourth considers the wide variety of methods for data analysis and subsequent interpretation. Logical analysis can help to improve all of these activities.

To repeat, it is important to conceive of these activities as a continuous/simultaneous set of clusters, with constant interaction. This implies that there is no definite beginning or ending in some sort of research cycle, but a set of activities that can be broken into at *any* point—by the researcher, or, as is the case here, by the commentator on research. This point of view is important for us, as the core of this book (chapters 3 through 6) begins at what would be the end of a linear view of the research process. Beginning in chapter 3, we start with the most obvious or visible of the clusters—interpretation of results. From there we work into methods of analysis and into the other three clusters in reverse order from that by which Gurr introduces them. As we started to deal with the research process from a logic of inquiry perspective, initially the most obvious flaws appeared to be in the interpretation and analysis cluster.

FIGURE 1.1.   Depictions of the Research Process

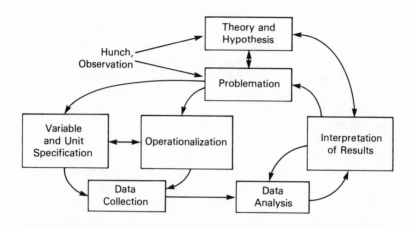

From Gurr (1972:16)   Map of the research process in politimetrics.

Application   Formulation
Part V   Part II

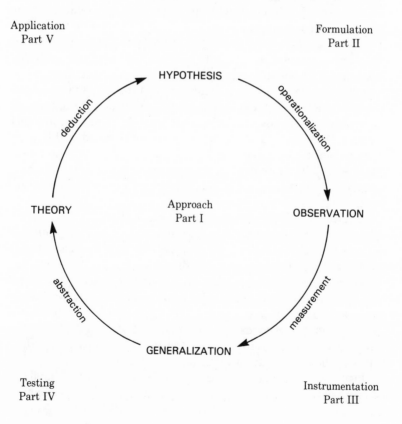

Testing   Instrumentation
Part IV   Part III

From Raymond (1975:42)

But as our analysis deepened we found that the flaws in analysis and interpretation derived from and were magnified by logical problems in the other clusters of activities.

This series of questions mirrors the intellectual history of our project studying the diffusion of violent conflict. Our initial attempts at research design confronted us with the question of what the empirical results of quantitative data analysis would *mean*. We thus began with a concern with how we would interpret our results. This led us to design research in such a way that we could demonstrate what those results meant. We soon realized that we needed a fuller conceptualization of war and diffusion, how to tell if they were present or absent, and what the logical relationships between them would be. It became clear that opportunity and willingness, and the idea of interaction opportunity would be central to this project, and that the operationalization of concepts and the collection of data needed to be consistent with the logical requirements of the analysis. Our first steps in empirical analysis were with the collection of data on borders, as borders were key to the interaction opportunity perspective. Initial analyses of borders and the relationship of borders and war clarified the logical problems in designing research to tap the existence of the diffusion of violence. As we attempted to work our way through these issues, the arguments presented in this book crystallized and were developed in a parallel project. We hope to demonstrate that the issues raised in this book are germane to the design and analysis of quantitative research projects, especially those dealing with phenomena such as war which are the interdependent outcomes of the behavior of two or more actors.

In terms of research design, by the time we finish our discussion we will be analyzing and critiquing the whole issue of *problemation* in the study of international politics. This includes the development and use of international relations theory—what questions international relations scholars are asking and how they arrived at those questions. Though beginning with flaws in analysis and interpretation, we found that in developing the arguments for this book, we had to "move backwards" through Gurr's clusters to deal with the increasingly broad ramifications of the problems uncovered, ending up with the problemation cluster.

Just as each aspect of the research triad must be dealt with, all the clusters of the research design process must be handled with competence, or else the whole process will fail. In this sense, all clusters are crucial to research. However, we feel that the problemation cluster may be first among equals, that it may be the most crucial of the research design activities. We suggest this possibility on the basis that the problemation cluster is the *translation* cluster. It is here that broad conceptions of how the world works, that is broad models and theories, are translated into puzzles, problems or questions. These, in turn, are translated into a research question or hypothesis (or set) and into research design issues.

By the end of chapter 6 it will be clear that many problems previously conceived of as methodological or as research design issues stem from logical failures in the translation cluster. For example, questions concerning inadequacies of data and the need to collect data appropriate to one's theory, may be less important than the need to consider how theory and logic affect the *quality* of the data one wants in terms of degree of accuracy, sampling frame, and so on (see chapter 5).

By the end of chapter 6 it will also be clear that much more effort needs to be devoted to understanding the nature of the broad theories/models/concerns that initially motivate scholars, so that the translation (research design) effort is relevant to those theories/models/concerns. It will also be clear that many of the problems of cumulation, research dead ends, and the failure to find compatible results have been due to logical flaws in theory and method, and more particularly to the linkages (translation) between theory and method.

'OPPORTUNITY' AND 'WILLINGNESS' IN ORGANIZING THE STUDY OF INTERNATIONAL POLITICS

The introduction of logical concerns raised the importance of the notions of necessity and sufficiency. Using these two concepts forces us to think about partitioning the world in at least crude ways: the presence or absence of dependent variables (Y and $-Y$), and the presence and absence of predictor variables (X and $-X$). We are forced to consider *different contexts*—the presence or absence of certain conditions. In doing so we have been made to realize that the *most general* questions or propositions might not hold because there are at least these crude partitioning factors that might limit their general applicability. At the least, we must consider that some factors and/or relationships are necessary, others sufficient, and others both necessary and sufficient.

In chapters to follow (especially chapter 5) we develop this idea much more fully. We argue that general propositions or "laws" will miss important processes and relationships that occur in various subsystems, subgroups, or more limited, context-specific sets of actors or patterns or interaction. Following Boynton (1982a, 1982b) we call these more restricted or specified propositions, "nice laws." That is, with the correct specifications (or "valid simplifications" accerding to Boynton, 1982b:33), nice laws can very usefully indicate patterns, correlations, processes, and explanations for some subsample of phenomena.

These views are not new. They are central to the enterprise of comparative analysis, where a key issue is whether or not we categorize phenomena accurately and place them in their proper contextual or comparative reference. Comparative research design is continually concerned with the generalizability of the inferences that may be drawn from the results produced. Consider, for example, the cube presented in figure 1.2 (from Starr and Most, 1985b). It illustrates that any datum, "fact" or variable can be defined on three dimensions: It is only one of many possible variables; it is selected from a particular polity or case; and it is drawn from a specific point in time. Clearly, reality can be "sliced" in several different ways. A case study can be conducted that focuses on a large number of variables at a single point in time. A cross-sectional, synchronic, study can be conducted in which the focus is on the relationships among variables in a large number of cases at a single point in time. A time-series, diachronic, design would focus on the relationships that hold through a large number of points in time in a single case. Each of these approaches partition reality differently; all have limitations in generalizability and in the applicability and utility of the inferences that can be drawn.

A number of students of empirical theory have raised this issue of context, and its limitations on the generality of analysis and inference, (see, for example, Ostrom 1982a, especially chapters by Boynton, Benjamin, Sprague, and Barry). As Ostrom (1982b:20) notes, "Boynton's chapter can be viewed as an inquiry into what is the 'right type of law' for social scientists. The right type of law, he argues, is highly specific and relates a limited number of variables to each other under stated conditions." Both Barry and Ostrom (1982b:22) quote John Stuart Mill as to the use of empirically deter-

FIGURE 1.2. The Analysts' Cube

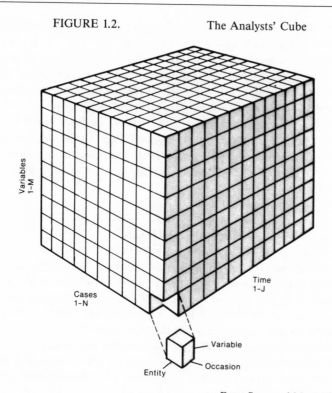

From Starr and Most (1985b:36)

mined patterns: "we cannot use them with any confidence as a basis of prediction unless we have reason to expect the underlying conditions to remain unaltered."

The analysis cube, and many of the following discussions indicate that underlying conditions, or context, does change and thus limits the generality of analysis. An important enterprise, then, must be a search for the "valid simplifications" provided by theory; the search for organizing concepts or principles. One last observation by Boynton (1982b:64) helps us introduce the ideas of opportunity and willingness: "What is an organizing principle that it may order particulars? It is that by which apparently incommensurable things are 'related to each other as just so many forms of one substrata.' "

In both the application of logic to research design as well as the development of a substantive theoretical approach to international relations, we wish to highlight both structure and process—the need to study the structure of a system or situation *and* the processes that operate within those structures. In addition, the logic of inquiry approach outlined here, with a focus on process within a framework of opportunity and willingness, forces the researcher to cut across levels of analysis. International phenomena must be conceptualized in terms of multiple levels of analysis, letting the logic of inquiry push the researcher into the relevant level or levels, rather than predetermining the appropriate level. As noted, we have applied opportunity and willingness and cross-level logic of inquiry to our study of the diffusion of violent conflict. Examples from, and references to this project will be used to illustrate the utility and feasibility of these approaches.

CHAPTER OUTLINE

In chapter 2 opportunity and willingness serve as our organizing principles as we attempt to apply logical analysis to the theoretical structure of international relations. We have used opportunity and willingness (which can also be interpreted as structure and decision or macro-and micro-factors) as a "pre-theoretical" structure that allows us to link context/contextual, environmental or structural variables to decision making/process variables and outcomes.

By the conclusion of the book we hope to have proven that opportunity and willingness have moved beyond "metaphor" and "analogy" and have developed into "model," if not fully into "theory" (see Snidal, 1985, for elaboration of each of these terms).[10] Integrative cumulation requires the organization of what we know around some sort of theoretical structure. We hope to demonstrate that opportunity and willingness as organizing principles, as principles that relate "apparently incommensurable" things to each other, can be useful in providing such a theoretical structure for the study of international politics.

After introducing opportunity and willingness in chapter 2, chapter 3 introduces the central logical arguments that form the basis for subsequent discussions. Chapter 3 argues that both the static cross-sectional research designs commonly used and the manner by which researchers have selected cases for their analyses are appropriate only for the examination of necessary conditions, even though researchers claim to be investigating sufficient relationships. The identification of answers to the sufficiency questions that they pose appears to be logically precluded by their case selection procedures and research designs.

Chapter 3 also argues that while many analysts have focused on linear and additive combinations of factors internal to states—national attributes—as possible sufficient conditions for their research, the general existence of such relationships appears to be logically precluded if the phenomena under investigation can be conceptualized as *interdependent outcomes* or *resultants* of the actions of at least two states (such as war).

Moving on from these issues, chapter 4 shows that simply identifying which factors determine international phenomena is inadequate. Equally important, and more difficult, are questions that concern *how* such factors are *logically* and *causally* related to one another and to the phenomena in question. We introduce the argument that the search for patterns that are generalizable through time and across space, hitherto the sine qua non of quantitative international relations, is illusory. While patterns may still exist, they are not likely to be of the variety, or even appear like the variety, of patterns for which analysts have been exploring.

In chapter 5 we argue that the development of various "islands of theory" in international relations will not yield a broad-ranging understanding of states' foreign policy behavior if analysts define those islands in terms of concrete, unabstracted, empirically oriented events-behaviors. International behaviors are shown to be alternative means that different international actors utilize in pursuit of their (perhaps heterogeneous) national goals, and under certain conditions may be *substituted* for each other. If this is the case, then all the behaviors that tend to be studied in fragmented fashion need to be conceived and studied from the outset *not* as separate and distinct phenomena, but rather as commensurable behaviors or component parts of abstract conceptual puzzles.

Additionally in chapter 5 we return to the utility of nice laws. If it is plausible to argue that states may pursue different goals for different reasons and with different degrees of effectiveness, then it may be useful to reconsider the efforts to search for a true, general, or universally applicable explanation of what states do. It might instead be more sensible to search for models or theories that are valid only under certain explicitly prescribed conditions.

Using the current debates over system polarity and war, and dyadic power relations and war, the discussion in chapter 6 focuses on the impact that international structural phenomena can logically be expected to have on the operation of dynamic, micro-level decision processes. Using both empirical and simulated data, the problems of micro-macro composition and micro-macro decomposition are discussed, as are procedures and conceptual approaches for making the linkages.

Chapter 7 includes discussions of: The ultimate end of our research, a new and more appropriate conceptualization of what it may mean to explain international relations and foreign policy phenomena, and conclusions about the types of theory and modes of research that appear best-suited for meeting the challenges of cumulation in the study of international relations. The limitations of "middle-range" theory and the need for renewed efforts to construct "grand theory," as introduced in chapter 5 are reviewed and discussed. We also review the need to gain closure on theoretical and empirical questions, the need for more dynamic and process-oriented approaches, and the need for increased emphasis on micro-macro/process-structure linkages.

2

OPPORTUNITY AND WILLINGNESS:
A Pre-Theoretic Framework

INTRODUCTION: THE NEED FOR ORGANIZING CONCEPTS

Over a decade ago one of the authors discussed the various complexities of studying international politics, and proposed a pair of organizing concepts to aid in that study.[1] These concepts—opportunity and willingness—cover both macro and micro approaches to the study of international relations. Opportunity is a shorthand term for the possibilities that are available within any environment. As such, it represents the total set of environmental constraints and possibilities; it sets up the macro-level of environmental and structural factors. Willingness is a shorthand term for the choice (and process of choice) that is related to the selection of some behavioral option from a range of alternatives. Willingness thus refers to the willingness to choose (even if the choice is no action), and to employ available capabilities to further some policy option over others. In this chapter we develop the argument that both the environmental/structural level and the decision-making/ choice level are required for a full description and explanation of international relations phenomena.

How does the development of such concepts contribute to our understanding of international relations, and, more specifically, to the arguments delineated in this book? There are a number of features to these concepts (but not confined to these concepts) that facilitate the further development of our arguments. Together, opportunity and willingness require the combination of both structure/environment and choice/decision process—and, as a consequence, argue against deterministic models of international politics. They also require attention to be given to the process of decision making, no matter what argument is made for system-level models. Thus, they concern the relationships between decision makers and their surrounding environments; how the environment constrains the activities of decision makers and how decision makers perceive that environment.

At their most basic level opportunity and willingness may be used both to help in partitioning the world, and by organizing our thinking in these terms, to help in bringing disparate phenomena together in an orderly manner. Our hope is that we will be able to move opportunity and willingness from their initial use as organizing concepts to a model for the study of international relations. First, then, we must demonstrate the need for organizing concepts. If these two concepts have utility as organizing concepts, we need to show how they might order a literature—hypotheses, models, findings, variables, and factors. To be manageable, this exercise needs to be related to some important concept or set of questions. However, to indicate how this might work for all of international relations would not be manageable (examples of applications across international relations may be found in the textbook treatment by Russett and Starr, 1985). Thus, we present a truncated exercise focusing primarily on international conflict and war. Because international conflict and war are used as the primary illustrations in the following chapters, a broad overview of the conflict literature will also be useful to the reader.

While the amount of research and commentary in the area of international conflict and war continues to expand (as it does in international political economy, transnationalism, and integration), the student of conflict has received little help in making sense of this vast literature. While the sophistication of specific models or theories in international relations—including the causes and processes of international conflict—also increases, there have been very few attempts to provide conceptually useful devices for organizing and integrating these literatures. Clearly such devices are needed for pedagogical reasons. However, they are also crucial, as noted in chapter 1, for helping students of international relations trying to theorize, conceptualize and design research.

This gap is a particularly serious one in the study of international conflict. The search for causes, explanations, correlations, and a representation of the conflict process, requires the scholar to investigate conflict at, and across, all levels of analysis—from psychological factors to the international system. In addition, scholarly investigation of conflict has been pursued from a variety of substantive disciplinary perspectives—economic, sociological, psychological, political, historical, anthropological, biological, and others. The analytical complexity and interdisciplinary nature of the study of conflict raises the serious problem of how to bring the various speculations, hypotheses, and findings about conflict together in ways useful to the student of international conflict. Again, this is a microcosm of the needs of international relations in general.

Investigators clearly require more help in grappling with the wide array of disparate materials which in some way should be relevant to the study of international conflict. In the early 1970s one could cite a number of major bibliographical works on the study of war, as well as several book-length research summaries.[2] A major mode of organization in the early reviews was disciplinary. Perhaps the first work intending to draw together a wide range of the previous knowledge of war was Quincy Wright's (1942) monumental study. Wright moves the reader through the then extant knowledge of war along mostly disciplinary lines, focusing on history and historical sources. Other discipline oriented summaries were Newcombe and Newcombe (1969) and Alcock (1972). In 1970, Singer (1970:532) observed that the most widely used "taxonomy" for the categorization of explanatory variables at that time was one based on disciplinary categories.

This method, however, was deficient in the synthesis and integration of the materials under review. Singer (1970:532) noted the major hazard in the use of standard disciplinary categorization schemes: "...one is struck by the frequency with which many scholars move quickly from such an itemization to a concentration on just *one* of the categories, and proceed to 'explain' the incidence of war almost exclusively in terms of a single cluster of variables. And, to nobody's surprise, the academics among us usually tend to select the variables of their own discipline." Much the same phenomenon can be found in the international political economy literature concerning dependency, and the preference of different ideological positions for models derived from economics, sociology, law, or political science.

A second major approach to the organization of the study of war has been the use of levels of analysis. Waltz (1954) introduced a three tiered scheme (three images) for investigating the causes of war—human behavior, the internal structure of states, and the nature of the international system. This has proved to be a durable organizational scheme (evident in works from M. Haas [1972, 1974]; to Dedring [1976]; to Gurr [1980]). Singer's (1980,1981) general systems theory approach uses a more complex set of levels. These are similar to Rosenau's (1966) five pre-theoretical factors which have influenced many pedagogical and research treatments of international politics in general (see, for example, Russett and Starr, 1985). North and Willard (1983) also start with Waltz's three images, but add a fourth based on "nested relationships" which resembles the Sproutian basis for opportunity and willingness developed below.

Seemingly unrelated materials can be ordered in such a way that their relationship to each other becomes clear within the broad conception of either opportunity or willingness (or the ways in which they relate to each other). But opportunity and willingness should help us go beyond additive cumulation. In terms of integrative cumulation, we need theoretical tools that provide *linkages* among all the various findings, concepts, models (see also North and Willard, 1983, for a discussion of linkages). Opportunity and willingness permit us to add new pieces of evidence and theory to existing material (additive), but they do more by forcing students of conflict to think across all the levels, stages and processes involved in international conflict (integrative).

At another level opportunity and willingness become the pre-theoretical basis for a conceptual framework dealing with the study of international conflict and international relations as a whole. At this level we begin to develop an explanation of what conditions are *necessary* for the occurrence of events (in this case, war). That is, opportunity and willingness are pre-theoretical in that they represent conceptions and clarifications that are preliminary, but required, before the development of more sophisticated theories of international politics. Boynton (1982:38) notes the importance of such ordering concepts: "First, the ideas of a science prescribe *how to look* at empirical phenomena. The empirical world is just what it is. One might speak of either divining or imposing on the stuff of experience the order we seek. We seek an order to experience, and that order is to be found in a theory that says, 'Look at the phenomenon in this way; when you do you will see the order that has been eluding you'" (emphasis added).

THE ECOLOGICAL TRIAD: DECISION MAKERS AND THEIR ENVIRONMENT

The general notions of opportunity and willingness derive directly from the works of Harold and Margaret Sprout (1956, 1965, 1968, 1969) dealing with the ecological relationships embedded in world politics.[3] It should be noted, however, that the Sprouts did not present their ideas specifically as a way to organize a disparate literature—either for international relations as a whole, or a specific subset of that literature. We will show in this, and following chapters, that their ideas can be subsumed under opportunity and willingness.

The Sprouts have provided us with a useful set of concepts for dealing with the relationships between macro and micro phenomena. They have presented us with the notion of the "ecological triad" composed of an entity, its environment, and entity-environment relationships (1968:11–21; 1956:17–19; 1969:42). The advantages of this framework, like those of general systems theory, derive from its applicability to any number of levels of analysis. That is, whether our focus is on a single decision maker, a small group of decision makers, a foreign policy organization, a government as a whole, or the state as international actor, the concept of the ecological triad argues that we need to look at the ongoing policy/choice processes within that entity, its context or environment, and then the interaction between the entity and the environment.

Three types of relationships between the entity and environment discussed by the Sprouts are of particular interest: environmental possibilism, environmental probabilism, and cognitive behaviorism. These relationships were developed by the Sprouts as alternatives to environmental determinism, where, by definition, decision makers are incapable of choice given the characteristics of the environment, or "milieu" (Sprouts, 1969:44). Environmental possibilism, according to the Sprouts (1956:39), returns the initiative to the decision maker. The environment is seen to be a number of factors which limit human opportunities, which constrain the type of action that can be taken as well as the consequences of that action. While the limits set by the environment may be wide or narrow, it is assumed that the limitations are discoverable (Sprouts, 1969:44).

The essence of environmental probabilism "is explanation or prediction by means of a generalized model, of the average, or typical persons's reaction to a given milieu" (Sprouts, 1956:50). It is based on assumptions of motivation and knowledge of the environment. As decision makers view their environment, the characteristics of that environment provide cues as to the probability of certain outcomes. The environment not only presents the decision maker with what is possible, but what course of action is more (or less) likely under those particular circumstances.

Entity-environment relationships based on possibilism and probabilism can be summarized by Russett's idea of "menu" (Russett, 1972b:112–113; see also Russett and Starr, 1985:19–25)—the analogy of a diner (entity) within a restaurant looking at a menu (environment). The menu provides a number of behavioral/choice possibilities, not determining the diner's choice, but limiting it; (the essence of opportunity). The probability of that choice is then affected through factors such as price, size of portion, side dishes, the restaurant's reputation for certain meals, and other factors related to the motivations, tastes and values of the customer/decision maker.

Finally, cognitive behaviorism is the Sproutian term for "the simple and familiar principle that a person reacts to his milieu as he apperceives it—that is as he perceives and interprets it in light of past experience" (Sprouts, 1969:45). On this basis, the Sprouts stress the importance of the "psychological milieu" of decision makers.[4] The Sprouts' position here, is that entity-environment relationships are based upon the way in which decision makers perceive the environment. How decision makers *see* the world or environment, the content of their *image* of the world—is the central matter of importance in terms of creating policy, planning, or decision making. The "real" world has an impact only after making decisions and taking actions; but again, this feedback from the real world needs to be perceived.[5]

Opportunity and willingness overarch these three ways of viewing entity-environment relationships. Environmental possibilism is particularly related to the "opportunities and limitations which are implicit in a state's milieu." (Sprouts, 1969:42). Cognitive behaviorism, as an introduction to the perceptual processes of the psychological milieu in which decisions and plans are made, is concerned with the same phenomena that produce the willingness to choose one policy/behavioral option over another (e.g., the decision to go to war). Cognitive behaviorism (and, to a lesser degree environmental probabilism) and willingness both focus on decision-making processes and the factors involved in those processes. The argument that both opportunity and willingness must be taken into account in the study of international phenomena derives in part from the understanding that *all three* parts of the triad—entity, environment, entity-environment relationship—must be studied in order to cover all the jointly necessary conditions for explanation of phenomena.

In contrast, for example, some studies of perception or psychological factors appear to assume that the "objective" world is of little relevance. Similarly, the bureaucratic politics approach, based on Allison's (1971) organizational politics and governmental politics models, has been used to focus entirely on the domestic environment. These studies have been criticized because they ignore the international context. Students of macro-quantitative and international systemic phenomena have made parallel simplifying assumptions. These include the assumption that the possibilistic (and, to a lesser extent, the probabilistic) constraints of the international environmental context override the variables involved in the policy-making process (for example, Waltz, 1979, criticizes any theory/model that works below the level of the international system as "reductionist"). The assumption is that governmental systems and their decision makers, when faced with certain systemic environmental possibilities, will behave in generally similar ways within some range of probability. This simplifying assumption was used to justify exploratory study of the systemic environment before theories of entity-environment linages were developed. Singer (1972, 1970), for example, argued that we needed to discover the variance explained by such environmental or structural variables to see what degree of control or leverage was left to decision makers.

It should be clear that the ecological triad calls for the study of *both* entity and environment, and most importantly, how the two are related. The ultimate entities—single decision makers or small groups of decision makers—are surrounded by factors that structure the nature of the decision, the options available, the consequences, costs and benefits of those options. Individuals, then, make choices within a complex set of *incentive structures*. This can be captured only by looking at all three parts of the ecological triad. Opportunity and willingness, as compared to other approaches for ordering international relations or international conflict literature, encompasses all three aspects of the triad.

OPPORTUNITY

One way of looking at the environment is to see it as creating and constraining opportunities for activity. The primary use of opportunity in the following chapters is in its conception as the "*possibil-*

ity of interaction." The same conception of opportunity has been presented in our work on the effects of borders as interaction opportunities in the diffusion of violent conflict. In that work we quickly moved from models and analyses that investigated the possible effects of diffusion on a global scale to investigating subsets of units that had high levels of interaction. We began by looking at geographic proximity because proximity provided the opportunity (or possibility) of high and sustained levels of interaction. If wars were to diffuse, we needed to investigate mechanisms that provided the opportunities for mutual interest, concern and importance. The initial studies looked at borders, subsequent analyses incorporated alliances (see Most, et al., 1987; Siverson and Starr, 1988). Thus, opportunity means that the possibility of interaction exists. In terms of war, opportunity means that interaction exists between individuals of one national state and those of another so that it is *possible* for conflicts to arise.

The logic of the diffusion of violent conflict is based on the possibility of interaction in turn creating the possibility of conflictual interaction (in turn creating the possibility of violent interaction; see, for example, Most and Starr 1975, 1976, 1980, 1981, 1985). These studies drew upon the existing literature on the proximity of international actors and the effects of contiguity on the interaction of nations. Thus, literature on geopolitical factors affecting the interaction of states directly relates to opportunity, and led to our use of borders as a primary, and initially employed, indicator of the "opportunity for interaction."[6] Our comments about borders (Starr and Most, 1976:588) summarize the operative elements of opportunity:

> So that we are not misunderstood, it should be reemphasized that we recognize that a border does not necessarily *cause* either conflictual or cooperative internation interaction. The argument is only meant to imply that a border creates a certain *structure* of risks and opportunities in which various interactions appear to be more or less likely to occur.

Opportunity as interaction possibility is, then, linked to environmental possibilism in two basic ways. First, it closely parallels the idea that what humans do is constrained by the actual possibilities in the "objective" environment. At certain times in history entities were denied the possibility of interaction with others due to spatial and geographic factors; interactions later made possible by technological innovation. Technology, then, can become an agent of inter-action possibility, allowing states to transport information and objects (trade and/or military capability) across natural obstacles and distance in ways not possible before the technological innovation.

Interaction opportunity also means that countries such as Bolivia and Burma *cannot* become engaged in conflict over contiguous borders or territorial issues, because no such border or territory now exists. Thus that possibility, or opportunity, for this kind of war does not exist. This is one reason we have been concerned with borders created by colonial possessions in our diffusion studies— while nineteenth century Britain did not share contiguous land borders with the home territories of France, Germany or Italy, the con-tiguity of their colonial territories in Africa (and elsewhere) created the possibilities for a variety of interactions; including the opportunity for conflict over territory or border violations.

The Sprouts (1969:53) relate environmental possibilism to "capa-bility analysis," which is, "the calculation of the opportunities and limitations implicit in the milieu." This is a second link between op-portunity and possibilism—the existence of capabilities that permit the creation of opportunities (as will be noted, capabilities also af-fect willingness). Here we are again taking into account the often crucial impact of technology. Technology can help produce capabil-ities that modify distance and other aspects of the physical oppor-tunities presented by geography (e.g., Boulding's [1962] "loss-of-strength gradient"). Capabilities, then, not only may pro-mote, but actually permit interaction. Before the Second World War (and prior to the series of Law of the Sea Conferences begin-ning in the 1950s), navies and merchant fleets had to exist before nations clashed over commercial rights, colonies, or the rights of passage on the high seas. Technological capabilities must first exist before the issues of airspace or satellite overflights can become part of the international agenda, and generate conflicts—both among those who have the capabilities, and those who do not.

The two points raised above indicate the dual nature of capabili-ties and possibilities. Initially, some capability—technology, ideol-ogy or religion, form of government, manner of organizing people to some task, etc.—must be created/invented so as to be part of the range of possibilities available to at least some members of the in-ternational system. Examples are the creation of Islam or Marxism, the invention of nuclear weapons or the ballistic missile, or the establishment of the United Nations. A second dimension in the relationship of capabilities and possibilities is the *distribution* of such capabilities in the international system. At one level all international actors share the same menu of possibilities—no one could have nuclear weapons to fight World War I because they had not yet been invented; the United Nations could not send peacekeeping forces to separate United States and Mexican forces in 1846 because such an organization did not yet exist. At another level international actors may have very different menus of possibilities—the wealth, technological talent, and resources needed to take advantage of the nuclear possibility are not evenly distributed. The availability of the United Nations to contemporary states is much more evenly distributed. It is here that environmental probabilism becomes relevant to opportunity. While there is no possibility that a very poor country lacking the requisite resources and expertise to create nuclear weapons could build them, there is still some probability that such weapons could come into their hands because they do exist somewhere in the system and could be transferred to them.

It is important that these two dimensions of opportunity (based on capabilities and possibility) be recognized and distinguished. The uneven distribution of capabilities means that some states will have the ability (opportunity) to take some actions, become involved in some situations that others will not have—in Russett's "menu" analogy: some people will not go into a certain restaurant because they know they do not have enough money. They *could* go in, because the restaurant is there—it exists—but the probability is such that they will not because they lack the capabilities to take advantage of the opportunity. Various types of national economic and military capabilities can influence the types of interaction that may be undertaken. In turn, these interactions can expand the *range* of interaction opportunities with other states creating new possibilities. This dynamic, for example, has been developed and demonstrated in the work on "lateral pressure" (see Choucri and North, 1975; North and Choucri, 1983; Ashley, 1980); it is also central to Galtung's (1964) structural theory of aggression.

Again, "menu" is a useful summary metaphor. One can't eat the meal without being in the restaurant; or give one's order to the waiter; or have the busboy spill water on your silk suit. Thus, the restaurant must exist, and one must be able to get in. In defending the Correlates of War Project's initial focus on contextual or environmental variables, Singer (1970:537) noted that, "A nation, must, in a sense, be in the 'right' setting if it is to get into war." This "right setting" involves the opportunities and possibilities created by the systemic environment—for example, the configuration of power distributions, alliances, intergovernmental organization membership, and other "ecological" variables. Similarly, in our studies of spatial diffusion we have conceptualized environmental conditions as differential treatments that can be studied systematically. That is, we have looked for environmental conditions such as the presences or absence of having a bordering state at war; or an alliance partner at war. Sprague (1982:116), discussing very different substantive phenomena, makes the same point regarding context (or menu): "Social structure enters the theory as determining probable reinforcement schedules: in other words, social structure furnishes *experimental conditions* realizing differing reinforcement phenomena" (emphasis added).

There is yet one more way to look at opportunity. For the purpose of designing analyses, for example studying the impact that common language has on promoting or constraining conflict between groups, Richardson (1960a) would calculate the *statistical* opportunities for conflict that existed. He then had some objective benchmark against which to evaluate the factor under consideration, and the impact it might have had on conflict through history. Richardson recognized that the issue of measuring the effects of variables on violent conflict—increasing or decreasing the likelihood of "deadly quarrels"—was a methodologically difficult one, depending on the range of statistical opportunity for some event to occur.

It is fitting to end this brief overview of opportunity with Richardson's (1960a:288) analogy between war and murder. He simply notes that very few foreigners are murdered within any given country because there are fewer of them to murder. There is just less opportunity. Most murder opportunities arise from close contact and interaction, so that murder victims are most likely to be killed by close relatives or friends. It is much less probable that a person will murder someone he or she does not know, and almost impossible to murder someone with whom there is no contact.

WILLINGNESS

The concept of willingness is more easily handled, being central to the study of decision making and choice. Cognitive behaviorism and environmental probabilism are both relevant to willingness. The dynamics of choice (e.g., the final decision to go to war) are embedded in a decision maker's image of the world, or definition of the situation. Willingness is intimately related to a decision maker's calculations of advantage and disadvantage, of cost and benefit, that decision makers consider on both conscious and unconscious levels.[7] Hence, willingness is related to the congeries of factors (psychological, cognitive, role) that make up the idiosyncratic prism through which individuals process information about their environments. Especially in regard to war, and the calculation of costs and benefits (as in expected utility), decision makers must try to anticipate and approximate the reactions/behavior of others, and see their own behavior constrained within a range of opportunities presented by the environment (governmental, domestic, and international).

An example that illustrates many aspects of willingness, is the common situation where decision makers claim (or commentators argue) that there was "no other alternative" than to go to war. This is an obvious reference to willingness and choice. One becomes more willing to accept the war option, and such acceptance becomes more psychologically satisfying, when other alternatives are severely limited, or eliminated from the decision maker's image of the situation or choice calculus (similar arguments are made in regard to the "preventive motivation" in Levy, 1987). Deutsch (1969:60) has noted that, "Governments frequently—though not always—decide to go to war when they believe themselves to be constrained by the lack of *any acceptable* political alternative to war" (emphasis added).

Such a position removes the probabilistic element of choice, and permits the justification that there was "no other" course of action but war. Thus, willingness may be based on a process whereby the environment is perceived as deterministic rather than probabilistic—the supremacy of cognitive behaviorism over environmental probabilism. Note that the effects of selective perception are varied, and may open up options as well as constrain them. It has been suggested that a creative set of images can suggest courses of action not apparent in the objective situation, but which may work. Returning to the menu analogy, such creative people may ask the waiter for something *not* on the menu—*and get it*.

Willingness thus deals with the variety of (socio-) psychological, perceptual, informational and other processes by which humans perceive their environment. The work in this area covers all aspects of human choice, and the full range of international relations phenomena.[8] These are the processes by which decision makers *recognize* opportunities, and then translate those opportunities into alternatives that are weighed in some manner; willingness means the decision to choose among those alternatives and accept the costs and benefits accompanying that option. The willingness to choose war may be based upon real (relatively accurate) perceptions, or distorted and selective perceptions of security and insecurity, threat, hostility, fear or anxiety. These perceptions may be the result of processes such as displacement, defensiveness, prejudice, conformity or obedience (see, for example, M. Deutsch, 1973; Stagner, 1967; White, 1970; Jervis, 1976; and Milgram, 1974).

ORDERING CONCEPTS: EXAMPLES FROM THE CONFLICT LITERATURE

The reader should already be able to see how various sections of the conflict literature can be sorted and related through opportunity and willingness. In this section we present additional examples. We also indicate the scope of these organizing concepts by indicating how Waltz's three images can be subsumed under opportunity and willingness, just as the Sprouts' concepts were shown to be included within them. Waltz's three images may not only be interpreted in terms of opportunity and willingness, but can be linked together in a more general manner by our two concepts, which have a broader applicability.

Waltz's first image deals with human nature. The views presented under the first image assume that willingness to go to war is always present, as man is viewed from a "realist" perspective and seen to be, by nature, aggressive. Thus, willingness always exists, and we should be looking to those opportunities that trigger this willingness. Radical/Marxist views of predatory free-market modes of dominance and dependence contain similar assumptions about the willingness of the leaders of Western economies and MNCs to exploit LDCs.

On the other hand, Waltz bases his discussion of the third image on the anarchy of the international system and the security dilemma it engenders. The nature of the international system is such that the opportunity for war is always present, so that we should be looking for those factors that bring about the willingness to exploit these opportunities.[9] Structural analysts of dependencia make similar arguments concerning the structure of the world economy.

The second image, the nature of the state (which can be expanded to include the nature and impact of the range of domestic factors) can be seen as containing elements of both opportunity and willingness. As noted, internal capabilities must also be mobilized—people must be convinced to bear the costs of such a mobilization and sacrifice for the foreign policy goals of decision makers. Nationalism, and related mechanisms are used by leaders to mobilize populations and commit them to specific courses of action. Before decision makers can choose a course of action they must understand domestic costs, and the degree to which potential resources, both material and human, can be converted into usable power. The willingness of decision makers to take some foreign policy action is thus also related to the perceived willingness of the society to suffer the costs of that particular foreign policy activity.[10] It is clear, then, that questions of governmental and individual legitimacy, political culture, public opinion and their relationship to the domestic political system, all act to affect willingness.[11]

Following from the relationships between Waltz's third image and opportunity, we can categorize systemic level studies concerned with the configuration of the international system (e.g., Kaplan, 1957; Rosecrance, 1963), its patterns of power and distribution of activity (e.g., Bueno de Mesquita, 1975; Sabrosky, 1985), as those dealing with opportunities. The literature on balance of power and alliances (e.g., Liska, 1962; Claude, 1962; Siverson and King, 1979; Wayman, 1984), on the comparison between bi-polar and multipolar systems (e.g., Rosenau, 1969:291–345; Morgan and Levy, 1986; chap. 6 below), and geopolitical studies, especially in terms of geography affecting interaction (e.g., Spykman, 1944), are all concerned with the structure of opportunities and their relationship to behavior. Nations may exist in a system with powerful neighbors or weak ones; with many neighbors or few; with one, two, or many alliances; with one, two, or many centers of power; with neighboring states that are at peace or with bordering states that are at war. All of these are part of the structure or possibilities, and thus opportunities, presented to any international actor by the international system.

Opportunity may also be seen as a connecting link between various international phenomena and war. One example is the concern with the role of major powers in the onset of war (e.g., Modelski,

1972; Levy, 1983). Much of this argument centers on the greater scope of major power interaction. To be a major power means continual involvement in global and regional politics, and thus to engage in large numbers of interactions that create the opportunity for conflict (e.g., McClelland and Hoggard, 1969; Starr, 1975). Some observers have merged this notion of interaction opportunity with general cycles of warfare among major/hegemonic powers into theories of general or global war (see, for example, Gilpin, 1981; and for useful overviews, see, Levy, 1985; Modelski and Morgan, 1985). As noted, studies of contiguity, borders, and contagion are concerned with opportunities for interaction—with positive relationships occurring between borders and war (e.g., Starr and Most, 1978; Wilkinson, 1980).

Another topic, seemingly unrelated to those noted, but also reliant on the logic of opportunity for interaction, is the literature on conflict resolution that discusses avoidance or the separation of parties, through devices such as United Nations peacekeeping forces (e.g., Boyd, 1971; E. Haas, et al., 1972; E. Haas, 1983). Again, the underlying logic concerns attempts to reduce the opportunity for interaction, in this case physically preventing the armed forces of the parties from getting to each other. Similarly, we can interpret the writings on alternative world futures as addressing the problem of changing the configuration of international units, so that opportunities are reduced (see especially the works of the World Order Models Project, particularly Falk, 1975; Mendlovitz, 1975).

The study of regionalism and integration is also concerned, in part, with reducing the number of "we-they" distinctions within some geographic area, and the forging of one unit where there were many. This concern with group identity, the we-they aspect of human organization, the need to form groups and the consequences of such "subspeciation" as the tendency to perceive outgroups as threatening (as "enemies"), is central to the study of social conflict. These writings, from sociology, social-psychology, anthropology and ethology (e.g., see Coser, 1956; Sherif, 1966; Stein, 1976) deal with the processes by which opportunities for friction and conflict arise because there are distinctive groups.[12] The integration and regionalism literatures are directly related to this aspect of opportunity, as they are concerned with ways in which *commonalities* can be created (e.g., Deutsch's idea of "community" based on responsiveness). These commonalities thus remove opportunities for intergroup conflict by removing the distinctions between groups and creating new, larger, loyalties. Such processes also address, at least on the regional level, the security dilemma that is the focus of Waltz's discussion of the third image.

Many of the items cited immediately above also deal with willingness. Such studies have both macro and micro consequences (and interactions). From the opportunity viewpoint, these studies indicate ways to create new actors or draw new boundaries, and thus new structures and new sets of opportunities for coalition, balancing, and acquisition of resources. But these new structures also mean a new or changing set of incentives. If we are concerned with changing attitudes, loyalties, and perceptions, then we are clearly dealing with willingness.

It is interesting (and important) to note that both Waltz's first image and third image—human nature and the international system—present similar notions of opportunity. Because humans lack the innate physiological mechanisms that prevent the use of violence on other humans, the *possibility* for violence and violent conflict is present. Similarly, the formal "anarchy" of an international system composed of separate and sovereign states makes *possible* the outbreak of organized violence between states.[13] In both cases there are no a priori mechanisms for *preventing* violent conflict. Both images are necessary for violent conflict to occur; neither is sufficient.

It was noted that the second image, or national level of analysis, may apply to both opportunity or willingness, with most treatments of the second image tending to deal with willingness. It was also noted that the vast range of decision-making literature, drawing from psychology, cybernetics, and organization theory, is concerned with how decision makers select among alternatives. The national level of analysis also deals with the domestic and governmental conditions that affect willingness by framing and delineating the possible set of alternatives, and suggesting the behavioral consequences of choosing among them.[14] Recalling that the ability to mobilize support and capabilities affects willingness, it is important to see studies of public opinion and war, studies of the media, studies of leadership as all relating to the domestic environment's effects on the structure of alternatives. Studies about peace movements and peace action, or about activities such as the draft resistance in the United States during the Vietnam War are related to ways that may reduce the willingness of leaders to go to war through lack of societal support. These studies are paralleled by the literature looking at the impact of interest groups, PACs, and single-issue groups that affect foreign policy across all issues (e.g., the reputed strength of the pro-Israeli lobby today, and the pro-Taiwan lobby in the 1950s and 1960s).

On the societal (and small group) level, a number of studies are also concerned with the ways in which socialization, education and group pressures might act to create (or decrease) willingness for conflictual actions. Work on the military-industrial complex, C. Wright Mills-like elite studies, or Janis's notion of "groupthink" (1982), for example, deal with how the societal or group environment affects the decision maker as environed entity. Related studies of ideology and nationalism move away from the decision maker, but are also involved with influences on the decision maker's perceptual screens/belief systems, and how ideological inputs can affect the images that are created. Images that attribute hostility, threat, and the label of the "enemy" (e.g., Gladstone, 1959: White, 1970) are ones that greatly increase willingness to go to war. All of the contexts or environments within which decision makers exist provide stimuli that influence how decisions makers see the world and affect willingness to use violence or other foreign policy tools.

Since deterrence is a psychological relationship, the vast literature on deterrence and nuclear strategy is directly concerned with willingness. Deterrence relies on affecting the calculations of others so that they are *un*willing to take certain actions. Writings on international bargaining and bluffing, commitment, and especially credibility are central to the willingness of decision makers to go to war (e.g., Schelling, 1960, 1966; Snyder and Diesing, 1977; Morgan, 1983; Huth and Russett, 1984). The concept of credibility is a particularly interesting combination of opportunity and willingness. The credibility of a threat requires the communication of both the capabilities (opportunity/possibilism) and the intent/willingness to carry out that threat (e.g., see Singer, 1963).

Willingness deals with the incentives and disincentives for action. This was noted above in the brief reference to the literature on expected utility. The application of game theory to the study of international relations and international conflict deals directly with the manner in which environmental structures, relationships, and payoffs, provide incentives or disincentives for action. The key to the Prisoner's Dilemma (and all its relatives such as the security dilemma, the Tragedy of the Commons, and free-riding in situations marked by collective goods characteristics) is the temptation to defect from cooperation deriving directly from the incentive structure of the situation. Studies of ways to escape the Prisoner's Dilemma (e.g., Axelrod, 1986) concern not only the security dilemma and security issues, but the whole set of free-rider and commons situations in international economic and ecological issues.

Any factors that promote temptation (such as technology that increases the importance of haste as in the pre-World War I mobilization situation, or in a nuclear first-strike), that are thus destabilizing in terms of arms races, arms control, or the first use of weapons, and that lead a party to defect, should be studied as part of willingness.[15] The growing attention to the Prisoner's Dilemma as central to many kinds of cooperation/coordination/conflict is reflected in recent works such as: Jervis (1978); Krasner (1983, especially in the chapter by Stein); Wagner (1983); Snyder (1984); Axelrod (1984); Lipson (1984); Keohane (1984); and Oye (1986, especially the chapter by Snidal).

In this brief overview we have tried to indicate the utility of opportunity and willingness as categories for ordering studies related to international conflict (with a few references to other areas of international relations). This scheme can encompass ordering schemes based on levels of analysis and accommodate those based on disciplinary divisions. We have tried to show that the underlying basis for relating various factors to war can be expressed in terms of either opportunity or willingness. In so doing, we have also provided a preliminary indication of how opportunity and willingness can demonstrate the linkages among apparently diverse topics, and deal with similar phenomena (e.g., borders and contiguity along with United Nations peacekeeping operations and the polarity of the international system).[16]

RELATIONSHIPS BETWEEN OPPORTUNITY AND WILLINGNESS: THEORY AND SUBSTANCE

While some scholars stress the nature of the international system (and thus opportunity) and others stress the aggressiveness of human nature or the flaws running throughout the decision-making process (and thus willingness), neither is a sufficient explanation. Clearly, while humans have always warred, *not all* groups have gone to war (Harrison, 1973:7). Similarly, opportunity and willingness should be viewed as jointly necessary conditions; neither alone is sufficient (see chapter 4). The questions that need to be pursued in-

FIGURE 2.1. Opportunity/Willingness and War

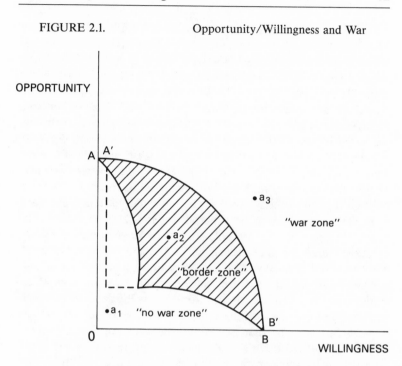

volve what sorts of opportunities trigger what sorts of willingness, under what conditions, and how often. Although opportunity and willingness may be viewed as independent, dependent, and/or intervening variables, let us begin with opportunity and willingness as the independent variable and the interdependent decision outcome of war as the dependent variable.

Figure 2.1 provides one possible graphic representation of this relationship. The shape presented is merely suggestive of the jointly necessary relationship of opportunity and willingness to war. Note first the two extreme cases where there is a high degree of opportunity or willingness, and none of the other (points A and B). At either of these points war could not occur. Thus, the area under AOB could be called the "no war zone." The shape of this area is only suggestive because we can say only that both opportunity and willingness must exist at *some threshold level* before war can occur. Not only may those thresholds vary from state to state, or across historical periods, the threshold for each may vary with the magnitude of the other.[17]

The idea of thresholds is illustrated by the shaded area in figure 2.1. Whereas point a^1 is located in an area where there is inadequate opportunity and willingness for war, and a^3 is located in a "war zone" where there is ample opportunity and willingness for war on both sides of a conflict, and thus the occurrence of war, point a^2 is located in an indeterminate "ambiguous zone." This is an area where either opportunity or willingness may have passed its threshold. If both have gone beyond the threshold, the war will occur. If only one has passed a threshold, then the question is how far must the other go to pass its own threshold. If we have compelling information that the threshold has been achieved in one area, then we must be very concerned with the other area. For example, in regard to nuclear war between the superpowers it is clear that each has passed the opportunity threshold—the knowledge of nuclear weapons exists, each has had the capacity to utilize that knowledge to build weapons, and each now has thousands of such weapons and systems to deliver them. Given that the opportunity exists, most attention over the years has been directed at willingness to use such weapons and the calculations/incentives built into various models of deterrence (e.g., mutual assured destruction). Continuing this example, disarmament can be seen as being directed to *removing* the opportunity for nuclear war by abolishing the nuclear weapons systems necessary for the possibility of such war.

The ambiguity/threshold element in the relationship between opportunity and willingness adds the important element of *process* to the scheme. The ambiguous zone is in some ways analogous to various pre-violence or pre-hostilities stages used in process models of conflict (e.g., Bloomfield and Leiss, 1969, use a pre-hostilities phase, as does Barringer, 1972). The search by some scholars for the factors that move a conflict from one stage to another could be reinterpreted in terms of the ambiguous zone, and the interplay between opportunities, their perception, and the subsequent increase in willingness. Escalation models (e.g., Wright, 1965; Rummel, 1979: part 4; or even Richardson's arms race model) all include structural elements of opportunity which are then plugged into a psychological dynamic.

Perhaps the more interesting and difficult question concerns the possible relationships between opportunity and willingness. One can begin with two simple possibilities: Opportunity can lead to the development of willingness, and willingness can lead to the development of opportunity. How may opportunity affect willingness?

Drawing on the work of Midlarsky (1975), our discussion of borders and diffusion notes that opportunities for interaction can create feelings of insecurity, threat or hostility that may lead to willingness. The existence and location of resources, as elements of opportunity, may lead to increased willingness, (à la lateral pressure models). More generally, Galtung's (1964) notion of rank disequilibrium, where entities have mixed rankings of "topdog" and "underdog" across a variety of factors, is an argument based on capabilities/opportunities (topdog factors) promoting willingness to aggression. This is related to Blainey's (1973:103–104) argument that other opportunities such as rising prosperity (or the availability of newly important resources) could create "bullish optimism," confidence, or feelings of superiority in decision makers which could lead to willingness for war. To note as above—opportunities create incentive structures of cost and benefits; of risk and opportunity; of more and less probable behavior.

There are also ways in which willingness could help to develop opportunity (i.e., "get the waiter to bring something not on the menu"). Willingness, in terms of strongly held images of hostility, fear, revenge, and the like, can bring about misperceptions (or better, selective perceptions) of the activities of other states. Such perceptions can, in turn, lead to behavior on the part of the perceiving decision maker's that provides the interaction opportunities necessary for war. Escalation processes, the security dilemma, and the classic conflict spiral are all examples of this dynamic (e.g., see Jervis, 1976; Axelrod and Keohane, 1986:228–232). Thus, fear of losing a share of available territory could lead to a race for the acquisition of colonies. Subsequent to a colony-race, colonial borders have been created that are now interaction opportunities, and which have been major conduits for the diffusion of war in the post-1945 period (as shown in Starr and Most, 1978; Most and Starr, 1980). This same process occurs in arms races where willingness driven by the security dilemma leads to the creation of capabilities that enhance opportunities or conflict. Given the psychological climate of the security dilemma (fear and hostility), there is a greater probability that willingness and opportunity will combine for war.

Perhaps there is renewed interest in the security dilemma (looking at arms races but going into other security and economic areas as well) because it incorporates the dynamics of the conflict spiral (e.g., North, Brody and Holsti, 1964). The conflict spiral process, one that escalates and is reinforcing, in turn holds a deadly fascination because it seems to be a phenomenon where both opportunity and willingness could be at initially *low* ("no war zone") levels, yet could lead to war. Here, we need not start with either opportunity or willingness already above some war-threatening threshold—but see how initial perceptions may begin a process that could bring both into the ambiguous zone or war zone.

Willingness may also, more directly, create the immediate opportunities that have been called the "trigger" events that actually begin wars. The American instigated border clash that began the Mexican War in May, 1846 is one example. American willingness to have war led to the positioning of troops in such a way almost to ensure that hostile interactions would take place. Willingness created the specific interaction opportunity, or immediate cause, of the war.

As developed in later chapters, while both the opportunity-to-willingness and willingness-to-opportunity relationships exist, several arguments suggest that opportunity-to-willingness is the more prevalent and important. Situations of ample opportunity may require lower levels of willingness to cause war. In effect, this means that figure 2.1 should be less symmetrical, as suggested by the dotted line to the left of the "ambiguous zone." Using the dotted figure, ample opportunity for war exists (e.g., Waltz's arguments regarding the anarchic nature of the system; or Naroll's 1969, study of deterrence across history indicating that "prominent" powers become involved in war regardless of their policy stance). It seems that the more interesting, and manipulable element is the development (or dampening) of willingness within broader incentive structures.

However, as in our conceptualization of diffusion and a later application to the internal-external conflict literature (e.g., Most and Starr, 1980; Starr and Most, 1985b) we must consider *negative* as well as positive relationships. Various opportunities may lead to the *reduction* of willingness. Perhaps the best example is in the impact of changing technology in weaponry. If changing technology can provide offensive or defensive weapons with a clear advantage, the calculations of willingness to initiate conflict or use those weapons, may change and have a dampening effect. Clearly, nuclear weapons and intercontinental delivery systems have *increased* the opportunity to wage war—all states are now possible targets, targets that can be destroyed with a speed never before possible and without having to defeat their armies on the battlefield. Yet the deterrence and strategy literature also indicates that in superpower relationships there has been *less* willingness to go to war than among great powers in other time periods. This was directly discussed as the "fear in the arms race" factor noted by Smoker (1964). The vastly increased costs of war dramatically reduce willingness despite increased opportunities (in speed and range of weapons delivery).[18] Similarly, a lack of willingness may lead to reductions in opportunity (e.g., the dismantling of alliances or colonial empires). There may also be a "negative reinforcement effect" where lessons are learned from past behavior, and willingness at an earlier juncture leads to a *lack* of willingness on subsequent occasions due to the costs of a policy and its outcomes, particularly domestic costs (see, Starr and Most, 1985a).

CONCLUSION

It is obvious that the relationships between opportunity and willingness are complex and must be worked out in greater detail. Opportunity and willingness can help order the implications and contributions of an apparently disparate literature. It should be clear, however, that various studies deal with phenomena that relate to both opportunity and willingness. It should be equally clear that opportunity and willingness do not create mutually exclusive boxes, and that once a study of factors or variables is used to help understand one, it may also be useful in understanding the other. Anything that affects the structural possibilities of the environment(s) within which decision makers must act, also affects the incentive structures for those decision makers. Capabilities, for example, make some actions possible (opportunity) and at the same time make some actions more attractive and others less attractive (willingness).

The relationships between opportunity and willingness will be developed as we move through the logical issues involved in the conceptualization and study of international politics. In turn, opportunity and willingness will help us in this endeavor by pushing us to cross levels of analysis and artificial disciplinary boundaries. We have also noted how opportunity and willingness naturally push us towards process-oriented conceptualizations of international politics in terms of abandoning deterministic models, of unavoidably looking at the decision-making processes of the states involved, and looking at events as the joint interdependent outcomes of two or more states.

While much of the original discussion of opportunity and willingness (Starr, 1978) was sketchy and incomplete, we have attempted, over the years, to fill out the initial framework and apply it to the development of our work across a number of substantive areas. In addition to war, the authors have applied opportunity and willingness to general discussions of the public policy process as it works within states (e.g., Most, 1979; Most and Starr, 1981) and the foreign policy process in general (e.g., Papadakis and Starr, 1985). In addition, these concepts have been integral in developing and applying logical analyses based on necessity and sufficiency first to international conflict, and subsequently to international relations theory as a whole.

While more needs to be done, it should be evident that opportunity and willingness has not been one of those "pre-theoretical" treatments presented to the scholarly community with calls for consideration, and then abandoned by its progenitors. Many of the rather inchoate notions first published in 1978 have now been clarified and developed into a more explicit and useful framework.

3

BASIC LOGIC AND RESEARCH DESIGN:
Conceptualization, Case Selection, and the Form of Relationships

In the opening chapter, various perspectives on the nature of international relations theory, and impediments to the development of such theory, were reviewed. We asserted that lack of attention to basic questions of logic in the development of research design and theory was a major culprit in the lack of theoretical progress and research results. In this chapter we begin to develop the logical basis of inquiry asserted earlier. More specifically, this chapter focuses on two general problems of logical analysis as they apply to the study of international conflict. For the most part unrecognized, these problems act as impediments to the development of a base of verifiable and generalized knowledge about international relations. Again, using war as an illustrative case, we argue that scholars who are interested in understanding and explaining international conflict should recognize that:

1. The attainment or the isolation of answers to the questions they pose is often logically precluded by their method of selecting cases.

   That is, while they have been posing questions of sufficiency ("If some X_1, X_2,..., then war") and using statistical procedures applicable to such queries, they should recognize that their procedure of working backward from the reports of conflict that appear in various war lists limits their focus to an examination of possible necessary relationships ("Only if some X_1, X_2,..., then war").

2. The question of how the determinants in the process that leads to war are related to one another and to conflict itself is as important as which factors are the determinants.

That is, while they have focused on identifying the determinants of war and have tended to use simple linear and additive formulations, they should recognize that the tasks of specifying the form of the relationships among their predictors and the linkages between them and the dependent variable are no less important.

These contentions are not entirely original. As the discussion below suggests, certain elements of both problems are well understood in the literature on experimental and quasi-experimental research. A discussion of the points seems warranted, however, precisely because they are rather basic, logical problems that generally seem to have escaped the attention of most international relations analysts. Indeed, the problems reviewed here are worthy of discussion because they are by no means limited to research on international conflict. They seem endemic, for example, to much of the work on alliances, the determinants of public policies, and research on causes of bureaucratic-authoritarian rule in developing countries.

PROBLEM 1: CASE SELECTION AND THE CONCEPTUALIZATION OF WAR

Three preliminary points are essential for an understanding of the first problem. The first is that researchers who are concerned with the factors that lead to the outbreak of international conflict are, in actuality, like most students of international relations, analysts of events data.[1] Although they often say that they are concerned with some *process* that leads to war, they begin their work by developing (or borrowing) reports of war occurrences and by focusing on war occurrences—events—that are at best only the "traces" or "residues" of conflict processes. While they have debated the validity and reliability of those lists,[2] each analyst eventually selects one or more data sets and proceeds to focus on those occasions in which wars are therein reported to have actually occurred. This is the case for practically all social science inquiry into war, inasmuch as they use the basic data sets collected by Quincy Wright, Lewis F. Richardson, the Correlates of War Project (COW), Stockholm International Peace Research Institute (SIPRI), Istvan Kende, or the various events-data projects such as Cooperation and Peace Data Bank (COPDAB), World Events Interaction Survey (WEIS), or Comparative Research on the Events of Nations (CREON).

Put differently, each such analyst begins with some list of wars $(Y_1, Y_2, \ldots, Y_n)$ and works backward in order to explore and understand the factors $(X_1, X_2, \ldots, X_m)$ that preceded the reported events and that may have contributed to their occurrence. In some instances, explicit hypotheses are developed; in other work, brute statistical procedures are employed. In either situation, the focus of the analysis is on identifying those factors that alone or in combination were sufficient for the outbreak of war—that is, they search for (or test) relations of the form: "If X_1, X_2, \ldots, and/or X_m, then war."

All of this seems perfectly straightforward. If one is interested in why wars occur (or any event resulting from interdependent choice), then it is a matter of course that one should focus on the actual occurrences of such events. To do otherwise would seem like a waste of time. The point to be argued below, however, is that these reasonable and accepted procedures may be deceiving. Analysts are likely to be led astray by attempts to explain wars (or any phenomenon Y) by working backward from such events in order to isolate their sufficient antecedents.

The second preliminary point entails considering the three propositions shown in figure 3.1 that posit linkages between two hypothetical factors X and Y.[3] In each, X (the antecedent) is related to Y (the consequent). As will be recalled from logic, however, the nature of the X/Y relationships is slightly different in each proposition. In the first, X is posited as a sufficient but not a necessary condition for Y. Whenever X occurs, Y follows, but Y may not invariably be preceded by X. Some other factors (V or Z) could also produce Y.

In the second statement, X is posited as a necessary but not sufficient condition for Y. Whenever Y occurs it must have been preceded by X, but Y may not always occur whenever X does. Some other additional factor (Z) may also need to be present before Y will occur. Finally, the third statement in figure 3.1 posits X as both a necessary and sufficient condition for Y. Whenever X occurs, Y will follow; whenever Y occurs, it must have been preceded by X. Note that the body of this section and the next focuses on dichotomous factors X and Y. They are either present (X, Y) or absent (-X, -Y). The important point for the reader to remember is that this perspective is adopted only in order to maximize logical clarity. As the discussion eventually suggests, the same problems develop if analysts are working with indicators that have higher levels of measurement.

FIGURE 3.1.   Necessary and Sufficient Relationships
between X and Y: Possible Causes of Y

a). If X, then Y.

> X is sufficient, but not necessary for Y.
>
> X always leads to Y; Y not always preceded by X.
>
> All cases in the double-hatched area are Y.
>
> Some cases in the single-hatched area may be Y.

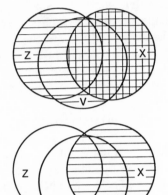

b). Only if X, then Y.

> X is necessary, but not sufficient for Y.
>
> X does not always lead to Y; Y is always preceded by X.
>
> Some cases in the single-hatched area may be Y.

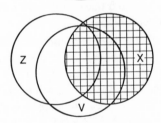

c). If and only if X, then Y.

> X is both necessary and sufficient for Y.
>
> X always leads to Y; Y is always preceded by X.
>
> All cases in the double-hatched area are Y.

V, Z = alternative possible causes of Y.

An Exclusive Focus on Occurrences of the Independent Variable: Sufficiency but Not Necessity

Finally, consider the third preliminary point, the logical reverse—and actually the better understood—aspect of the first problem. Scholars frequently focus on a certain phenomenon and utilize that factor as an independent variable in their analyses. Such a design is common in the policy evaluation literature: Given some policy innovation or change (X), what is its impact (Y)? Scholars who focus on arms races or conflict spirals pose much the same query: given an arms race (X), what is its effect on the occurrence of war (Y)?

Suppose now that an analyst is interested in such a question. Suppose also that a complete list of *all* of those instances in which X has

TABLE 3.1   Sampling on Only Examples With the Occurrence of an
Independent Variable

CASES INCLUDED

PATTERN I
Case 1   X   Y
Case 2   X   Y
Case 3   X   Y

PATTERN II
Case 1   X   Y
Case 2   X   -Y
Case 3   X   -Y

POSSIBLE PATTERN IN OMITTED CASES
Case 4   -X   Y
Case 5   -X   Y
Case 6   -X   Y

Key:

X: The occurrence of some independent variable
-X: The nonoccurrence of some independent variable
Y: The occurrence of some dependent variable
-Y: The nonoccurrence of some dependent variable

ever occurred is compiled and that the researcher elects to include only those cases in the sample. What types of linkage or relational queries can logically be considered? By examining all of those occasions in which X occurred but only those cases, the analyst will be able to test the question of X/Y*sufficiency*. If X was invariably followed by Y (as in pattern 1 in table 3.1), the investigator will have some reason to conclude that the evidence is consistent with the proposition that X was indeed a sufficient condition for Y.[4] The X/Y hypothesis will not be rejected. On the other hand, if X did not tend to be followed by Y (as in pattern 2), the analyst will be in a position to conclude that X was not a sufficient condition for the occurrence of Y. The X/Y hypothesis will be abandoned.

The problem, of course, is that the analyst who selects cases in this fashion (i.e., focuses exhaustively on the occurrences of the independent variable X but also exclusively on only those occurrences) cannot draw any conclusions about whether or not X is a necessary condition for Y. The principle of selecting only on X and omitting cases of non-X (-X) will lead the researcher to overlook and exclude from analysis any cases in which Y occurred *even though* it was not preceded by X. The analyst's design would be appropriate for testing whether or not X is a sufficient condition for Y (statements in group a, figure 3.1) as has been said, but it would not be appropriate for considering the necessary conditions of the dependent variable Y (statements in group b, figure 3.1).

An Exclusive Focus on Occurrences of the Dependent Variable: Necessity but Not Sufficiency

The problem just delineated is well recognized in the policy evaluation or policy impact literature and has led, of course, to the elaboration of the simple "pretest/posttest with control group design" (Campbell and Stanley, 1963; Zetterberg, 1966). Analysts who are interested in some X/Y relationship must eschew an exclusive focus on cases in which X was present; other cases—*control group(s)*—in which X did not occur (-X) must be included in the analysis. The concept of control group is important for it forces the investigator to consider the possibility of -X and -Y cases. If, in the rare instance that no such cases could be found after a thorough search, the investigator would be able to draw some very strong conclusions about the results. Only through the use of such control groups can the researcher escape the logical problem noted above and pose questions of both the sufficiency and the necessity of X for Y.

The point that appears to be less well understood is that the difficulty reviewed in the previous section has a symmetrical opposite. If the analyst who is interested in an X/Y relationship elects to include all of those cases in which the dependent variable Y occurred but focuses only on those cases, something approaching either pattern 1 or pattern 2 in table 3.2 might be obtained. By examining the cases in such a sample, the analyst can determine whether or not the occurrences of Y were invariably preceded by X. If they were (as in pattern 1 of table 3.2) there will be reason to conclude that X was a necessary condition for Y. The X/Y hypothesis will not be rejected. On the other hand, if Y was not always preceded by X (as in pattern 2 in table 3.2) there will be reason to conclude that X was not a necessary condition for Y. The hypothesis could then be rejected.

The analyst who elects to focus exclusively on "successful" occurrences of the dependent variable Y and attempts to work backward from such events to discover their antecedents (X_1, X_2,...,

TABLE 3.2 Sampling on Only Examples With the Occurrence of a
Dependent Variable

CASES INCLUDED

PATTERN I
Case 1 X Y
Case 2 X Y
Case 3 X Y

PATTERN II
Case 1 –X Y
Case 2 –X Y
Case 3 X Y

POSSIBLE PATTERN IN OMITTED CASES
Case 4 X –Y
Case 5 X –Y
Case 6 X –Y

Key:

X: The occurrence of some independent variable
–X: The nonoccurrence of some independent variable
Y: The occurrence of some dependent variable
–Y: The nonoccurrence of some dependent variable

X_m) will not be able, however, to test the question of whether or not
any given X_1 is sufficient for Y. In excluding those cases in which Y
did not occur, the analyst cannot be certain that the sample has not
also excluded cases in which X did appear but was followed by Y. A
focus on the full universe of cases in which Y as a dependent variable has occurred—is appropriate for assessing the possible necessary conditions of Y (statements in group b, figure 3.1), but such a
design is *in*appropriate for probing the sufficient conditions of Y
(statements in group a, figure 3.1). In terms of the study of war, for
example, this requires that "peace" (meaning negative peace which
denotes only the absence of war) must also be studied—that the dependent variable include nonwar outcomes as well. This can be
done by looking at cases of some independent variable X—e.g., crisis, alliance formation, arms races—that is not followed by war. Alternatively, one might select periods of time when the relevant
populations—e.g., all major powers, specific sets of dyads, specific

TABLE 3.3   Consequences of Selective Sampling for Hypothesis
            Testing

PATTERN I

Case 1	X	Y
Case 2	X	Y
Case 3	X	Y
Case 4	X	-Y
Case 5	X	-Y
Case 6	X	-Y

PATTERN II

Case 1	X	Y
Case 2	X	Y
Case 3	X	Y
Case 4	-X	Y
Case 5	-X	Y
Case 6	-X	Y

Key:

    X: The occurrence of some independent variable
   -X: The nonoccurrence of some independent variable
    Y: The occurrence of some dependent variable
   -Y: The nonoccurrence of some dependent variable

regions—experienced no wars, and investigate the presence or absence of the independent variables under consideration (see further discussion of this point below and in note 6).

Consider now an additional complication. Suppose that the universe or full population of cases displays the X/Y relations shown in pattern 1 in table 3.3 and that two analysts are attempting to understand the nature of that X/Y relationship. The first investigator elects to focus on only those cases in which Y appears: the second decided to consider only those cases in which X occurs. Following his strategy, researcher 1 would fail to reject the X/Y hypothesis; in that analyst's sample, Y was invariably preceded by X. Researcher 2, in contrast, would reject the hypothesis; in that sample, X was not invariably followed by Y. The two researchers, focusing on the same body of evidence but doing so in different ways, would be led to different conclusions.

The results are reversed, of course, if pattern 2 in table 3.3 resembles the "true" X/Y relationship. An analyst selecting on Y would reject the hypothesis; an investigator sampling on X would fail to reject it. Once again, even though the full body of evidence is the same, two analysts can produce diametrically opposed findings if they happen to focus their analyses in different ways.

Generalizing Problem 1

All of this is important, it should now be apparent, because most researchers who are interested in the onset of international conflict fail to understand the problem. In attempting to explain why nations go to war, they often in effect focus on conflicts that are reported to have occurred—successful occurrences of the dependent war variable—and work backward. Using a design or case selection procedure that is appropriate only for probing possible necessary relationships, they proceed to examine questions of sufficiency and utilize statistical techniques that are appropriate for such queries. They fail to match the cases they consider with the questions that they ask and the methods that they employ.

The tendency to pose questions of sufficiency but to design studies that actually are suited for test of possible necessary conditions is widespread throughout the literature where hypotheses are constructed in the "If-X–then-Y" fashion, with Y being some form of war or violent conflict. Such a design was almost standard for both quantitative studies of comparative foreign policy and the research on conflict that appeared from the 1950s through to the mid-to-late 1970s. Much of the work of the Dimensionality of Nations Project and the early analyses of the Correlates of War Project fit the pattern.[5]

In an analysis focusing on the possible relationship between domestic political instability and foreign conflict behavior of the African nations during the 1964–1969 period, for example, Copson (1973) excludes all nonconflictual foreign policy events from the investigation. In a second study concerning the question of whether or not "serious disputes between nations engaged in an arms race have a significantly greater probability of resulting in all out war than those between nations exhibiting more normal patterns of military competition," Wallace is in effect probing whether or not arms races and disputes have an interactive effect (dispute/arms race) on war (1979:244). He does this, however, by considering only the ninety-nine major power disputes that are reported to have occurred between 1816 and 1965. While it should be noted that he is cautious in concluding only that it is difficult to argue that the dispute/arms race combination plays no role in leading to the onset of war, the force of that conclusion is undercut by his failure to include examples of the "no dispute/arms race" combination. Yet another illustration of this tendency is the work of Garnham who proceeds to investigate the probability of "lethal international violence" by studying only "all pairs of contiguous nation-sates which experienced lethal international violence during the period 1969–73" (1976:380–381). A list of further examples would be almost endless. An early effort by one of the authors fits the pattern (Starr, 1972). In fact, even certain chapters in Richardson's otherwise pathbreaking *Statistics of Deadly Quarrels* (1960a) fails to avoid the trap.

Failure to recognize the necessity/sufficiency distinction has not only affected research design, but the quality of the critical evaluation of research as well. Without reviewing the range of criticism in detail, we may note one of the charges against the expected utility research reported in Bueno de Mesquita's book, *The War Trap* (1981a). This is the complaint of "over prediction." That is, a number of critics have found it problematic that states have positive expected utility far more often than they initiate conflicts. The correct response, which is noted clearly at several points in his chapter 1, is that Bueno de Mesquita is concerned with *necessary* conditions, and not with issues related to possible *sufficient* conditions.

Bueno de Mesquita's argument can be simply restated as: "only if decision makers have positive expected utility $[+E(U)]$, then do they initiate conflict." Given our discussion above, such an argument implies that while conflict initiations should *always be preceded* by positive expected utility, positive expected utility *may not always* lead to a conflict initiation. The point to stress is that Bueno de Mesquita's hypothesis does not expect a conflict initiation to occur simply because $+E(U)$ is present.

Consider the following cross-tab type table which provides a set of relationships between X (expected utility) and Y (conflict initiation):

		Expected Utility	
		≤ 0	> 0
		(-X)	(X)
Conflict	Yes (Y)	(1)	(2)
Initiation	No (-Y)	(3)	(4)

Recall that the necessary relationship, only if X then Y, means that X's could sometimes occur but not lead to Y's. The alleged over prediction problem of the expected utility model arises because there are numerous cases falling in cell 4. The issue, however, is not how many cases fall in cell 4. If $+E(U)$ is necessary for conflict initiation, then the hypothesis does not depend on cell 4, and the number of cases in that cell is irrelevant. The issue revolves around how many cases there are in cell 1. Necessity implies that cell 1 should be empty. Reviewing *The War Trap*, one sees that despite a large number of analyses of war, alliance and other phenomena, cell 1 *is* practically empty, with less than a handful to be found there.[6] Given this discussion, and the range of examples noted, it is hardly surprising that the results of research efforts have not always seemed to add up or shed much light on the solution to the puzzle of war.

The difficulty here is not avoided, it should be noted, by analysts who reject a dichotomous operationalization (e.g., war/nonwar) in favor of continuous variables such as the duration of the conflict, its extent of deadliness, the number of combatants and so on (e.g., see Singer and Small, 1972; Small and Singer, 1982). If a researcher elects to operationalize the war concept in terms of the number of battle deaths incurred, for example, the sample will include the set of events in which the deaths range from some maximum number and some minimum that is greater than zero. The events of cases included in the analysis would consist exclusively of state behaviors in which deaths resulted. Inasmuch as there is an effectively limitless number of cases through time and across space in which state behaviors do not result in deaths, however, it follows that the behaviors included in the study would be nonrepresentative of the full universe of state behaviors. Unless and until the minimum number of deaths is reduced to zero, all nonsuccessful occurrences of the dependent variable (i.e., nonwar events in which deaths equal zero) would be excluded. The analyst would in effect, therefore, still be focusing exclusively on successful occurrences of the dependent variable (i.e., on indicators of actually occurring wars).[7]

The logical problem outlined above is exacerbated by problems of conceptualization (see chapter 4). The concept "war" as it is used in much of the literature is a curious "one-tailed" concept which has no well-understood or measured opposite. While analysts will occasionally pay passing attention to the notion of a continuum between "peace" and "war,"[8] they appear to have no clear conception of what war is not or of what they have when they are confronted with nonwar events. As a result, each researcher focuses on wars as one tail in the distribution of state behaviors. The investigator's sample is nonrepresentative of the universe of state behaviors, includes only Y's (which may or may not be coded as being of varying magnitude, duration, or intensity), and excludes all examples of the lower end of the distribution of behaviors (-Y's or nonwar events).

The importance of studying nonwar is also crucial, of course, when working forward from war lists to an understanding of the effects of impacts of international conflict. There may be no need to belabor the obvious, however. Both of the more *general* logical principles should be clear:

1. Scholars can work forward from a given list of events to test whether or not those occurrences are necessary conditions for some subsequently occurring phenomenon if and only if the events in the sample reflect the full range of possible variation in such events.
2. Scholars can work backward from a given list of events to isolate the conditions that were sufficient for causing them if and only if the events of the sample reflect the full range of the possible variation in such events.

Put more contextually, working forward to understand the consequences for which war is necessary logically entails the inclusion of examples of both war and peace as the independent variable while an understanding of the conditions that are sufficient for war logically entails the inclusion of both war and peace as the dependent variable.

It is possible to identify researchers who seem to be doing these things.[9] Their work avoids the specific problem under review here and suggests how others might proceed. In some instances, these researchers are looking for thresholds and escalation processes that will indicate why crises do and do not stop short of violent conflict; in other cases, the analysts are developing general scales that include various forms of violent and nonviolent conflict and cooperative events. In this body of research at least, the investigators are concerning themselves with situations in which war does and does not occur and with a more dynamic, process-oriented perspective on the study of international conflict. It should be clear, even from these initial comments on the impact of logical analysis, that a process perspective increases the chances of avoiding basic logical design problems, while static, cross-national, attribute analyses decrease such chances.

PROBLEM 2: SPECIFYING THE "FORM" OF THE RELATIONSHIP

An understanding of the constraints imposed by existing case selection procedures and conceptualizations of war is important, but a second—again rather basic and logical—problem should also be considered. Put simply, researchers who have been concerned with the causes of international conflict have tended to begin with war lists and focus on identifying the factors that preceded the reported events. They have focused on the question, "Which predictors have the greatest potency?" They have done too much hypothesis testing. In too many instances, students of war have failed to think through the processes that they posit; they have failed to model them or to specify the initial conditions under which the relationships should be expected to hold. In many cases, analysts have relied too heavily on bivariate, linear (or multivariate, linear additive) statistical techniques that are designed to assess sufficiency relationships; they have generally failed to probe nonlinear or interactive effects. Much of this is equally applicable to the comparative study of foreign policy (see Hermann, Kegley and Rosenau, 1987; Papadakis and Starr, 1987).

All of these problems, failures, and limitations are recognized in the literature, especially in the discussions of cumulation. It is generally admitted that such difficulties are important. Along with other factors that space precludes mentioning, they seem to have inhibited the development of a theory to explain international conflict.

That said, however, the point here is that researchers on the causes of war and their critics have also overlooked the important question of the *logical forms* of the relationships they study. While it is important to consider just what linkages hold, when, where, and why, there is also a need to consider the basic issue of the different types of logical linkages or connectives that may pertain among their predictors and between those factors and their conflict measures. Efforts to answer the potency question, to model processes, to utilize nonlinear or interactive multivariate statistical techniques, and so on are likely to become more productive once analysts recognize that there is a need to understand the basic, logical means by which—how—predictors relate individually to one another and collectively with the dependent variable.

The point that one's theoretical perspective is important for understanding will be illustrated below in general terms. For the moment, however, it may be useful to contrast the differing results obtained in several actual analyses, all of which focus on the general question of the diffusion or spread of war. Consider first an investigation by Altfeld and Bueno de Mesquita (1979) in comparison with two studies by Siverson and King (1979, 1980). The two teams of scholars focus, at some stages at least, on much the same problem: the effects (if any) that alliance ties have on third-party decisions to join ongoing wars. They use much the same data bases and spatio-temporal domains. They arrive, however, at what seems to be strikingly different conclusions. Using simple Yule's Q's in their 1979 study and discriminant analysis in their 1980 effort, Siverson and King conclude that (1) "A nation having an alliance with a belligerent is five times more likely to become involved in war" (1979:44), and (2) "the characteristics of a nation's alliance configuration influence whether it will participate in a war alongside its alliance partners" (1980:13). However, after applying a rational choice model of "how decision makers choose sides, or neutrality, in ongoing wars" first to a sample that includes all third parties between 1816 and 1965 and then to a sample that includes only those third parties that had bilateral alliance ties with an initial antagonist, Altfeld and Bueno de Mesquita conclude the opposite that "the 'allied' subset and the analysis that includes all cases...yield similar results" (1979:87, 103).

The importance of theory and its impact on the interpretability of one's findings is perhaps even more apparent in the author's own research on war diffusion. At one stage, the application of simple stochastic models led to the conclusion that there was little evidence to suggest that states' war participations, as reported by the Correlates of War Project, tended to diffuse during the 1945–1965 era (Most and Starr, 1976). That more-or-less atheoretical finding contrasts sharply with a result obtained in a subsequent, more theoretically informed, analysis: States that shared a border with a warring nation were nearly five times more likely to become involved in war themselves than countries whose bordering nations were all at peace (Most and Starr, 1980). The stochastic modeling effort bordered on crude empiricism. It neither revealed nor taught us very much. Once the question of how wars might possibly diffuse had been thought through and the rudiments of a more sophisticated theoretical formulation had been put in place, however, we understood much better just what to look for. It should be clear that it was the improvement in our theoretical formulation and the greater attention to logic that lent us the increased leverage on the problem of war diffusion and led to the new result.

The importance of theory and the need for a more self-consciously logical approach can be demonstrated more clearly, perhaps, by considering a hypothetical example in which an analyst is in possession of a theoretical formulation that is complete in every way except insofar as it leaves open questions regarding the logical forms of the relationships. More formally, let us consider the situation where:

1. A researcher who is interested in the occurrence of some phenomenon Y has, from the full range of possible factors that might have been considered, correctly concluded that it is X_1 and/or X_2 that "cause(s)" Y.
2. The two predictors have a determinative, rather than probabilistic, impact on Y so that whenever the appropriate combination of X_1 and/or X_2 occurs, Y will follow.
3. The researcher's indicators of the three concepts are all valid and reliable.
4. The analyst has recognized and overcome the problem reviewed in the previous section. The sample includes both instances of Y and -Y.

All that the investigator needs to do in this situation is to specify the *forms of the relationship* that hold among the two (or three) variables. The investigator needs only to delineate the "true" linkage between the antecedent(s) and the consequent in the hypothesis ("If. . ., then. . ." or "Only if. . ., then. . .") and the relationships between the factors X_1 and X_2 in the antecedent clause ("and" or "or"). (A number of $X_1/X_2/Y$ possibilities are shown in figure 3.2.)[10]

Consider the pattern in the data on X_1, X_2, and Y, which is shown in part A of table 3.4. How might analysts in the situation just described attempt to understand it? The predilection would probably be to begin with the two bivariate/sufficient hypotheses a1 and a2. (Readers interested in diagrammatic presentations of those hypotheses and the others shown in table 3.4 may consult the correspondingly sequenced diagrams in figures 3.1 and 3.2.) Alternatively, a linear additive, multivariate/sufficient hypothesis might be examined (proposition e). Under the impetus of the critics mentioned above, analysts might even plump for a hypothesis in which X_1 and

FIGURE 3.2.   Elaboration of Necessary and Sufficient
                       Relationships: Possible Causes of Y

d). If X_1 and X_2, then Y.

Independently not necessary;
jointly not necessary; jointly
sufficient.

(X_1X_2) always leads to Y; Y not
always preceded by (X_1X_2), by
X_1 or by X_2.

All cases in the double-
hatched area are Y.

Some cases in the single-
hatched area may be Y.

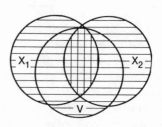

e). If X_1 or X_2, then Y.

Independently not necessary;
jointly not necessary; independently sufficient.

X_1 or X_2 always leads to Y;
Y not always preceded by
(X_1X_2), by X_1 or by X_2.

All cases in the double-
hatched area are Y.

Some cases in the single-
hatched area may be Y.

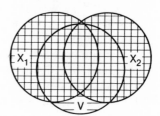

f). Only if X_1 and X_2, then Y.

Jointly necessary; in-
dependently not sufficient;
jointly not sufficient.

(X_1X_2), X_1 and X_2 do not
always lead to Y; Y always
preceded by (X_1X_2).

Some cases in the single-
hatched area may be Y.

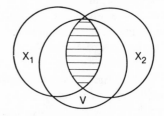

g). Only if X_1 or X_2, then Y.

Independently necessary; independently not sufficient;
jointly not sufficient.

(X_1X_2), X_1 and X_2 do not
always lead to Y; Y always
preceded by X_1 or X_2.

Some cases in the single-
hatched area may be Y.

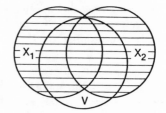

h). If and only if X_1 and X_2 then Y.

Jointly necessary; jointly
sufficient.

(X_1X_2) always leads to Y; Y
always preceded by (X_1X_2).

All cases in the double-
hatched area are Y.

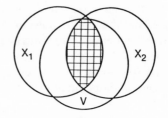

V = alternative possible cause of Y.

X_2 are posited to have an interactive/sufficient effect on Y (proposition d).

A minor and a major point should be recognized in this. The minor point is that, while researchers would have tended almost automatically to test hypotheses a1, a2, d, and e, those possible sufficiency relationships could not logically have been examined had not both Y's and -Y's been included in the sample. The second point, more germane to the focus of this section, is that analysts would be likely to ignore the other types of ways—and in the example at hand in table 3.4, the actual ways—in which X_1, X_2, and Y might be interrelated. Hypotheses b1, b2, c1, c2, f, g, h, i1, and i2 would in all likelihood be overlooked even though all of those posited linkages are logically possible.

Consider the problem from a different perspective. What is the likelihood that analysts might be able to induce the existence of complex, logical linkages from the pattern in part A of table 3.4? The task may appear facile, but in fact it is not. Knowing everything that needs to be known—except the nature of the logical connectives—the analyst would have considerable difficulty in making sense of the data. If we assume that the investigator's logical horizons are expanded so that the range of possibilities suggested is fully recognized, hypotheses a1, a2, c1, c2, and e would lead an analyst to conclude that neither X_1 nor X_2 is related to Y. (This would be especially troublesome, of course, if the researcher thinks only of propositions a1, a2, or 3; the two factors X_1 and X_2, which in fact have a "true" and truly determinative impact on Y would be discarded and excluded from further analyses.) Propositions d, h, i1, and i2 would lead to the inference that moderately strong associations exist. In all of these propositions, the researcher would be rejecting—or at the very least underestimating the significance of—relationships that are "nearly true." The investigator would be on the verge of abandoning a focus on X_1 or X_2, or at the very best concluding that what is in fact a perfectly determinative relationship is probabilistic.

The analyst could also err in the opposite direction, however. Hypotheses b1, b2, and g are all strongly supported by the pattern in part A of table 3.4. The difficulty here, of course, is that those propositions are only partially valid. The analyst could end up embracing (or only failing to reject) what is in fact a false hypothesis. Only one proposition actually fits the data: Only if X_1 and X_2, then Y (proposition f).

TABLE 3.4   Alternative Hypotheses and Consequences of Logic in
Design

PART A

Case 1 X^2 X^1 Y
Case 2 X^2 $-X^1$ $-Y$
Case 3 $-X^2$ X^1 $-Y$
Case 4 X^2 X^1 $-Y$

PART B*

	Hypotheses	Proportion of Occurrences in Part A	
a1.	If X^1, then Y.	1/3	33.3%†
a2.	If X^2, then Y.	1/3	33.3%
b1.	Only if X^1, then Y.	1/1	100.0%‡
b2.	Only if X^2, then Y.	1/1	100.0%‡
c1.	If and only if X^1, then Y.	1/3	33.3%
c2.	If and only if X^2, then Y.	1/3	33.3%
d.	If X^1 and X^2, then Y.	1/2	50.0%
e.	If X^1 or X^2, then Y.	1/4	25.0%
f.	Only if X^1 and X^2, then Y.	1/1	100.0%‡
g.	Only if X^1 or X^2, then Y.	1/1	100.0%‡
h.	If and only if X^1 and X^2, then Y.	1/2	50.0%
i1.	X^2 as an explicit control:		
	If X^2: If X^1, then Y.	1/2	50.0%
	If $-X^2$: If X^1, then Y.	0/1	0.0%
i2.	X^1 as an explicit control:		
	If X^1: If X^2, then Y.	1/2	50.0%
	If $-X^1$: If X^2, then Y.	0/1	0.0%

Key:

  X^1: The occurrence of some independent variable
  $-X^1$: The nonoccurrence of some independent variable
  X^2: The occurrence of some second independent variable
  $-X^2$: The nonoccurrence of the second independent variable
  Y: The occurence of some dependent variable
  $-Y$: The nonoccurrence of some dependent variable

---

*   Readers interested in diagramatic presentations of hypotheses of
    types (a) through (h) may consult the correspondingly sequenced
    Venn Diagrams in Figures 3.1 and 3.2. Slightly different explications
    of those relationships are shown in note 10.
†   In "If..., then..." hypotheses, the reported scoring is based on the
    occurrences of the antecedent. In "Only if..., then..."
    propositions, it is based on the occurence of the consequent. In "If
    and only if..., then..." statements, it is based on the simultaneous
    occurrence of both.
‡   The pattern displayed by the universe of cases in Part A is consistent
    only with proposition f. Simple truth tables can be used to
    demonstrate that if (f) is true, however, statements b1, b2, and g are
    also true. See: Kemeny, Snell and Thompson (1966).

Thus, even within the very simplified situation implied by the assumptions above, the analyst is likely to face an enormously difficult task. Relax those assumptions, and the complexity of the difficulties begins to become clear. An understanding of the causes of international phenomena such as conflict will undoubtedly require the development of a theory that is basically true, involves the correct concepts, has valid and reliable indicators of those concepts, and is tested on a sample that is representative of the full range of the possible variation in the dependent variable. Such developments are not likely to come easily. Even with them, however, the analyst will still need something more that is all too often entirely overlooked or presumed by those who rely on existing statistical techniques. The analyst will still need to pay careful attention to basic logical issues. It will be necessary to specify the proper linkages between the antecedents and the consequents and to denote correctly the relationships among the factors in the antecedents even if those logical associations cannot readily be tested using standard statistical procedures.

The importance of this point and the attention given here to necessary relationships is perhaps underscored by Bueno de Mesquita in one of the few studies that explicitly recognizes the differences between investigating necessary and sufficient factors in the outbreak of war. As he carefully observes, his work constitutes a test of "necessary, but not sufficient, conditions for the initiation of serious interstate conflicts, including war" (1980a:917). The authors' work on diffusion adopts a similar perspective. It focuses on the relationship between two specific factors and the outbreak of war but suggests that a focus on the possible sufficiency of either one of them independently or jointly should not be expected to add up or make sense. It would not yield a solution to Zinnes's puzzle regarding the causes of war. The thesis that is expected to make sense, organize reality, and provide at least a partial solution to the puzzle suggests that the two factors should have a jointly necessary and sufficient impact on the initiation of war. Thus, it is possible to imagine, formulate, test, and—if the work completed is indicative—actually discover support for complex necessary relationships.

CONCLUSIONS

At least six lessons appear to follow from the discussion. Analysts who are concerned with developing an understanding of the factors leading to such phenomena as the outbreak of international conflict should recognize the following:

1. Case selection procedures or conceptual limitations define what queries can be tested.
2. While the samples or cases that are commonly considered by analysts who study the causes of international conflict logically permit only the investigation of the factors that are *necessary* for the occurrence of such events, analysts have overlooked that limitation, mismatched their cases with their questions, and attempted to test possible *sufficient* hypotheses.
3. Because many of the existing analyses have mismatched cases and questions in this fashion (i.e., have attempted to test possible sufficient hypotheses on samples that are appropriate for probing only necessary linkages) the status of the findings produced in such work would appear to be in serious doubt.
4. The failure to include cases that reflect the full range of the possible variation in their dependent war variables limits scholars to the assessment of only necessary relationships and thereby precludes their use of standard statistical procedures, regardless of how many predictors are employed or whether they are entered in additive, multiplicative, linear, or nonlinear fashion.
5. Even if case selection and conceptualization problems are overcome, the existing statistical procedures limit analysts to probing only a very limited range of the linkages that are logically possible.
6. Because the statistical techniques that are commonly employed by quantitative analysts of international relations and conflict have biased them toward an almost exclusive focus on possible sufficient relationships, there is a need for both a better understanding of alternative types of logical linkages (what types of relationships are possible) and improved substantive theoretical knowledge (what types of relationships are probable).

In short, logic and conceptualization in the design of research are crucial. In regard to war, analysts must study peace as well as war and refocus their attention on conflict processes. The points are basic. The fact that they have been generally overlooked suggests yet another explanation for the apparent failure to solve the puzzle of the war proneness of states. As noted in the opening chapter, the logical problems identified here are closely related to problems of conceptualization—the translation of the idea of war into more specified questions, indicators and data. The relationships among theory, logic, and data (the research triad) are pursued further in the next chapter, where logical tools are applied to a further conceptualization of war.

4

CONCEPTUALIZING WAR:
Attributes and Process

INTRODUCTION
In this chapter we wish to demonstrate how the application of logical analysis can help clarify concepts central to the study of international relations. As noted above, this will be facilitated through the use of one example that can be investigated in depth. Thus, following on the two central concerns addressed in chapter 3, the purpose of this chapter is to focus on two additional problems that appear to have hindered the development of a solution to the "puzzle" regarding the war proneness of nations. Specifically, we suggest that scholars who are interested in understanding and explaining interdependent outcomes such as international conflict should recognize:

1. While many analysts have focused on linear and additive combinations of factors internal to individual nations—national attributes—as possible sufficient conditions for war, the general existence of such relationships is logically precluded by the way in which analysts have defined wars.

   That is, given the way in which the concept of war has been traditionally defined in the literature, it seems more plausible to expect that certain multiplicative or interactive combinations of nations' attributes may serve as necessary, but not sufficient, conditions for war.

2. While scholars are trained to search for generalized patterns that hold both through time and across space and often seem to believe that the isolation of such associations is the sine qua non of the systematic analysis of international conflict, the existence of such patterns seems unlikely.

That is, given the already existing theoretical and empirical understanding, it seems probable that different relationships may hold under different conditions. Scholars who fail to recognize this possibility and who instead insist on testing what they hope will be universally applicable propositions are likely to have considerable difficulty in understanding and explaining the causes of war.

Again, the contentions involve rather basic, logical issues that are neither original nor complex. Bits and pieces of both have been hinted at by a number of other researchers. Once again, however, a discussion of the points seems warranted precisely because they involve rather elementary problems that generally seem to escape the attention of most quantitative analysts of international relations, and those who focus on the causes of international conflict. Given that this literature generally professes to be interested in discovering the *causes* of war, the question of necessary and/or sufficient conditions is thus critical to research design.

Three points are preliminary to an understanding of the problems. The first reviews the importance of theory and logic in the study of war. The second concerns the question of how scholars have tended to conceptualize international war and other war-related phenomena. The third concerns the analytical approaches that have been adopted by a number of analysts in their efforts to understand and explain such events.

Theory and Logic and War

As a preliminary illustration of the importance of logic, theory, and design (as well as the relationships between opportunity and willingness set out earlier), suppose first that four analysts are attempting to understand why states go to war. The first focuses on states' opportunities or capacities to fight and posits that increases in a state's war-fighting capacity (O) are sufficient for increases in its level of participation in war (Y). The second is concerned with the willingness of states to fight and postulates that increasing "war moods" (W) lead to increasing war participation (Y). The third analyst attempts to synthesize hypotheses 1 and 2 and hypothesizes—in simple additive fashion—that increases in a state's war-fighting capacity (O) *or* in its willingness to fight (W) tend to increase its level of participation in war (Y). The last researcher, in turn, attempts a somewhat different synthesis of hypotheses 1 and 2. Here, the postulate is the states' war-fighting capacities and their willingness to

TABLE 4.1   A Preliminary Illustration

(A)	
HYPOTHESES	**COMMON FORMS OF EXPRESSION***
H1: If increasing (high) war-fighting capacity (O), then increasing (high) war participation (Y).	$Y = a + b(O) + e$
H2: If increasing (high) willingness to fight (W), then increasing (high) war participation (Y).	$Y = a + b(W) + e$
H3: If increasing (high) war-fighting capacity (O) or increasing (high) willingness to fight (W), then increasing (high) war participation (Y).	$Y = a + b1(O) + b2(W) + e$
H4: If increasing (high) war-fighting capacity (O) and increasing (high) willingness to fight (W), then increasing (high) war participation (Y).	$Y = a + b(OW) + e$

(B)†			
Case 1	–O	–W	–Y
Case 2	–O	W	–Y
Case 3	O	–W	–Y
Case 4	O	W	Y

* Any of the propositions could be expressed in a variety of different forms. The linear depictions shown simply appear to be of the type most commonly used in the literature.

† Coding for all three variables—opportunity (O), willingness (W) and war (Y)—are dichotomous, with the negations (–O, –W, –Y) indicating the absence of the variable in question.

fight interact; states initiate conflicts that lead toward (Y) if they are *both* willing (W) and able (O) to fight.

Suppose next that each analyst specifies the preferred hypothesis in the manner shown in part A of table 4.1 and proceeds with its testing. For the purpose of argument, let it also be assumed that each analyst manages to develop operational indicators of the concepts which are perfectly reliable and free of measurement error.

For the purpose of clarity, assume that these indicators are dichotomous codings. Finally, let it be assumed that the data fit the pattern shown in part B of table 4.1.

The first hypothesis would be rejected. States do not always fight when they have the opportunity or capacity to do so (see case 3). The same holds true for the second hypothesis; states do not always go to war when willingness is high (see case 2). Hypothesis 3 would similarly be discarded; being willing or able to fight does not mean that states actually do fight in the illustration at hand (see cases 2 and 3). Only hypothesis 4—in which both high willingness and high opportunity are postulated to interact—would be supported by the pattern (see case 4).

While the illustration here is purely hypothetical, it appears to have at least one important implication. Analysts' theories are important for understanding and explaining why wars occur, and a critical component of those theories is *specification of the logical connectives*, which are expected to pertain among the predictor variables. Illustrating arguments set out in the opening chapter, we repeat that analysts' theories must specify the correct concepts. The operational measures of those concepts must be valid and reliable. The theories will need to be tested on samples of cases in which war had not occurred. Equally important, the theories must specify the logical nature of the expected relationships. The search for bivariate correlations and the application of simple linear additive (multiple regression) formulations may not suffice. The question of how factors are logically interrelated can neither be presumed nor ignored.

Conceptualizing War: What It Is and What It Involves

In light of the above, the importance of clear conceptualization is obvious. In reading the literature on the causes and consequences of international conflict, however, one is struck immediately by the fact that scholars appear to share no common understanding of why wars are important to study, what such events represent or indicate, or of how to operationalize and measure the very phenomena that so concerns them. A number of definitions and operationalizations of various forms of international conflict that exist in the literature, and that appear to form the foundations on which others have attempted to build, is presented in the Appendix of this chapter. In so doing, we have not even attempted to delineate the many approaches to "intervention" which appears to be the most recent incarnation of the war literature.

At a broad conceptual level, there are a number of different perspectives on the characteristics of war that are most important for us to study. One such perspective is Wright's view of war as a special "legal state" that exists between countries. Another stresses "war as a process"—the occurrence of stages of conflict that increasingly exhibit coercion, the threat of violence, and finally, the use of violence (e.g., Rummel, 1979:part 4). A third general perspective views war as a set of "consequences." One variant of this approach stresses the somatic violence, death, and destruction that war produces (e.g., Richardson or the Correlates of War Project); a second variation emphasizes the political consequences that wars have for the international system. The contrasting perspectives thus stress different aspects of war, raise different questions about the nature and causes of war, and color the operational definitions of war. Such differences strongly influence just what it is that actually concerns the researcher. Different analysts study wars for different reasons. Wars are taken by different analysts as indicators of different overarching concepts.

At a somewhat more empirical level, of course, scholars also differ over how wars should be operational and measured. Wright (1942) criticizes the procedures by which Sorokin (1937) identifies such events. Singer and Small (1972) find problems with both Wright's and Richardson's war selection procedures. Duvall (1976) and Starr (1976) raise questions about Singer and Small's operational criteria. A debate rages over whether or not it is even possible to code war data from historical sources (Singer, 1976; Small, 1976, 1977; Schroeder, 1977; Alexandroff et al., 1977). Kende (1971, 1978) adopts new measurement rules and develops lists of wars that contrast sharply with those provided by his predecessors. Eckhardt and Azar (1978a) use still another set of operational rules for identifying what they call "major international conflict." If anything, the comparisons of the various war lists that have been presented by Singer and Small (1972:chap. 5); SIPRI (1970); Most and Starr (1976, 1977); Eckhardt and Azar (1978a); and Beer (1981:chap. 2) are striking precisely because they indicate the lack of agreement about just what constitutes a "war," a state's participation in it, its duration, and so on. These variations in the operational criteria by which researchers identify the occurrences of war, assess their magnitude, measure their duration, and so on are clearly important. They have critical impacts on the results obtained in actual empirical analyses (Most and Starr, 1980). They have an impact on shifts in research foci, e.g., the current concern with intervention. It is likely that such a shift from war to intervention occurred because of the *fuzziness* of the war concept—that is, an "intrinsic ambiguity" in the phenomena (Cioffi-Revilla, 1981:130). Intervention, then, would appear to be useful as a "fuzzy set" approach to war.

While scholars thus quite clearly diverge on what wars represent, how to operationalize and measure them, and so on, it is important not to overlook the fact that a number of them appear to share a loose, but nevertheless common, abstract conceptualization of just what constitutes a "war." Scholars such as Wright (1942:app. XX); Richardson (1960a:6–9); Coser (1956:55–56); Schelling (1960); Boulding (1962:4–5); North (1968:226); Kende (1971, 1978:227); Singer and Small (1972:chap. 2); Blainey (1973:159); Feraru (1974); Pearson (1974:434); Midlarsky (1975:4); Gochman (1976:557); Snyder and Diesing (1977); Eckhardt and Azar (1978a), and others generally appear to understand wars to be events that involve:

—at least two parties, one of which is a state[1]
—conflictual goals[2]
—parties that are aware of their conflicting goals
—parties that are willing to attain a goal that they recognize conflicts with the wishes of the other(s)
—situations in which at least one party is willing to use overt military force to attain its goal
—situations is which least one party is able to resist another's use of overt military force to the extent that it avoids "immediate" defeat, suffers a minimal number of casualties, and/or inflicts minimal number of casualties on the other(s)[3]
—situations in which no party that is willing to use overt military force can attain its goal with only a single use of force or with a series of such acts that are highly dispersed over time

The outlines of this apparently consensual definition are clear: A war is a particular type of outcome of the *interaction* of at least dyadic sets of specified varieties of actors in which at least one actor is willing and able to use some specified amount of military force for some specified period of time against some other, resisting actor and in which some specified minimal number of fatalities (greater than zero) occur. Unlike situations involving structural violence, wars involve what Galtung (1969) terms "complete influence relations"—an influencer, an influencee, and a mode of influencing—in which the mode is military force and at least some fatalities result.[4] To the extent that all involved parties are states, wars are the *resultants* of attempts by one to use particular means of influencing another, resisting state.

Efforts to Understand and Explain the Causes of International War

Bearing this consensual definition in mind, consider how Zinnes conceptualizes the search for a solution to the puzzle regarding the question, "Why are some nations war prone?" Observing that "some nations go to war more frequently than others, but almost every nation has engaged in war at some time," she argues that:

> This suggests that international violence is probably not the result of special conditions but rather the consequence of certain attributes of nations. . . . It must be the case that an attribute of these nations—e.g., their power—makes them more prone to engage in territorial conflict. . . . Since all nations find themselves in conflict situations at some point in time, it must be the case that the attribute which makes nations conflict prone must vary over nations; some nations must have the attribute more than others (Zinnes, 1980:327).

Although Zinnes proceeds to review a number of studies that have tried but failed to identify general linkages between various national attributes and war, she notes that at least one set of studies appears to proffer the beginning of a solution to the puzzle:

> Borders are an attribute, borders produce contact, contact generates conflict, conflict leads to international violence. It would seem that the puzzle is on its way toward a solution (Zinnes, 1980:330).

Several aspects of the way in which Zinnes attempts to solve the war puzzle are worthy of note. First, like so many of those researchers whose work she attempts to synthesize, she focuses on the state level and utilizes the "state as actor" as her unit of analysis. She seems to reason—again as others have hypothesized in actual empirical work—that there must exist some characteristic or trait of states such that its presence (or presence in high degree) is sufficient for war: If some $X_1, X_2 \ldots, X_n$, then war. Finally, Zinnes appears to expect that the relationship(s) between the various X_i and the dependent war variable should hold both through time and across space.[5] The search—or perhaps better put, the solution to the

puzzle—entails the identification of sufficient relationships between states' attributes and their war involvement that are accurate,
parsimonious, causal, and (most important) generalizable.[6]

PROBLEM #1: NATIONAL ATTRIBUTES AND WAR

Having rehearsed the preliminaries, it becomes possible to move
on to a consideration of the first problem and the contention that
sufficient relationships ("If . . ., then . . .") cannot logically exist
between the attributes or characteristics of individual states and
their war involvements.[7] The ways in which scholars typically define, conceptualize, and operationalize "international war"
preclude—for simple and readily understood logical reasons—the
existence of such linkages. To the extent that international war is
viewed as an outcome of the interactions of at least dyads of states,
no single or combination of characteristics of any one warring
party can logically be expected to act as sufficient conditions for
that party's war involvement.

A First Cut

An understanding of why this is the case can be developed by
supposing for the moment that there exists some national attribute
such that having it (or having it to a prescribed degree) is sufficient
for making a state aggressive or war ready. Call that attribute
"power," "capacity," or the "opportunity" to wage war. While we
have not engaged in a lengthy conceptualization of power, we need
to outline our position on terminology. We specifically omitted reference to power from the discussion of opportunity and willingness
in chapter 2 because the many different meanings, aspects, and
views on power would have only obfuscated the presentation. Instead, we used the Sprouts' notion of "capabilities" as one way to
judge whether an international actor possessed the physical means
or ability to perform some foreign policy action—whether the possibility or opportunity were available to that actor. We understand
that such a perspective covers only one of the many facets of the notion of power. Recall that the whole perspective on power dealing
with influence and influence relationships was considered under
willingness.

In addition to opportunity, suppose also that one is able to identify reliably and without measurement error those states that possess this attribute and that are therefore war ready. The question,

then is: Could possession of the attribute and therefore the status of being war ready logically be expected to serve as a sufficient condition for war involvement? The answer is that it could not.

That this is the case can be understood by considering the situation described in part A of table 4.2 in which two parties (i and j) are coded according to whether or not they possess the hypothetical factor (in the example at hand, the minimal capacity that would allow them to fight) that makes them war ready. The first point to note in the illustration is that war between i and j could not occur by definition under the conditions described by cell 1; neither party could fight even if it wanted to do so. In cells 2 and 3, one or the other could fight. Given the definitional stipulation that wars are at least dyadic phenomena, however, a war could not result in these situations either because of one party's inability to resist. (In cell 3, for example, the ith actor might not need to apply military force at all if j has no capacity to resist. Alternatively, i might be able to use only a very small detachment of its forces in an attack on j that would be too short or too bloodless to be classified as a "war." One could thereby have the "process" and the "system change" consequences that some see as being related to war, *but there would be no war*.) War between i and j would thus be possible only under the conditions described by cell 4, in which both actors have some minimal war-fighting capacity. Note that all of these relationships can also be presented in terms of "paths," as shown in part B of table 4.2. Such a representation may, in addition, help us relate the present analyses to the complementary "political reliability" analyses of Cioffi-Revilla (e.g., 1984). Our discussion of table 4.2 is important, it should be understood, because i's capacity to fight is "high" *both* when it does fight (cell/path 4) and when it does not (cell/path 3). Party i would never be in a war when it is totally unable to fight, but it is not always in a war when it can fight and is (by the presumption above) war ready. Being war ready—or possessing whatever attributes make for being war ready—is not sufficient for actual war involvement. The reason for this, moreover, appears not to be explainable solely on the basis of i's attributes; something about j—the ith actor's potential opponent in a war—is also important. War between i and j is possible only when i and j are both able to fight. (See part C, table 4.2.)

This then appears to be a basic point. When war is conceived as the outcome of the interactions of at least two parties, the attributes of all of those parties—not just one of them—must be considered in

TABLE 4.2   Simple Interaction Possibility

Key:

Oi: The existence of some minimal war-fighting capacity in nation i
      (e.g., an "army" consisting of at least one uniformed soldier)
-Oi: The nonexistence of some minimal war-fighting capacity in
      nation i
Wi: The existence of some minimal willingness to fight in nation i
      (e.g., a wish or desire either to launch or resist an attack)
-Wi: The nonexistence of some minimal willingness to fight in
      nation i

Oj: ...stence of some minimal war-fighting capacity in nation j
-Oj: ...nexistence of some minimal war-fighting capacity in
      j
Wj: ...istence of some minimal willingness to fight in nation j
-Wj: ...nexistence of some minimal willingness to fight in
      j

(A)

	-Oj	Oj
-Oi	1	2
Oi	3	4

(B)

Actor i minimum war-fighting capacity (O_i)	Actor j minimum war-fighting capacity (O_j)	
0	0	(1)
	1	(2)
1	0	(3)
	1	(4)

(C)

O_i	O_j	War	
0	0	0	(1)
0	1	0	(2)
1	0	0	(3)
1	1	1	(4)

*   For the purpose of this illustration, all variables are coded
    dichotomously with 0 denoting the total absence or lack of a
    war-fighting capacity and 1 signifying its presence e.g., an "army"
    consisting of at least one soldier.

one's attempts to understand and explain when wars will and will not occur. Again, the notion of a process depending on interdependent outcomes of interactive components is similar to "political reliability" analyses. Cioffi-Revilla (1984:14) notes that: "Political Reliability Theory focuses on the multiple-step structure of political processes, or on the multiple-component structure of political systems. The central characteristic of all reliability models is that the political reliability of the overall process or system is viewed as crucially dependent upon the likelihood that the required steps will take place, or that the necessary components will work." In our discussions, the outcome of the reliability process is the actual outbreak of war, or the war involvement of some country. As we will see below, the complexity of the needed combination of elements is one factor that makes war a relatively rare event.

A Second Cut

The difficulty here is not at all obviated, it should be understood, by moving beyond the simple bivariate hypothesis to a more complex national attribute formulation. Consider, for example, an interactive/sufficient hypothesis in which a country's war involvement is posited to be related to two internal requisite conditions: First, a state must have the capacity or opportunity to become involved; second, it must perceive itself to be in conflict with some other actor so that it has the wish, desire, or the willingness to become involved.

This second national attribute hypothesis is certainly more sophisticated than the simple capacity or opportunity proposition discussed above. Because it implies a multiplicative or interactive relationship between states' opportunities and willingness to fight, there would be little reason to expect a generalized correlation between the size of an actor's military and its involvement in war. States that lack the capacity to fight and/or are unwilling to do so will not be capable of participating in a war. If decision makers want to launch an attack, the action may not actually occur unless they command some minimal war-fighting capacity. States which are themselves attacked may in general face similar requisites. Except in those instances in which country i attacks country j solely for the purpose of killing the citizens of j,[8] j may not be able to participate in a war—and indeed a war with significant numbers of deaths may not even result—unless j is both willing and able to resist.[9]

Although the reasoning of this argument might appear to be plausible, it too overlooks the problem. That this is in fact the case can be readily seen in table 4.3, in which parties i and j are now scored according to their level of opportunity (O) and willingness (W) to wage war. Even if one presumes for the purpose of argument that high levels of opportunity and willingness are sufficient conditions for war readiness, it seems clear that a given country's scores on the two factors have an indeterminate impact on its war participation.

While the ith actor can never participate in a war unless it has minimal war-fighting capabilities, for example, it is not always in a war when it does (see paths 9 through 16). While the ith actor can never participate in a war unless it is willing to use its capacities, the fact that it is willing to fight does not imply that it will fight (see paths 5 through 8 and 13 through 16). While the ith actor must be both willing and able to fight, it is not always in a war when it is willing and able to do so (see paths 13 through 16).

Consider again the ith state's characteristics on paths 13 through 16. They are invariant. In all such situations, country i has high opportunity and high willingness. It is thereby (again, by presumption) war ready. Even though that is the case, war between the ith and jth actors is by definition possible only in the situation described by the sixteenth path on which *both* parties possess the prescribed minimal levels of opportunity and willingness to fight.

Although the ith state is war ready on paths 13 through 15, war will not—again, by definition cannot—erupt with j. Because that second actor is unable and/or unwilling to resist any pressures that are brought to bear on it by the ith actor in these situations, actor i might be able to accomplish its ends *without* having to resort to overt or extensive uses of force. It could, for example, use economic sanctions, diplomatic jawboning, and so on. Alternatively, i could resort to threats—but not the actual use—of force (e.g., the equivalent of gunboat diplomacy). In still other situations, i could attempt to coerce j by deploying only small contingents of its military forces or by ordering its forces to engage j in a small scale/short duration encounter (e.g., by shooting at, or actually downing a few of i's aircraft). At another level, the ith actor could even undertake a small scale/short duration incursion into the territory of j.

Such acts by i could accomplish ends identical to any that might be attained by actually going to war against j. Because none would entail the use of sufficient military force, for sufficient periods, and

TABLE 4.3　A More Complex Interaction Possibility

	(A)			
	$[(-O_j)(-W_j)]$	$[(-O_j)(W_j)]$	$[(O_j)(-W_j)]$	$[(O_j)(W_j)]$
$[(-O_i)(-W_i)]$	1	2	3	4
$[(-O_i)(W_i)]$	5	6	7	8
$[(O_i)(-W_i)]$	9	10	11	12
$[(O_i)(W_i)]$	13	14	15	16

(B)

Actor i minimum war-fighting capacity (O_i)	Actor i willing to fight $(W_i)(b)^\dagger$	Actor j minimum war-fighting capacity (O_j)	Actor j willing to fight $(W_j)(b)^\dagger$

```
                                                         ┌── 0   (1)
                                              0 ─────────┤
                                           ┌─────────────┘── 1   (2)
                              0 ───────────┤
                          ┌───┘            └─────────────┐── 0   (3)
                          │                 1 ───────────┤
                          │                              └── 1   (4)
                          │
          0 ──────────────┤
              │           │                              ┌── 0   (5)
              │           │                 0 ───────────┤
              │           └─────────────────┘            └── 1   (6)
              │                          1 ──┤
              │                              └───────────┐── 0   (7)
              │                                1 ────────┤
              │                                          └── 1   (8)
          ────┤
              │                                          ┌── 0   (9)
              │                                 0 ───────┤
              │           ┌─────────────────────┘        └── 1   (10)
              │           │                    1 ────────┐── 0   (11)
              │     0 ────┤                      1 ──────┤
          1 ──┤     │     └─────────────────────┐        └── 1   (12)
              └─────┤
                    │                                    ┌── 0   (13)
                    │                           0 ───────┤
                    └────────────────────────────┘       └── 1   (14)
                                               1 ────────┐── 0   (15)
                                                  1 ─────┤
                                                         └── 1   (16)
```

TABLE 4.3   A More Complex Interaction Possibility (Continued)

O_i	W_i	O_j	W_j	War	
			(C)		
0	0	0	0	0	(1)
0	0	0	1	0	(2)
0	0	1	0	0	(3)
0	0	1	1	0	(4)
0	1	0	0	0	(5)
0	1	0	1	0	(6)
0	1	1	0	0	(7)
0	1	1	1	0	(8)
1	0	0	0	0	(9)
1	0	0	1	0	(10)
1	0	1	0	0	(11)
1	0	1	1	0	(12)
1	1	0	0	0	(13)
1	1	0	1	0	(14)
1	1	1	0	0	(15)
1	1	1	1	1	(16)

*   For the purpose of this illustration, all variables are coded dichotomously with 0 denoting the total absence or lack of the factor in question and 1 signifying its presence.

†   Conflict between i and j may be said to be present only when both actors hold conflictual goals, each is aware of the incompatibility and each is willing to attain a goal which is incompatible with the wishes of the other (see Boulding, 1962).

with sufficiently deadly consequences, however, none of them would be likely to be classified as a war by most researchers. Once again, therefore, there could be process and possible system consequences without a change in either the legal state or somatic violence.

The explanation of such "nonwars" would derive only partially from characteristics of the ith actor. It possesses all of the postulated attributes of actually warring states, and is therefore presumed to be war ready both when it does and does not wage an actual war. The explanation of nonwars also involves attributes of the jth actor. When i is war ready (paths 13 through 16), nonwars occur because the potential opponent, j, is unable and/or unwilling to use its own military force to resist any attempts by i to influence its behavior. Unless one is willing to entertain the possibility of unrealistic violence in which i kills citizens and soldiers of j even though they are unable or unwilling to resist (see Coser, 1956), war between i and j is in fact not even a logical possibility whenever *either* actor is unable and/or unwilling to fight.

Even if the hypothesis of an *intra*national interactive effect between opportunity and willingness is valid to the extent that having high levels of both is sufficient for being war ready, the consensual definition of war suggests another series of interactive relationships at the international level that involve characteristics or attributes of each of the opposing parties in such a conflict. As a result, it is not at all clear, and certainly not logical to expect, that attributes of individual countries (opportunity and willingness being only two possibilities) should be sufficient for, or covary with, such states' degrees of war involvement. The only world in which such covariations would exist would be one in which each and every war-ready actor is counterposed with at least one other war-ready party. Short of such a world, the occurrence of war should not be expected to covary with individual states' levels of opportunity or capacity or even with the outcome or product of individual states' levels of opportunity *and* willingness.

This means, of course, that scholars would be likely to be led astray if they were to test any of the following hypotheses:

1. if O_i, then war
2. if W_i, then war
3. if O_i or W_i, then war
4. if O_i and W_i, then war

While all four of these hypotheses are of the "If ..., then ..." variety in which one or more attributes is posited as a sufficient condition for the occurrence of war and together they constitute the standard way in which scholars probe for underlying relationships, none of them would be supported by the empirical evidence. Scholars examining the ith actor's capacities, its willingness, or even the interaction of those two factors with a view toward discovering whether or not they are sufficient for war would be led to the conclusion that such variables are not important for determining that actor's war participation. Because they would be searching for sufficient relationships and for covariations that are consistent with that type of logical connective, they would be likely either to abandon a focus on capacity, willingness, and their interaction, or to conclude that such factors are at best only marginally important.

A few less abstract examples may be helpful for understanding the point. Consider first the Soviet invasions of Hungary in 1956 and Czechoslovakia in 1968. The first is coded as a war by Singer and Small (1972) and Kende (1971); the second is not. The difference between the two cases, however, does not appear to be that simple; it is not just that the first resulted in a large number of fatalities whereas the latter did not. Unless one is willing to posit that something internal to the USSR was distinct in the two cases—e.g., altered levels of willingness and/or opportunity—the difference appears to have been the result of differences in the willingness or capacities of the Soviet Union's opponents. One event was a war and the other was not, and the factor(s) that effected those contrasting outcomes probably had nothing to do with characteristics of the Soviet Union; it seems likely that they had more to do with the other sides of the two dyads. In the simplest terms, the Hungarians were more willing and able to resist. They fought harder and longer than did their counterparts in Czechoslovakia twelve years later.

The United States interventions in Vietnam and the Dominican Republic (1965) present a similar analytical puzzle. In Vietnam, the United States encountered significant opposition. In the Dominican Republic, whatever resistance that actually did exist was quickly overrun. As a consequence, Vietnam is classed as a war by the Correlates of War Project, whereas the Dominican intervention is not.[10] The United States appears in retrospect to have been war ready in both instances, however. Once again, therefore, it would appear that the fact that the United States actually became involved in a war in Vietnam but not in the Dominican Republic must be explained by variables pertinent to both the United States and its opposition. If anything, a paradox emerges from a consideration of the two cases. In the case of the Dominican Republic in 1965, the United States may have been so willing and able to fight a war that actually fighting one turned out not to be necessary. Put differently, the United States use of overt military force in the Dominican Republic may have been so "successful" from its point of view that an extremely deadly and long-term conflict did not result. Again, the

process of coercion or "compellence" that occurred was so successful that its objective was achieved without somatic violence. Although the international political consequences and processes were
the same as with war, no war was coded.

PROBLEM #2: A PATTERN OR PATTERNS

The discussion in the previous section suggested that attributes of
individual states cannot serve as sufficient conditions for their war
involvement and that it is therefore unlikely that there will be any
crossnationally generalizable correlations between such attributes
and war participation. The argument in this section reaches a similar conclusion by a different route. Even if the argument above is invalid, some additional simple logic and a good deal of existing
theory suggest that it might *still* be unrealistic to expect general correlation relationships between nation-level characteristics and war
involvement.

Accepting that the consensual definition of war precludes the
possibility that a state's attributes can logically serve as the sufficient conditions for its war involvement, and, therefore, that correlations between such phenomena are unlikely, one could still search
for possible necessary linkages between national characteristics and
war. Logically, at least, the consensual definition leaves open the
possibility of such patterns. It permits possible necessary relationships of the general form:

5. only if O_i, then war
6. only if W_i, then war
7. only if O_i or W_i, then war
8. only if O_i and W_i, then war

The propositions in this set are, of course, logically distinct from
those listed in the preceding section. None posits a sufficient relationship between national attributes and war such that each time a
given X_i or a combination of X's occurs, war follows. Instead, the
propositions in this second set suggest not that wars follow given
$X_i(s)$, but rather, that wars are preceded by given $X_i(s)$. As has been
said, the consensual definition of war does not preclude the possibility that such linkages may exist and, indeed, the evidence in table
4.3 suggests that hypothesis 8 above—an interactive/necessary
postulate—would be supported.

The Attackers and the Attacked

While an examination of possible necessary relationships thus makes logical sense given the consensual definition of war, the existence and importance of another problem should be noted. Consider once again the situation described by path 16 in table 4.3. Because both actors possess the minimal levels of opportunity and willingness, a war between them is at least theoretically possible. Just when, however, would a war break out? Who would attack whom, and what patterns would be likely to hold between the attributes of i and j and their participation in war? The answer could vary, of course, but deterrence and balance of power theories might lead the analyst to expect the following possibilities:[11]

1. Country i might choose to attack j if its own levels of opportunity and willingness are especially high and j's—while still above the minimum—are low. To the extent that it does so, i's war participation occurs when its opportunity and willingness or war readiness are especially high. Nation j's participation in contrast occurs when its war readiness is quite low (although above the minimum needed).
2. Country i might not choose to attack j when both actors are especially willing and able to fight. For both parties, therefore, high levels of war readiness might coincide with peace.

If deterrence and balance of power theories are valid empirically, their operation—particularly in item 2 above—could produce the patterns shown in table 4.4 (note that these two possibilities mirror the power preponderance and power parity debate discussed in detail in chapter 6). Those patterns, in turn, would be likely to be virtually indecipherable to the analyst who develops and tests sufficient *or* necessary hypotheses with a view toward identifying generalizable patterns that hold both through time and across space. While the search for such patterns is the sine qua non of the systematic analysis of war, such patterns might not exist—and indeed, should not be expected to exist—if states do in fact deter one another and attempt to create (or disrupt) balances of power. Why is this?

Country i may sometimes fight when it is especially war ready, but at other times it may not. Country j, on the other hand, may sometimes fight when it is not especially prepared for war, but may avoid such conflicts when it is best prepared to wage them. Put differently, i may fight only when it is most able to do so, while j may

TABLE 4.4　A Deterrence/Balance Illustration*

(A)					
Actor i minimum war-fighting capacity (O_i)	Actor i willing to fight $(W_i)^\dagger$	Actor j minimum war-fighting capacity (O_j)	Actor j willing to fight $(W_j)^\dagger$	Actor i capacity level (O'_i)	Actor j capacity level (O'_j)

```
                                                        0   (1)
                                                  0 <
                                                        1   (2)
        1 ——— 1 ——— 1 ——— 1 <
                                                        0   (3)
                                                  1 <
                                                        1   (4)
```

(B)							
O_i	W_i	O_j	W_j	O'_i	O'_j	War	
1	1	1	1	0	0	0	(1)
1	1	1	1	0	1	1	(2)
1	1	1	1	1	0	1	(3)
1	1	1	1	1	1	0	(4)

* For the purpose of this illustration, variables O_i–W_j are coded dichotomously with 0 denoting the total absence or lack of the factor in question and 1 signifying its presence. O'_i and O'_j are coded as a 0 if the actor in question has only marginally more than the minimum war-fighting capacity and as 1 if that minimum is significantly exceeded.

† Conflict between i and j may be said to be present only when both actors hold conflictual goals, each is aware of the incompatibility and each is willing to attain a goal which is incompatible with the wishes of the other (see Boulding, 1962).

(1) i and j may both be deterred from initiating conflict even though both exceed the minimal capacity to fight to only a marginal degree.

(2) War may result, with j attacking i.

(3) War may result, with i attacking j.

(4) i and j may both be deterred from initiating conflict even though both have high levels of war-fighting capacity.

wage war only when it is least able. At the same time, when j is most able to launch an attack, it may actually do so. Given identical initial conditions, however, j may refrain from attacking.[12]

The pattern looks chaotic if one views all of this from the national attribute perspective and is looking for a single set of generalizable relationships, but it of course makes perfect sense. The internal attributes of i and j are important for determining when they will and will not participate in a war, but they are only part of the story rather than the whole of it. Once again, an understanding of when i wages war with j seems likely to require a focus on both of the actors. Even if the researcher does this, however, it is not necessarily the case that there must exist some universal pattern between states' attributes and their war involvement.

It should be added, of course, that it is often difficult to determine which parties are the attacker and which are the attacked. Even though that is the case, however, the argument in this section goes beyond the attacker/attacked illustration. It suggests first that it might be at least worthwhile to consider possible differences in the processes that lead states to participate in wars. (Deterrence and balance of power theories constitute only one of a variety of arguments that suggest such differences.) More important, perhaps, the argument in this section suggests that analysts overlook something useful if they implicitly equate identities or similarities in states' attributions ("sameness") with patterned relationships. While that equation of course underlies most statistical analyses, it should be clear that under certain conditions at least, patterns could hold even though—and perhaps because—states' attributes are distinct. Again, deterrence and balance of power theories suggest only one set of a variety of possible reasons why this could be the case.

GENERALIZING THE PROBLEMS

It may be helpful to review a number of the implications that appear to follow from the foregoing.

The Validity of War as an Indicator

It seems clear that a number of scholars are concerned with the causes of international war because such interactions have an intrinsic appeal that attracts their interest. War in and of itself is regarded as a concept; the only serious questions that arise are those that are concerned with data availability and measurement reliability.

For other researchers who are concerned primarily with under-standing and explaining the factors and processes that contribute to countries' high or increasing degrees of aggressiveness or war readi-ness, however, the important question of indicator validity also arises. They need to consider whether or not war—defined as the outcome of certain types of at least dyadic interactions—can serve as a valid indicator of the concept. One implication of the foregoing is that it may not. Wars, per se, are outcomes; the more one focuses on large-scale outcomes of great magnitude or of long duration, the more one appears to move away from individual countries, their acts, and their degrees of aggressiveness or war readiness.

At least some threats, negative sanctions, skirmishes, border inci-dents, and so on might have been wars if the acts by the initiating parties had been resisted—and resisted to a sufficient degree—by some opponent. The Clausewitz dictum that "war is nothing but a continuation of political intercourse, with a mixture of different means" needs to be reversed. Normal politics in which states unilat-erally employ both nonlethal (nonviolent) and relatively nonlethal means—e.g., economic leverage, propaganda, aid, small-scale sor-ties of short duration, covert subversion, cooptation, and so on—may be a continuation of war. Each state may have a certain range of means for pursuing its ends in international relations and there may be at least some potential for the substitution of different means. Thus states that are willing and able to go to war—and that have all of the internal attributes or characteristics of countries that actually do fight—could find that their goals can be achieved by nonviolent means, by hit-and-run skirmish maneuvers, or by em-ploying overt force with such efficiency that the opposition is over-whelmed before a war can result. To go a step further, one might even hazard that states that are most willing and able to fight may be among those that fight least often because they have a wide range of options for decreasing others' war-fighting capacities (op-portunities) and/or willingness to fight. To the extent that such tac-tics are employed successfully, neither a war nor even a "complete influence structure" need develop.

The point should therefore be clear. If war is taken as an empiri-cal indicator of some more general overarching concept, there is likely to be considerable slippage between the concept and the em-pirical observation as long as wars are conceptually defined as the outcomes of the interactions of a least two parties. Questions con-cerning the reliability of the various war lists are, and should continue to be, important. That said, however, it should be added that questions concerning their validity are at least equally important.

The Case for Studying Nonwars

If the argument above is sound, and if the attributes of an individual country cannot in fact serve as the sufficient conditions for its war involvement, it follows quite clearly that an understanding of those factors that are sufficient for countries' aggressiveness or for their being war ready will require an expansion of researchers' foci and the placing of war in a broader foreign policy context.[13] Both the war and the nonwar ("peace"/"successful" war) ends of the conflict-peace continuum need to be studied. In addition to studying the actions of states that do result in war, a focus on both nonconflictual/cooperative and conflictual (covert and overt) acts that do not lead to war is needed. Note that we have reached this conclusion by alternative, but complementary, routes in chapters 3 and 4.

War and the Level-of-Analysis Problem

It should be apparent by now that both of the problems under discussion here derive in large part from a tendency on the part of many analysts to confuse what Singer (1969) terms "levels of analysis." In attempting to discover the attributes or characteristics of individual countries that are sufficient for their involvement in war, researchers have in effect been attempting to relate such factors to a phenomenon that occurs—and by definition, can only occur—at least at the dyadic level. They have been ignoring Singer's observation that "we cannot afford to shift our orientation in the midst of a study" (1969:28).

However, the problem runs even deeper than this suggests. In its simplest terms, it raises questions about Singer's oft-quoted conclusion that it really does not matter which particular level is chosen as long as the analyst makes a choice and stays with it throughout the course of a given study.[14] In point of fact, as Singer really implies, it does appear to matter if researchers are serious about understanding the factors that serve as sufficient conditions for states' war involvements. A focus on war as the aggregated outcome of the behavior of individual states precludes the development of an understanding of the conditions that are sufficient for any one state's decision (problem 1) and may—for reasons related to problems of disaggregation to the state level—simultaneously fail to provide the basis for even correlational insights (problem 2).

Foreign Policy Outputs/International Outcomes

It is possible to be more specific. K. J. Hosti argues that the difference between foreign policy and international politics is "roughly the difference between the *objectives* and *actions* (decisions and politics) of a state or states, and the *interactions* between two or more states" (1972:21). If this is so, much of the problem with searching for attributes or characteristics of states that are sufficient for their war decisions stems from the use of a state-level, basically foreign policy approach to probe a phenomenon that is international in nature and is by definition a resultant outcome or interaction. To the extent that analysts are serious about understanding those factors that are sufficient for countries' aggressiveness, therefore, there is a need to focus directly on more unilateral foreign policy outputs. In other words, because a war is the result of at least dyadic interactions and the characteristics of any one country cannot logically determine that outcome, there is a need to redefine or at least reoperationalize the dependent variable, reducing its interactive nature and increasing its unilateral aspects.

That said, we need to stress a point already presented. While the focus here is on the ways in which analysts have attempted to understand the occurrence of wars, such events are of course only one of a variety of interactive phenomena that concern international relations scholars. As noted in chapter 5, if the interactive nature of war precludes the possibility that characteristics of any one state could serve as sufficient conditions for such events, the same could be said for *any* interactive international relations phenomenon.

War and the Solution(s) to Zinnes's Puzzle(s)

Noting once again that the search for relationships that are generalizable across countries has increasingly become the sine qua non of the systematic study of international conflict, it should be reemphasized that such associations and patterns may not in fact exist. One state may become involved in a war while another state with identical characteristics does not. Similarly, different countries with different attributes may both participate in wars. Both logic and theory suggest that generalizable sufficient relationships should not be expected to exist between states' attributes and their war involvement. The naive cross-national approach has not and does not seem likely to take us very far toward solving Zinnes's puzzle.

This does not imply that wars are more or less random occurrences. Stable patterns and relationships may in fact exist. It may simply be that we have not yet learned how to recognize them. One possible way for understanding them might be to concentrate on variables drawn from the same level of analysis as wars themselves and to indicate aspects of dyadic structure or interaction. An example of such a strategy is Bueno de Mesquita's use of expected utility. Another is the authors' work using symmetrically defined borders as indicators of countries' dyadic interaction opportunities. Work on the power preponderance hypothesis (to be discussed in detail in chapter 6) is in the same vein. Alternatively, analysts might develop interactive process models involving the capabilities and intentions of both actors and use them to explore the dynamics of states' interactions as they move through some conflict with one another. Such work might involve a version of the "conflict spiral" (North et al., 1964), stages of conflict (as, for example, those developed by Bloomfield and Leiss, 1969; and Barringer, 1972), or the "international conflict helix" (Rummel, 1979).

Efforts of this type might lead more quickly to a solution to the puzzle, but again, one should be cautious. Analysts may in fact be confronted with the single puzzle for which a single solution does exist, but there may also be several puzzles, each with its own solution. There may be one process that leads to war, but states that are part of that process may have widely divergent attributes. There could even be distinct processes leading to war, with different ones operating under different conditions, displaying different patterns, and being driven by different factors. A much closer analysis of different contexts, conditions, and *subsets* of international phenomena, and the "nice" laws that deal with them, is thus needed. We turn to such an analysis in the next chapter.

APPENDIX TO CHAPTER 4

CONFLICT AND CONFLICT-RELATED DEFINITIONS

Wright   *War*

"... a state of law and a form of conflict involving a high degree of legal equality, of hostility, and of violence in the relations of organized human groups, or, more simply, the legal condition which equally permits two or more hostile groups to carry on a conflict by armed force" (1964:7).

"... all hostilities involving members of the family of nations, whether international, civil, colonial or imperial, which were recognized as states of war in a legal sense or which involved over 50,000 troops" (1942:app. XX).[a]

Richardson   *Deadly Quarrels*

"... any quarrel [in which there was malice aforethought and] which caused [at least 317 deaths] to humans." Such deaths may include (*a*) armed personnel killed in or as direct result of fighting, (*b*) civilians, belonging to belligerent populations, killed in or as a direct result of fighting, and (*c*) deaths among armed belligerent personnel as a consequence of disease or exposure (1960a:6–9).[b]

Singer and Small

Interstate Wars

Hostilities involving one or more members of the interstate system which resulted in at least 1000 battle fatalities among all of the system members involved.[c] In order to qualify as a participant in a given war, a nation must be (*a*) a qualified member of the interstate system, (*b*) "have had regular, uniformed, national military personnel in sustained combat," and (*c*) have at least 1000 "armed personnel engaged in active combat in the war theater" or suffer at least 100 fatalities (Singer and Small, 1972:chap. 2).[d]

Kende

Wars

Any armed conflicts in which all of the following obtain: (*a*) activities of regular armed forces (military, police forces, etc.) at least on one side—that is, the presence and engagement of the armed forces of the government in power; (*b*) a certain degree of organization and organized fighting on both opposing sides, even if this organization extends to organized defense only; and (*c*) a certain degree of continuity between armed clashes, however sporadic (1978:227).

Eckhardt and Azar

Major International Conflicts

". . . those events which had been coded on points thirteen to fifteen of the international scale, including very hostile war actions, territorial occupations, and many deaths (15); limited hostile acts with minor costs (14); and subversion, small air or border clashes, and skirmishes or blockades (13)" (1978:77; see also the presentation of the full 15-point International Interactions Scale in Table 1 of Eckhardt and Azar, 1978b).

Boulding

Competition

A situation which exists "when any potential positions of two behavior units are mutually incompatible" (1962:4–5).ᶜ

Conflict

"... a situation of competition in which the parties [of which there are at least two] are aware of the incompatibility of potential future positions and in which each party wishes to occupy a position that is incompatible with the wishes of the other" (1962:5).

Snyder and Diesing

International Crises

"... sequence(s) of interactions between the governments of two or more sovereign states in severe conflict, short of actual war, but involving the perception of a dangerously high probability of war" (1977:6).

Pearson

Foreign Military Intervention

"... the movement of troops or military forces, under orders or with some official leadership, by one independent country (or concerted group of independent countries) across the border of another independent country (the 'target'), or action by troops already stationed in the target country.... [While]... any organized border crossing by military units will be called an intervention. . . only instances in which the intervening country's troops or forces are actively employed (as opposed to long-term encampment on bases with no direct military action) inside the target to affect policies or conditions through the use or open demonstration of force will be considered. . . . [I]nterventions may be hostile (opposing target government or aiding rebels) friendly (supporting government or opposing rebels) or neutral" (1974:434–435).

Galtung

Violence

". . . present when human beings are being influenced so that their actual somatic and mental realizations are below their potential realizations" (1969:168).

NOTES TO APPENDIX

a. In compiling his list of wars, Wright also includes "some other incidents. . . in which hostilities of considerable but lesser magnitude, not recognized as legal states of war but which led to important legal results such as the creation or extinction of states, territorial transfers, or changes of government" (1942:636).

b. Richardson explicitly omits counting deaths in the following categories: of civilians by exposure; of civilians by infectious disease; and the number of "missed babies" which might otherwise have been born. The first two classes are excluded because the loss of life results from accident and negligence, rather than from intention. The missed babies are excluded on the grounds that it would be too difficult to estimate their numbers. On yet another category of deaths—accidental deaths of neutrals—Richardson is unclear.

c. Singer and Small identify members of the interstate system in the following fashion: For the period, 1861–1919, a state is said to be a member if it has at least 500,000 population and its capital city has diplomatic missions (of at least the chargé d'affaires rank) from Britain and France. For the period, 1920–1965, a state is said to be a system member if (a) it is a member of the League of Nations or the United Nations, or (b) has at least 500,000 population and a diplomatic mission from any two major powers (Singer and Small, 1972:19–22).

d. In addition to the political status and fatality criteria, it is worth noting that Singer and Small consider—but do not actually employ—another criterion: "...we might have required that the system member's forces be involved in active combat for some minimum period of time in order to exclude brief skirmishes and isolated engagements" (1972:36).

e. Two goals are said to be incompatible "if each excludes the other, that is if the realization of either one makes impossible the realization of the other" (Boulding, 1962:4).

5

FOREIGN POLICY SUBSTITUTABILITY AND "NICE" LAWS:
Integrating Process and Theory

INTRODUCTION: WORKING TOWARDS A "REDUCTIONIST" (MICRO-ANALYTIC) APPROACH

Before moving ahead, let us briefly summarize the main points developed so far. In the two previous chapters we focused on what we thought of as four simple but nevertheless generally overlooked, and related, problems which appear to have impeded the integrative cumulation of knowledge in the study of international relations, specifically about the causes and consequences of international conflict. We argued that researchers who are concerned with developing verifiable, replicable and generalizable explanations of international conflict need to recognize that:

1. While analysts have argued that they are concerned with the conditions that are sufficient for the occurrence of war, both the static cross-national research designs that they have commonly utilized and the manner by which they have selected cases for their analyses are appropriate for only an examination of the necessary conditions for such conflicts. The identification of answers to the sufficiency questions that they pose appears to be *logically* precluded by their methods.

2. While many analysts have focused on linear and additive combinations of factors internal to states—"national attributes"—as possible sufficient conditions for war, the general existence of such relationships appears to be *logically* precluded by analysts' conceptualization of wars which envisions such phenomena both as *independent outcomes* or *resultants* of the actions of at least two states and

also as occurrences that are fundamentally tied to important micro- or decision-level considerations.

3. While scholars have focused on identifying *which* factors are the determinants of international conflict, equally important—and perhaps, difficult—questions concern *how* those factors are *logically* and *causally* related to one another and to conflict itself.

4. While scholars are trained to search for generalizable patterns that hold through time and across space and often seem to believe that the isolation of such associations is the sine qua non of the systematic analysis of international conflict, the existence of such patterns seems unlikely. While patterns may still exist, they are not likely to be of the variety—or even *appear like* the variety—of patterns for which analysts have been exploring.

One conclusion of those discussions is that analysts should focus their research on the dynamics of state- and decision-level interaction processes.

In the present discussion, we attempt to extend that conclusion by demonstrating in somewhat more elaborate fashion just why decision- or micro-level concerns—decision makers' willingness to utilize overt force and the choices that they make—are likely to be critical for explaining and understanding war. We begin again with another pair of fundamental logical problems which raise questions about the ways in which scholars have conceptualized international relations and international conflict at the most basic level. The first has to do with the potential for what we refer to as *foreign policy substitutability;* it suggests that through time and across space, similar factors could plausibly be expected to trigger different foreign policy acts. The second problem concerns the potential existence of "sometimes true," *domain specific laws.* It is the logical opposite of the substitution problem and suggests that different processes could plausibly be expected to lead to similar results. Neither problem appears to be well understood in the current literature; if anything, standard research practices suggest that both problems are ignored entirely. Nevertheless, both possibilities are potentially important.

Taken together, the problems suggest that scholars who are interested in developing a cumulative base of integrative knowledge about foreign policy and international relations phenomena should recognize two fundamental points. First, the development of various "islands of theory" will not yield a broad-ranging understanding of states' foreign policy behaviors if analysts define those islands in terms of concrete, unabstracted or empirical foreign policy phenomena. If international behaviors can be alternative means that different states utilize in pursuit of their (perhaps heterogeneous) national goals and *under at least certain conditions* states may *substitute* one means for another, then all of the behaviors that tend to be studied in fragmented fashion need to be conceived and studied from the outset—*not* as separate and distinct phenomena, the understanding of which will eventually be integrated—but rather as commensurable behaviors of component parts of abstract conceptual puzzles.

Second, applications of the standard general approach for testing models and hypotheses are likely to produce misleading results and lead analysts to reject theories and models that are "good," "nice," and "useful" even if they are not general or universally "true." Scholars may err if they necessarily equate laws with empirically observable regularities and *universal* truths. If it is plausible to argue that states may pursue different goals, for different reasons and with different degrees of effectiveness, then it may be useful to reconsider the efforts to search for a "true," "general" or universally applicable explanation of what states do. It might instead be more sensible to search for models or theories that operate, hold, or are valid only under certain explicitly prescribed conditions. In saying this we hold with a basic point made by Morton Kaplan two decades ago (1967:158): "One cannot build a theory of international relations. . . upon a theory of foreign policy; nor can one begin with a theory of international relations and derive theories of foreign policy from it. Each attempt would assume a general theory that encompasses both viewpoints."

While we believe that a number of implications follow from the discussion, three in particular are given special emphasis. First, we conclude that there is a need to reexamine some of the "grand" theoretical approaches extant in the "traditional" literature; there is a need to develop a new synthesis of tradition and science and of grand, middle, and narrow-range theory. Second, there is a need to pay more careful attention to epistemological issues. Finally, we conclude that the most fruitful avenues for theorizing and research are likely to be at the micro-level in which the focus is on decision making, expected utility calculations and foreign policy interaction processes.[1]

We wish to argue that, contrary to arguments that an understanding of international politics requires a systemic approach, it appears that such phenomena are in fact amenable to theory and research on the national/decision-making level. Work that is conducted exclusively at the system-level *cannot* suffice for the development of a systematic understanding of either foreign policy or international phenomena. At a minimum, system-level concerns need to be complemented by research that focuses on decision-making processes and the means by which decision makers select from sets of alternatives within a dyadic (or multi-adic) framework. Decision makers, the goals that motivate them, and the choices that they make—whether or not they are value-maximizing selections—must be considered at some point.

COMMON RESEARCH PRACTICES

Let us begin this discussion by reviewing several basic research practices and procedures that have increasingly come to characterize much of the current quantitative research on foreign policy and international phenomena.[2]

Empirical 'Puzzles' and Empirically-Defined Islands

Recent theoretical and quantitative empirical research on foreign policy and international relations has tended to focus at the middle level in an apparent effort to develop "islands of theory" or solutions to middle-range puzzles. While scholars argue that they are ultimately concernd with understanding why states do what they do, they have eschewed efforts at grand theory. They have commonly specialized their research, with different ones becoming arms race experts, alliance theorists, war analysts, students of arms transfers, specialists on the uses of foreign economic policy, experts on international negotiation/conflict resolution processes, and so on.[3] Some have asked why states go to war. Others have dealt with why alliances form or dissolve. Possible explanations and effects of arms transfers have been analyzed by a third group of researchers. Still others have focused on arms races and so on.[4]

Some scholars specialize and focus on one phenomenon or type of event because the subject seems to them to have an intrinsic appeal. The phenomenon is, in and of itself, regarded as a concept; the typical goals are to understand its causes or consequences. Other analysts have focused on one phenomenon or type of event for rather different reasons. Viewing their chosen empirical behavior or event as an indicator of some more overarching concept, they appear to have reasoned that an understanding of the given empirical phenomenon would eventually inform them about the concept; e.g., scholars who focus on war from the perspective of Galtung's structural theory of aggression.[5] To put the point somewhat different, analysts have reasoned that progress toward an understanding of conceptual relationships comes most rapidly if they focus narrowly, concentrate on a given empirical phenomenon, and study it in isolation. At a minimum, this specialized work eventually yields an understanding of the phenomenon in question. An island of theory emerges; an island of understanding is established. If, in the meantime, other analysts have been successful in investigating other concrete behaviors and they have thereby been able to produce islands of their own, eventually it would be possible to go further. The "war" island would be liked with other middle-range theories of alliance behavior, arms transfers, defense expenditures, and so on. This theoretical synthesis or "bridging" of the islands of middle-range theory would provide a more abstract, broad-gauge, or overarching understanding of foreign policy and international behavior.

Empirical Generalizations' Laws and "Always-True" Theories

The tendency to define puzzles or research questions in terms of particular, concrete empirical phenomena and to focus on one—but only one—type of event at a time combine with the fact that most systematic or scientific foreign policy and international relations scholars seem to think of social laws and theories as being either true or false (see Coleman, 1964:516). As we have noted previously, the search for empirical generalizations seems to have become the sine qua non of at least the quantitative international relations scholar. To understand or explain some phenomenon such as an overt military attack, for example, is to identify the factor(s) that alone or in various combinations correlate with the occurrences of attacks or that seem generally useful—according to some statistical criterion—for postdicting the occurrences of attacks in the data set being utilized. Although a few exceptions can be noted, the most common view is that a "good" explanandum is one that is generally associated through time or across space with attacks; a "less than good" explanandum is one that is not. Research proceeds by identifying and retaining the former while rejecting and abandoning the latter.[6]

On first consideration, these practices seem largely commonsensical. None of them seem to be at all problematic. Indeed, the practices seem so uncontroversial that they are seldom discussed in current literature. As we will see in the next section, however, researchers may be led astray if they narrowly focus their research on only one type of empirical foreign policy behavior, define problems or potential islands in terms of such concrete phenomena, search exclusively for empirical-level generalizations, and equate laws with universal truths.

PROBLEM #1: THE OVERLOOKED POTENTIAL FOR POLICY SUBSTITUTION

The division of labor, the focus on unabstracted, concrete or empirical phenomena, and efforts to create middle-range islands of theory on the basis of such work seem unproblematic, as we have said. Unfortunately, however, such practices are likely to lead to a more abstract understanding of why states do what they do *only if* states' empirically distinct foreign policies and behaviors are never the alternative means that decision makers utilize in pursuit of their (perhaps heterogeneous) national goals. If foreign policies can indeed be alternative routes that foreign policy decision makers adopt in order to attain their goals, then it would seem plausible that decision makers who are confronted with some problem or subjected to some stimulus could, *under at least certain conditions, substitute one such means for another.* If that is the case, it would appear to follow in turn that any factor, stimulus or problem that triggers *some particular* type of empirical foreign policy response could, under different conditions, trigger other, *apparently* distinct, *apparently* incommensurable behaviors. If the argument here is valid, to put the point differently, *similar* factors could lead to *distinct* concrete or empirical foreign policy responses.

The confounding effects of this potential for foreign policy substituability can not be overemphasized. For example, realists have argued that states seek the goal of security in the Westphalian self-help system. To the extent that that is the case, that states do indeed pursue such a grand or meta-conceptual goal (Y), and that in principle they have a variety of partially substituable alternative means—war (y_1), alliance formation (y_2), arms importation (y_3), arms increases (y_4), and so on—for attaining the goal, then it would appear that a given presumed causal factor (x_1; e.g., an opponent that is increasing its arms) could logically be expected to be sufficient for explaining why the decision makers of a given state are willing to adopt *some* y_i. If the stimulus (x_1) could be expected to trigger y_1 adoptions by some decision makers but could lead others to adopt distinct behaviors, y_2, y_3, ..., y_n, however, an understanding of which particular y_i would be adopted by different decision makers who are deciding under different conditions would involve a consideration of how those actors make comparisons across, and eventually choices from, the range of available options, y_1, y_2, ..., y_n. It would require analysts, in other words, to focus on more than a single type or form of foreign policy behavior. It would require analysts to rethink the strategy of focusing on particular empirical phenomena and their efforts to construct middle-range islands of theory on the basis of such concrete, unabstracted phenomena.[7]

Two examples should help to clarify these points. First, let us imagine a simple, totally deterministic, world in which development of a problem (X) is invariably sufficient—but perhaps not empirically necessary—for an effort to resolve the problem (Y). Wherever and whenever X occurs, Y follows. The only complication is that efforts to resolve the eproblem (Y) can take any of three different empirical forms (y_1, y_2, y_3) which are not necessarily mutually exclusive (i.e., an actor could respond to X by adopting any one or any combination of the solutions, y_i). Presuming that (1) x_1 is a valid and reliable indicator of X; (2) y_1, y_2, and y_3 are valid and reliable complementary indicators of Y; and (3) letting x_1 and $-x_1$ denote the presence or absence of the problem X while y_i and $-y_i$ denote the presence or absence of a given attempt to resolve the problem, consider the following possible case structure:

Case 1	x_1	y_1	$-y_2$	$-y_3$	Y
Case 2	x_1	$-y_1$	y_2	$-y_3$	Y
Case 3	x_1	$-y_1$	$-y_2$	y_3	Y
Case 4	x_1	y_1	y_2	y_3	Y
Case 5	$-x_1$	$-y_1$	$-y_2$	$-y_3$	$-Y$
Case 6	$-x_1$	y_1	$-y_2$	$-y_3$	Y
Case 7	$-x_1$	$-y_1$	y_2	$-y_3$	Y
Case 8	$-x_1$	$-y_1$	$-y_2$	y_3	Y

Analysts who recognize the complementarity of the y_i and focus on abstract attempts to resolve the problem (Y)—rather than on the specific empirical forms that such solutions take—would not be at all confused by this pattern; each time x_1 appears, Y follows. Because Y also appears when x_1 is not present, however, this analyst would conclude that X, as indicated by x_1, is sufficient (but not necessary) for Y. Other analysts who focus narrowly and specialize in attempts to understand the occurrence of any one—but only one—of the concrete y_i behaviors would run the risk of overlooking the relationship. The occurrence of x_1 sometimes does—but other times does not—precede any particular y_i. In short, X, as indicated by x_1, would *not* appear to be sufficient (or necessary) for any one of the y_i.[8]

A consideration of the hypothetical interactions among actors m, i, and j in columns 1–3 in part A of table 5.1 may further clarify the problem. The mth state increases its defense spending in each alternative "round." Countries i and j "respond" by increasing their own expenditures (at t2), offering to form an alliance (at t4), dissolving an alliance or seeking foreign arms acquisitions respectively (at t6) and respectively seeking to negotiate or attack (at t8).

Recognizing that the illustration is purely hypothetical and quite clearly does not exhaust the full range of states' possible foreign policy behaviors, the basic point should be obvious: the situation would appear chaotic to analysts who ignore or overlook the substitutability potential and focus on only a single type of behavior. The typical arms race theorist who focuses on reciprocated increases in defense spending would discover that increases by one state sometimes do, but other times do not, lead to similar responses by others. The alliance theorist would discover that an increase in defense spending antecedes efforts to form an alliance in one instance but that other such increases precede the breakup of an alliance or states' complete inactivity in the alliance sphere. The war theorist and the expert on arms transfers would encounter similar complexities. Stepped up defense spending precedes an attack in one case but also antedates conciliatory efforts in another; spending increases generally do not, but in one case does, appear to lead to an effort to import arms.

Thus, analysts who elect to focus on any one—but only one—of the behaviors shown in the figure would be likely to be led astray. The strategy would make sense only if decision makers in all states respond identically to identical stimuli and they do not have the capacity to substitute (a position taken explicitly or implicitly by some

TABLE 5.1   Hypothetical Action-Reaction Process

(A)					
Nations: m	i	j	I	p	q
			I		
t1 X_4			I		
t2	X_4	X_4	I	00	00
t3 X_4			I		
t4	X_5	X_5	I	00	00
t5 X_4			I		
t6	X_6	X_7	I	00	00
t7 X_4			I		
t8	X_8	X_9	I	00	00

Key:

X_4: Increase Defense Spending
X_5: Offer to Form an Alliance
X_6: Dissolve an Alliance with nation k
X_7: Seek to Import Arms
X_8: Seek to Negotiate Outstanding Grievances
X_9: Initiate an Attack on the Threatening Nation
00: No Behavior

(B)					
Nations: m	i	j	I	p	q
t1 X_2			I		
t2	X_2	X_2	I	00	00
t3 X_2			I		
t4	X_2	X_2	I	00	00
t5 X_2			I		
t6	X_2	X_2	I	00	00
t7 X_2			I		
t8	X_3	X_3	I	00	00

Key:

X_2: Increase National Defense Capacity (C)
X_3: Decrease National Defense Risk (R)
00: No Behavior

TABLE 5.1 (Continued)

	(C)					
Nations:	m	i	j	I	p	q
t1	X_1			I		
t2		X_1	X_1	I	X_1	X_1
t3	X_1			I		
t4		X_1	X_1	I	X_1	X_1
t5	X_1			I		
t6		X_1	X_1	I	X_1	X_1
t7	X_1			I		
t8		X_1	X_1	I	X_1	X_1

Key:

X_1: Decision makers attempt to have $C > R$

	(D)					
	Period-End Status					
Nations:	m	i	j	I	p	q
t1	$C > R$	$C < R$	$C < R$	I	$C < R$	$C > R$
t2	$C < R$	$C > R$	$C > R$	I	$C < R$	$C > R$
t3	$C > R$	$C < R$	$C < R$	I	$C < R$	$C > R$
t4	$C < R$	$C > R$	$C > R$	I	$C < R$	$C > R$
t5	$C > R$	$C < R$	$C < R$	I	$C < R$	$C > R$
t6	$C < R$	$C > R$	$C > R$	I	$C < R$	$C > R$
t7	$C > R$	$C < R$	$C < R$	I	$C < R$	$C > R$
t8	$C < R$	$C > R$	$C > R$	I	$C < R$	$C > R$

system-level theorists, which is perilously close to environmental determinism). If that is not the case—if the behaviors of decision makers in different states could in fact take a variety of forms—then there would be no reason to expect a systematic, sufficient relationship between any initial condition and *any other* specific form of foreign policy behavior. To the extent that decision makers have some latitude in their choice of options and they are sometimes able to substitute one such alternative for another, a given factor could be expected to lead to, stimulate or "cause" a variety of empirically distinct foreign policy acts, events or behaviors.

The substitutability phenomenon, then, provides a possible answer to the most puzzling of Zinne's puzzles (1980:323). In response to her question—"Do nations interact?"—she examines the work on arms races and concludes that, "...the overall and overwhelming result is that nations *do not interact* in this domain." She does not find interaction in this specific security area in which substitutability could have important effects. In the studies that do discover interaction, however, the focus is not exclusively on armaments, but rather on *overall* interaction patterns which are based on a wide range of hostile/cooperative events.

Although a thorough understanding of the best apparent solution to this difficulty must await the consideration of a few additional points, its basic outlines can at least be traced. *If* scholars are genuinely interested in understanding why states do what they do, they need to move beyond efforts to focus separately on particular concrete behaviors. Rather than asking middle-range questions about specific empirical phenomena, they should begin with that initial "grand" question with which they were allegedly concerned in the first place; rather than asking why countries arm, form alliances, import arms, negotiate, attack, and so on, they should begin by asking themselves what each behavior does—or at least could—represent.

Thus, we need to return to more generic conceptualizations such as "response to threat" or "response to uncertainty under the Westphalian security dilemma," that appeared in the traditional literature under the rubric of "security," "national interest" or the "balance of power." A whole range of activities that are presently discussed under headings such as trade, aid, international law, regimes, international organization and so on could be conceptualized more broadly as "adaptation for coordination or collaboration" or some similar overarching concept. Once broad conceptualizations are developed, analysts will be better able to probe the factors involved in the *choice* of specific foreign policy tools or behaviors. The point which should be emphasized, however, is that there is a need to reconceptualize *exactly what* it is that we want to study and *why*. Students of international relations have, in many cases, actually reified the operational indicators of international interaction. We have studied war *qua* war, alliances *qua* alliances, and tended to overlook the broader international processes and phenomena that such specific forms of behavior represent.

The results of the current narrowness are recognized in recent reviews of the alliance literature by Job (1981) and Ward (1982). Both note that there has not been much cumulation or theoretical development. Both seem to conclude that the alliance research is focused too narrowly—and rather unfruitfully—on questions such as the alliance-war relationship. While neither calls explicitly for reconceptual efforts, both suggest that the time may have come to move beyond the study of alliances per se and efforts to develop "alliance theory." Job in particular seems to suggest that the time has come to begin asking what alliances do (or under certain conceptualizations, could) "really" represent.[9]

The beginnings of one such unifying formulation are shown in appendix 1, following this chapter. The image is one of value-maximizing decision makers who perceive themselves to be confronted with a security dilemma. A perceived imbalance in the capacity-to-risk inequality (i.e., $C \leq R$) at any given point in time acts as the motive force; given an imbalance, decision makers are inclined or "willing" to attempt to reverse it by adopting some policy initiative that they expect will increase their defense capacity or decrease their risks. This "probable" behavior is expected to interact with what is "possible." Put simply, decision makers will be constrained by the range of available policy options; they will adopt a given policy alternative (such as war) if and only if they have both the "willingness" and "opportunity" to do so (along the lines of our earlier discussions of war).

While major elements of Realism and the security dilemma are thus specified in appendix 1, it should be underscored that those elements are being formalized around an expected utility framework that draws on the Sprouts' concept of "cognitive behaviorism" in a manner that is eschewed by Realist theorists. While the model is somewhat similar to the general Realist approach, therefore, it is also consistent with the Sprouts' rejection of environmental determinism, i.e., it seeks to map motivating factors through decision makers' perceptions *even if* all decision makers perceive alike and they do not make a (statistical) difference on what they refer to as foreign policy outputs. Mapping through decision makers is a *logical* requirement and not a statistical concern; nothing would happen (no relationships would hold) if decision makers did not exist.[10]

Assuming for the moment that the axioms in appendix 1 apply to states m, i, and j (that each has effectively unlimited implementation capability or opportunities to act) and that m views i and j as risks while i and j view m—but not each other—as possible sources of danger, the interactions among m, i, and j in part A of table 5.1 begin to become intelligible. The apparently diverse behaviors and acts become commensurable. If the formulation and the just mentioned auxiliary conditions had been in place at the outset, it would have been possible to deduce that each state would adopt *some* measure to increase capacity (C) or decrease risk (R) in each successive round (see part B of table 5.1). Each of those concepts would have brought together a number of hitherto apparently diverse behaviors. Within the context of the model, increases in defense expenditures, alliance offers and efforts to import arms could have been seen as commensurable; they could have been recognized as alternative indicators of decision makers' efforts to increase their defense capacity. Alliance dissolutions, offers to negotiate and military strikes could also have been rendered commensurable as efforts to decrease risk. It would have been possible to go further; efforts to increase capacity or decrease risk—along with the distinct empirical behaviors that each embraces within the formulation—could have been linked in turn to decision makers' efforts to manage their respective C-to-R inequalities (see part C of table 5.1).

With all of this in mind, consider the behaviors of actors p and q in columns 4 and 5 of table 5.1. While m, i, and j display a wide range of behaviors—presumably in an effort to manipulate their capacity-to-risk ratios—p and q remain completely inactive. Viewed at the raw empirical level, there appears to be no consistency whatsoever in the actions of the five countries. Each responds differently. Even for analysts who recognize the underlying unity of the actions of the first three actors, the behaviors of p and q would probably appear to be distinct departures from the expected pattern. While the acts of m, i, and j are consistent with the postulate that the decision makers in those states perceive a security problem and that they are therefore moving to undertake policy initiatives that will increase their defense capabilities or decrease their risks, as has been said, p and q appear to behave quite differently. They do nothing at all; the conceptualization does not seem to apply.

The point to be noted, however, is that states p and q could be imbedded in the pattern if one began with the model in appendix 1 and also knew that: (1) The decision makers of p view actor m as a potential threat which upsets their C-to-R ratio throughout the sequence, but they lack the capability to undertake any action to reset the equality (see postulates 1 and 5 in appendix 1); and (2) the decision makers of actor q do not perceive the acts of any of the other parties as threatening, perhaps because they are distant from or ideologically allied to them (see postulate 3). Given these auxiliary conditions, one would *expect* the empirical behaviorial patterns of p and q to appear distinct from those of m, i, and j. While the latter three would be expected to increase their defense capacities or decrease their risks if the model is "true," p would remain inactive because its decision makers' willingness to act would be frustrated by lack of capability (opportunity) while q would remain inactive because it simply is not motivated to act. The acts of all five states, m, i, j, p, and q in table 5.1, are in fact consistent with the postulate that decision makers are operating to establish favorable capacity-to-risk inequalities.

Another reason why actors p and q in this illustration are of interest derives from the so-called "empty cell" problem. Instead of ignoring the nonbehaviors of actors (the zeros or empty cells in data matrices), analysts might better attempt to utilize the important information that is conveyed by such nonbehaviors when they construct and evaluate their models.[11]

These observations raise an important point that is generally overlooked: Correlations and other such associations may not exist among empirical indicators simply because a given process is operating. *If* the security dilemma formulation shown in appendix 1 was "true," states could reasonably be expected to behave differently. The relationships among the theoretical concepts could be general, but even if that were the case, the outcomes of the decision processes of different states *could be* rather heterogeneous. Again, if the model is "true," different empirical behaviors could follow.

PROBLEM #2: THE OVERLOOKED POSSIBILITIES OF ALTERNATIVE TRIGGERS AND "SOMETIMES TRUE" LAWS

The problem created by the potential for foreign policy substitutability is exacerbated by analysts' practice of equating laws, theories and models with universal—or at least highly generalizable—empirical "truths." At one level, the problem arises because the operation of even universal laws may not invariably be evident empirically. Scholars already recognize some of the reasons why this could be the case.[12] Our concern here is with a more fundamental—and generally overlooked—possibility. Put simply, analysts may be led astray when they associate laws and theories with questions of universal truth or empirical generalizations because a given phenomenon may occur for a variety of distinct, totally incommensurable, reasons.

Just as the foreign policy substitution possibility suggests that a given factor may lead to different results (a one-to-many mapping), the *logical reverse* is also imaginable. Different processes may lead to similar results; different factors may trigger similar responses (a many-to-one mapping). If policymakers can use different options in their pursuit of similar goals (i.e., substitute), it is also quite likely that different decision makers may adopt identical options for different reasons or that they could sometimes employ similar means to pursue different goals.[13]

One aspect of the alternative trigger problem is implicit in part A of table 5.1 above; in this guise, at least, the difficulty is easily circumvented by employing existing procedures. As we showed in that illustration, the mth state's increases in each round could plausibly be expected to lead to different responses by the ith and jth states; in a process of foreign policy substitution, a given trigger could lead to different empirical reactions. The point to be noted here is that even though the mth state elects to increase its defense spending in each round, one should not necessarily expect to find any single empirical trigger for the selection of that option. Assuming that the leaders of the mth state are concerned with their country's security situation, then increases in defense spending by i and j, the formation of an alliance between them, the dissolution of an alliance, efforts by j to import arms, and certainly attacks by the jth state should *all* be expected to contribute to decisions by leaders of the mth state to increase their defense capabilities.

A second aspect of the alternative trigger problem is perhaps more important; in this form, the difficulty is less easily resolved. Imagine a world that is comprised of two sets of cases: those that are characterized by condition A and those that are not, i.e., a world in which there are A and –A cases. Presume that type A cases are those in which decision makers are concerned with maintaining their country's national security, while decision makers in –A polities pursue other goals. Imagine also that within the set of cases A, the development of an external risk (X or any x_i) is invariably sufficient for an effort to resolve the security problem (Y), but that external risk is not necessary for efforts to resolve the security problem because leaders are also concerned with through-time deteriorations in their defense capacities. Within the set of type A states, (1) Y follows wherever and whenever X (or any x_i) occurs, but (2) Y sometimes occurs in the absence of X (or all X_i). When A is not present, in contrast, (3) X (and the x_i) do not lead to Y, and (4) Y sometimes occurs in the absence of X (or all x_i).

Expressed simply, the hypothesis is of the form, "Given A, if X (or any x_i), then Y (or any y_i)," i.e., given A, X is sufficient but not necessary, for Y. If A were a measured variable rather than a theoretical postulate or axiom that is presumed to be either true or untrue, the proposition could be rewritten: "If A and X (or any x_i), then Y (or any y_i), i.e., A and X are jointly sufficient for Y." Seen in this fashion, axioms are simply dichotomous variables that analysts either choose or are forced to leave unmeasured. What this suggests is that, in general, axioms should *not* be viewed as assertions of universal truth. They should instead be seen as *antecedents* in complex "if...then" statements which in collapsed form would read: "If the specified axioms are true for a given case then the model should apply." Once this is seen, one can move quickly beyond debates over the universal truth or falsity of the assumptions themselves. The question of the truth or falsity of the model is put aside. One even moves beyond concerns for generality and becomes more directly concerned with (*a*) identifying cases in which the axioms are true and in which the model should therefore be useful, and (*b*) developing complementary models which hold under alternative sets of initial axioms.

Finally, let us make the usual presumptions regarding the validity and reliability of the indicators and consider the following possible case structure:[14]

Case 1	A	x_1	$-x_2$	$-x_3$	X	Y
Case 2	A	$-x_1$	x_2	$-x_3$	X	Y
Case 3	A	$-x_1$	$-x_2$	x_3	X	Y
Case 4	A	x_1	x_2	x_3	X	Y
Case 5	A	$-x_1$	$-x_2$	$-x_3$	$-X$	Y
Case 6	A	$-x_1$	$-x_2$	$-x_3$	$-X$	Y
Case 7	A	$-x_1$	$-x_2$	$-x_3$	$-X$	Y
Case 8	A	$-x_1$	$-x_2$	$-x_3$	$-X$	Y
Case 9	$-A$	x_1	$-x_2$	$-x_3$	X	$-Y$
Case 10	$-A$	$-x_1$	x_2	$-x_3$	X	$-Y$
Case 11	$-A$	$-x_1$	$-x_2$	x_3	X	$-Y$
Case 12	$-A$	x_1	x_2	x_3	X	$-Y$
Case 13	$-A$	$-x_1$	$-x_2$	$-x_3$	$-X$	Y

Case 14	–A	$-x_1$	$-x_2$	$-x_3$	–X	Y
Case 15	–A	$-x_1$	$-x_2$	$-x_3$	–X	Y
Case 16	–A	$-x_1$	$-x_2$	$-x_3$	–X	Y

Even for those analysts who recognize both the substitutability problem and the first type of alternative trigger problem and elect therefore to focus on Y and X rather than exclusively on the occurrence of any one of the y_i or x_i, interpretation of the pattern would not be a simple matter. That would be especially the case if they ignored the A/–A bifurcation of the set of cases and were concerned only with the X/Y relationship. Put simply, application of the standard procedures would lead them either to reject the hypothesis that X generally leads to Y or to underestimate the importance of that linkage.

Within the domain circumscribed by the presence of A (cases 1–8 above), however, X is sufficient for Y. Outside of that domain, X does not lead to Y (cases 9–16). The occurrences of Y in the –A domain must be triggered by something else. Knowing about X or any x_i would not help.

That said, however, the point should be clear. While the X/Y hypothesis is not general, it is nevertheless a perfectly sound—indeed, even "lawlike"—proposition *within its domain of applicability* (the cases in the set A). While one is ultimately interested in developing an explanation that applies to all sixteen of the cases above, no additional work, either theoretical or empirical, is necessary to account for the first eight.

Thus, there are two different ways to approach the cases above. One is to develop and test hypotheses that are expected at the outset to be general or applicable to the universe of cases. That method would be consistent with current practices and the standard approach. Generalizations are found by aiming directly at them. Unfortunately, that strategy seems to reduce to an all or nothing situation in which the analyst is forced to play to weakness; to explain completely any occurrence of a phenomenon, one must account for all occurrences.

The other strategy is to develop and test hypotheses that are expected to hold only under certain conditions (e.g., A or –A; when decision makers seek to maintain their national security and when they do not). While the analyst is ultimately interested in accounting for all occurrences of a phenomenon, the immediate, somewhat counterintuitive, strategy would entail an initial consideration of *what* relationships should hold *when* and a focus on only those cases in which the conditions pertain. Once those occurrences were explained, the effort would move on, perhaps developing very different models that are applicable to the other cases. This domain-specific theory approach would thus let the analyst *play to strength.* Rather than requiring the analyst to be able to account for the phenomenon Y both when decision makers are and are not concerned with their countries' security dilemmas, it would allow one to conclude that there are occurrences for which one can account (i.e., those in set A) and those whose explanation requires more theoretical and empirical research (i.e., those in the –A set). Rather than resting "progress" on the isolation of *the* explanation that holds for all, it would allow one to move ahead with efforts to identify *an* explanation that holds for some.

Let us consider now the unified actor/security dilemma formulation discussed above (see appendix 1). Among other things, that model specifies that decision makers are motivated to establish the inequality expressed in axiom 3a: Cnt > Rnt. It suggests that decision makers want to be unconditionally viable and would be consistent with their attempts to maintain at least local supremacy.

If we presume for the purpose of argument that at least some decision makers in at least some settings do in fact key their decisions on that inequality, we come up against an obvious problem. With very little in the way of data analysis, we know that there are (or in principle, could be) states that act to increase their defense capabilities and decrease their risks at given points in time *even though* they have already so *clearly* satisfied the inequality and established their unconditional viability that the acts of other states do not reverse the inequality. Because such states have already attained their goal, the motivation that assumedly drives decision makers is lost; the antecedent condition in postulate 4a (i.e., the condition Cntl < Rntl) would simply never be established. Even though the model could therefore be adequate in accounting for the behaviors of states such as m, i, and j in table 5.1, it would leave totally unexplained the behaviors of such already convincingly viable actors.

Still assuming then that the formulation in table 5.1 is useful for accounting for the decisions of some states but having concluded that it could not logically be expected to account for the decisions of all states, the researcher is in a difficult situation *if* the goal is to discover a single, general formulation that applies to all cases both through time and across space. Even though the axioms of the model could be valid for some cases and the model's postulates could also hold within that domain, current practices would lead the analyst to reject the model because neither it nor the relationships that it implies are universally "true." Put more squarely, a model that could be perfectly adequate for explaining what happens in some well-defined cases would be abandoned because it does not always apply or help to explain all cases.

The importance of this point becomes more apparent once one recognizes that a variety of *other motive* assumptions could be postulated to characterize decision making processes. (See Appendixes 2-4. These formulations are useful in that they indicate how our arguments and analyses can be applied to broader political and policy phenomena—that our discussions clearly go beyond war and international conflict.) One such motive assumption would be a variation on the national security model in appendix 1; rather than attempting to establish the Cnt > Rnt inequality, decision makers could be posited to seek the maintenance of the status quo so that the capacity-to-risk ratio at any time is at least equal to that of an earlier period. Such a modified national security formulation might be applicable to states that continue to increase their own defense capacity and reduce the threat engendered by their opponents even though they are already unconditionally viable; it might be consistent with the illusory question for "perfect" security or with the "security dilemma" of never knowing how much capability is "enough." It might also be appropriate for states that are only conditionally viable (e.g., most Third and Fourth World countries) that it would be implausible to pursue increases in national defense capability or decreases in external risk which would be sufficient to establish a favorable defense capacity-to-risk inequality.

In contrast to such national security motivations, one could posit cases in which decision makers ignore *external* exigencies and questions of national survival and focus instead—or at least more immediately—on *internal* pressures that concern their own survival in office. Put differently, one could imagine "domestic/ governmental viability" models in which decision makers seek either to maintain enough political strength to keep from being deposed by their domestic opposition (a domestic algorithm of the capacity-to-risk inequality in which the focus is on a government's capacity to resist internal threat and the degree of such threat) or they try to maintain at least their prior position vis-à-vis domestic threats.

The point here should be clear. A variety of goals, and indeed combinations of several goals, could be postulated *even if* it is the case that the anarchic international system requires self-help and over the long-run "rewards" states whose decision makers pursue national survival by adopting policies that increase national capacities and reduce those of other states and eventually punishes states that either ignore the demand or simply fail in their pursuit of it. Any of those motivating factors could provide a rationale for expecting that decision makers might increase their military expenditures, create alliances, dissolve them, import arms, open negotiations, launch preemptive military strikes, and so on (see appendix 5). Different processes—including a number that depart from an assumption of unified, value-maximizing decision makers—could lead to similar results.

A consideration of such alternative formulations suggests several important points. Consider first the partitioning role of axioms. While there are probably some actual cases in which decision makers pursue almost any goal that one might reasonably wish to posit, there are also likely to be instances in which decision makers are motivated by other concerns. To the extent that that seems plausible, it follows that such alternative motive forces or goals would not in any sense constitute the bases for rival or competing models. To be sure, one of the motive assumptions might be true for more cases than others. If so, the formulation that is appropriate for that axiom would be more useful than the other models; it would apply to more cases. The point, however, is that it would probably not be plausible to argue that any of the motive axioms is always true. Thus, it would not be reasonable to expect that any of the models is universally applicable. One would therefore not be inclined to conduct a *crucial* or *critical* test in order to discover which is the more general. One would instead be interested in exploring whether or not a given model applies to a given, well-defined, case or set of cases.

Second, if it is the case that different processes do indeed lead to similar concrete empirical behaviors, the concept that one such act would reflect could be different within different formulations. If the decision makers are dealing with a national viability or security dilemma for example (shown in appendixes 1 and 2), an increase in their defense expenditures or the formation of an alliance would be interpretable as—and more importantly, an indicator of—efforts to increase their own defense capacity or decrease the foreign risks with which they perceive it to be confronted; if they are seeking to resolve a simple governmental viability problem, on the other hand (see appendixes 3 and 4) those same acts would reflect efforts to increase their government's strength or decrease the degree to which it is threatened by domestic forces. Even though analysts at least sometimes tend to view acts as inherently or intrinsically falling on some fixed scale between conflict and cooperation or between friendly and hostile behaviors, therefore, it might make more sense to interpret decision makers' behaviors in the context of what they were attempting to accomplish.

Third, and perhaps most important, the argument here suggests that it may be useful to expect that true social laws may not *always* hold, operate or apply empirically. There may well be a variety of social laws, each of which is true but which should be expected to hold only under certain—perhaps very special—conditions. While it is possible that universals—always true laws—exist and we believe that scholars should continue their efforts to identify them, it is difficult to think of very many empirical universals that have been identified by even physical scientists. Thus, it may be useful to recognize that there could very well be laws that are in some sense "good," "domain specific," or "nice" even though the relationships that they imply are not necessarily very general empirically.[15] Rather than assuming that there need be a single, "always true," law which accounts for a given phenomenon whenever and wherever it has occurred or will occur, it may be more productive to think of laws each of which is always true under certain conditions (or within certain domains) but which is only "sometimes true" empirically because those conditions do not always hold in the empirical world. While the identification of universal relationships is still a worthwhile goal, it may be useful to consider other—equally important and perhaps more attainable—research objectives.[16]

Ultimately, of course, analysts may develop several models, each of which seems useful for explaining a given phenomenon under different conditions. When that occurs—when we understand why Y occurs in *both* the A and –A domains, to return to the example above—it may be possible to integrate or synthesize those "islands" of understanding. In the interim, however, we should play to strength; we should learn not to reject or disregard an explanation that is only sometimes true.

SOME CONSEQUENCES FOR THE STUDY OF INTERNATIONAL RELATIONS AND INTERNATIONAL CONFLICT

Cumulation and Theory

Let us return again to the relationship between cumulation and theory. Our discussion has attempted to delineate a particular impediment to cumulation: *The general failure to conceptualize questions and indicators broadly enough to capture the relationships and processes that scholars are actually interested in studying.* We have argued that the "islands of theory" extant in the international relations literature have been too narrowly conceived for answering the questions that have been asked; we have suggested that analysts' ways of theorizing—and perhaps even their expectations about the results of such efforts—may have been inappropriate for dealing with the problems at hand. Analysts have lost their perspective, perhaps as a consequence of the abandonment of grand theory, their efforts to develop middle-range formulations, or their adoption of the even narrower hypothesis-testing procedures which were fostered by the empirical "third wave" of the 1960s and 1970s.

While we have offered a number of specific recommendations about what should be done, two remedies should be reemphasized: First, scholars should endeavor to merge the rigor and systematization of scientific inquiry with the broader, "grand theoretical," conceptualizations of the traditional literature in which substitutability and domain-specific laws were at least implicitly recognized. Second, analysts should begin to pay more careful attention to basic epistemological issues (see also Bueno de Mesquita, 1980b, 1981a). Our central point is that existing research practices, drawn as they are from other disciplines that are concerned with other types of problems, should be utilized with circumspection. Even though scholars are often impatient with epistemological issues and find themselves anxious to get on with their analyses, they need to bear in mind that how they approach their problems—the manner in which they conceptualize them and the methods they utilize in their attempts to solve them—ultimately impinge on their results. If apparently distinct foreign policies could be states' responses to similar problems as a result of substitutability and similar foreign policies could be responses to different problems as a result of the operation of domain-specific laws, then we may need to rethink the accepted procedures.

These arguments relate to a similar issue regarding the lenses through which we wish to see the world. As social scientists we begin with the presumption that what we are interested in is prediction and/or explanation, and assume that there is a "reality" out there with which to deal. There are many problems with this assumption—e.g., "reality" has lots of detail if we take a close look, but much less if we pull back and look from a greater temporal or geographic distance. Singer (1969) has described this in contrasting the nation- and system-levels of analysis. We get the same result if we compare a time series comprised of daily observations with a time series made up of one observation per decade.

The obvious point is that all of these lenses provide us with images of "reality." The views are different, but they are all "real." The somewhat less obvious point is that the explanations of those different views might be different. For the more detailed pictures we would need a "fine" theory; for the less detailed pictures we would develop a "coarse" theory. These fine and coarse theories could very easily draw upon distinct sets of theoretical arguments and explanatory factors.

Micro-Level Decisional Analysis and Process

We have tried to do more than simply issue yet another call for "theory," for more fruitful merging of tradition and science, or for greater attention to the implications of our methods. As in earlier chapters, we have suggested here that a focus on *process* at a micro-analytical level of analysis could be fruitful for the study of international relations. We argue that both opportunity and willingness are fundamental for understanding the behavior of states. Each country's objective opportunities circumscribe the range of possible acts and behaviors that are available to its decision makers. Because the factors that create or preclude different options are differentially distributed across states and even within states through time, it follows that such concerns are, in some sense, likely to be important for understanding states' policy undertakings. A focus on such factors could provide insights into the basic parameters or limits of different states' foreign policies.

However, to the extent that analysts are less interested in the parameters within which states operate and are ultimately more concerned with understanding why states adopt certain options at particular times, we have carefully developed a complex argument to support our contention that a focus on states' attributes will not suffice. An attribute approach could tell us what it is possible for countries to do and therefore possibly what the aggregate probabilities are that certain types of events will occur in a given group or sample of states. A focus on attributes cannot tell us, however, what particular states will do or when they will do it. Certain objective capabilities may be *necessary* for a foreign policy initiation but they should not be expected to be *sufficient* for that undertaking unless, that is, decision makers are homogeneously willing to avail themselves of all their available opportunities. The problem, however, is that it does *not* seem reasonable to expect that all foreign policymakers in all nations pursue identical goals.[17]

In contrast to Waltz (1979:chap. 4) and other system theorists who argue that theories that deal with the individual-level or nation-level of analysis are reductionist and that as such those formulations are incapable of explaining international relations phenomena, therefore, we conclude that progress toward understanding foreign policy and international relations can indeed be made by focusing at the state/decision-making level. Waltz may be entirely correct in asserting that the environment—the anarchic/self-help international system—is important insofar as it "constrains" and "disposes" states to seek their own survival (1979:69, 72). It could indeed be the case as he argues that over the long run the exigencies of the system have evolutionary effects which are paralleled in micro-economics; states (like corporations) may ignore them, but they do so at their peril; in the long run, only states that attend to their environmental demands will survive. Different types of international systems could thus be conceptualized as constituting the A and –A domains discussed in the example in the previous section. Given an anarchic self-help system, decision makers are constrained or disposed to pursue survival; a particular set of micro-level behaviors and (in the long run) macro- or systemic-level outcomes hold. Change the system, move to a domain in which the legitimate use of power is centralized, and different micro- and macro-outcomes *could* follow.[18]

That said, however, two points need to be made. First, the type of system does *not* seem sufficient for deducing what states will seek or how they will behave. Waltz posits that systemic anarchy and the principle of self help will induce states to seek their own survival by increasing their own capacities while reducing those of other states; from the type of system, he infers a particular motivation or willingness.[19] The problem, of course, is that in the short run the system does not appear to dispose all decision makers or make them willing to pursue national survival as their main priority. Even though they may thus endanger long-run national viability as Waltz suggests, those states fall completely outside his formulation. Their decision makers are willing to do other things; their actual behaviors depart form what Waltz would predict. In other cases, of course, it could be argued that the system does animate decision makers and dispose them to pursue national security concerns. In at least some of these states, however, the will to adopt policies that enhance survival is outdistanced by the objective capacities or opportunities to act. Such states might try but fail; the actual behaviors of those countries would also depart from Waltz's predictions.

Finally, then, there are still other states—perhaps most especially the major powers—that might indeed be motivated by national security concerns and that also have the objective capabilities to act as Waltz predicts. Here too, however, a problem seems to develop. *Even if* Waltz is entirely correct about the ways in which the system constrains and induces such states, the possibilities that such states have for substituting options in pursuit of survival and national security (and, by definition, major powers would have the greatest latitude for such substitution), are left almost entirely unspecified. Hence, decision makers could use overt force, but they could also adopt any of a range of alternative behaviors, including the whole range of "almost-war" behaviors discussed in the previous chapter. Even if it were the case that all—or even all important—states pursue survival in a self-help system, therefore, it is not entirely clear that it would be possible to deduce the condition of that system, e.g., its stability, or more especially, its potential for largescale uses of force.

Waltz himself admits much of this, of course, when he observes that one should not *expect* a theory of international politics to explain or predict which countries will respond, when, and in what ways.[20] However, if that is the case—if system type does not permit the deduction of micro-level, foreign policy behaviors because the decision makers in some states are not motivated to seek survival, others fail, and those who are so motivated can substitute the precise means by which they proceed—then it is difficult to see how Waltz's reaggregation to the system-level could work.

The second point should be clear. Properly set out and specified, our own concepts of opportunity and willingness can reflect both the nature and structure of the international system and the ways in which that system constrains and induces national behavior. While Waltz focuses on structure and rejects process concerns, our own approach deals with *processes* that unfold *within structures*. In the short term, the formulation allows for the possibility that structures may very well impinge on processes, influencing to some extent the direction and precise outputs of decision makers. In the long term, however, processes can also have a generative effect on structures; they have the capacity to transform structure.[21] Our first use of process here, then, refers to how decision makers in different states choose from among alternatives. Our second use of process, in turn, refers to a focus on *interdependent outcomes* that derive from the interaction of decision-making units in different states (see chapter 4).

The first use of process permits a concern for actors' attributes, the system, their placement in the system, exigencies of the system, and so on. More importantly, however, it also rejects environmental (or even attributional) determinism. A central criticism of Waltz (1979) is that he has underestimated the cognitive links between social entities and their environments. He artificially separates the entity and the environment, and seems to ignore the third leg of the Sprouts' "ecological triad": the entity-environment relationship. This relationship almost always has a prominent cognitive component. The "enduring anarchic character of international policies" alone, which Waltz (1979:66) regards as the central factor in the analysis of international relations, *cannot* explain the variance in foreign policy behavior.

Indeed, while states' objective capabilities may define the range of possibilities as demonstrated in the following chapter, there is a need to consider both the processes by which decision makers choose goals and how they choose certain options over others in pursuit of those ends. This suggests that we might usefully follow Bueno de Mesquita's expected utility approach and study how decision makers select from among varying sets of available, potentially substitutable alternatives, paying particular attention to the cognitive or perceptual processes that we couch in terms of willingness and that the Sprouts cast in terms of cognitive behaviorism. The model in appendix 1, based on capacity-to-risk relationships (and the alternative models presented in the Appendixes 2–5), are *all* based on the idea of a general equilibrium-seeking decision routine.

Given disturbances that change some current state of affairs (e.g., that reverse a $Cnt > Rnt$ inequality to a $Cnt \leq Rnt$ condition or that lower a government's domestic viability by reducing its domestic strength or increasing its domestic threat), decision makers become willing to reestablish the status quo. Just as a variety of different empirical factors can cause such a disruption (alternative triggers), in principle decision makers have a variety of possible responses (substitution capability). What looks chaotic, unsystematic, and perhaps random at the empirical level becomes coherent, commensurable and simple at a more abstract level of logical analysis.

In summary, the discussion here has attempted to raise a series of issues regarding cumulation, conceptualization, levels of analysis and theory. While a number of points and conclusions have been developed, it should perhaps be especially emphasized in closing that Waltz's rejection of micro-level/analytical approaches seems too extreme. While he could be correct in arguing that a systematic theory can show and teach us many things, it also appears to be the case that one can work at the micro-level, avoid the "analytic fallacy," and develop theory that is useful for predicting and explaining foreign policy and international phenomena. Clearly, we need to consider how the willingness and opportunities of states interact to produce foreign policy behaviors. In the next chapter we turn to a fuller consideration of the international system. In the concluding chapter we consider more fully the substantive interaction of decision-making and systemic levels of analysis.

APPENDIXES TO CHAPTER 5

1: A UNIFIED ACTOR/NATIONAL SECURITY DILEMMA FORMULATION

Axiom 1: The decision makers of an nth nation are—or can be treated as—unified and value-maximizing actors who possess perfect information regarding all options and their consequences.

Axiom 2: At any given point in time, the decision makers in an nth nation perceive that they have a certain national defense capacity (Cnt) and are confronted by some degree of national risk or vulnerability (Rnt).[a]

Axiom 3: The decision makers of an nth nation are motivated or willing to establish the following inequality:

$$Cnt > Rnt$$

(I.e., the decision makers want to be unconditionally viable and maintain at least local supremacy.)

Postulate 1: Only if the decision makers of an nth nation command the necessary objective capability or opportunity (O) to adopt some unilateral policy initiative, then the adoption of that initiative.

Postulate 2: If the decision makers of an nth nation perceive that their nation's defense capacity has been neglected or allowed to deteriorate between t0 and t1, they will perceive that $Cnt0 > Cnt1$.

Postulate 3: If a given nation increases its national defense capacity between t0 and t1 and the decision makers in an nth nation perceive that action as a threat, they will perceive that $Rnt0 < Rnt1$.

Postulate 4: If Cntl < Rntl, then the decision makers of the nth nation will be motivated to adopt some policy initiative which is designed to increase Cn and/or decrease Rn at t2. (I.e., if the decision makers perceive that they are only conditionally viable at t1, then they will be willing to increase their capacities or decrease their risks.)

Postulate 5: If and only if the decision makers of an nth nation command the necessary capacity (or opportunity) to adopt some unilateral policy initiative and they are motivated (or willing) to do so, then the adoption of that initiative.

2: UNIFIED ACTOR/SECURITY DILEMMA, FORMULATION B[b]

Axiom 1: The decision makers of an nth state are—or can be treated as—unified and value-maximizing actors who possess perfect information regarding all options and their consequences.

Axiom 2a: At any given point in time, the decision makers in an nth state perceive that they have a certain national defense capacity (Cnt) and are confronted by some degree of national risk or vulnerability (Rnt).[c]

Axiom 3b: The decision makers of an nth state are motivated or willing to establish the following inequality:[d]

$$[\text{Cnt}/\text{Rnt}] \geq [\text{Cnt-1}/\text{Rnt-1}]$$

Postulate 1: Only if the decision makers of an nth state command the necessary objective capability or opportunity (O) to adopt some unilateral policy initiative, then the adoption of that initiative.

Postulate 2a: If the decision makers of an nth state perceive that their state's defense capacity has been neglected or allowed to deteriorate between t0 and t1, they will perceive that Cnt0 > Cntl.

Postulate 3a: If a given state increases its national defense capacity between t0 and t1 and the decision makers in an nth state perceive that action as a threat, they will perceive the Rnt0 < Rntl.

Postulate 4b: If [Cntl/Rntl] < [Cnt0/Rnt0], then the decision makers of the nth state will be motivated to adopt some policy initiative which is designed to increase Cn and/or decrease Rn at t2. (I.e., if the decision makers perceive that they are worse off at t1 than at t0, then they will be willing to increase their capacities or decrease their risks.)

Postulate 5: If and only if the decision makers of an nth state command the necessary capacity (or opportunity) to adopt some unilateral policy initiative and they are motivated (or willing) to do so, then the adoption of that initiative.[f]

3: UNIFIED ACTOR/GOVERNMENTAL STABILITY FORMULATION[b]

Axiom 1: The decision makers of an nth state are—or can be treated as—unified and value-maximizing actors who possess perfect information regarding all options and their consequences.

Axiom 2b: At any given point in time, the decision makers in an nth state perceive that their government has a certain degree of political strength (Snt) and is confronted by some degree of threat that it will be toppled by domestic forces (Tnt).[g]

Axiom 3c: The decision makers of an nth state are motivated or willing to establish the following inequality:[h]

$$Snt > Tnt$$

Postulate 1: Only if the decision makers of an nth state command the necessary objective capability or opportunity (O) to adopt some unilateral policy initiative, then the adoption of that initiative.

Postulate 2b: If the decision makers of an nth state perceive that their government's strength has been neglected or allowed to deteriorate betwen t0 and t1, they will perceive that $Snt0 > Snt1$.

Postulate 3b: If a given domestic opponent of the government increases its capacity between t0 and t1 and the decision makers in an nth state perceive that action as a threat to their government, they will perceive that $Tnt0 < Tnt1$.

Postulate 4c: If $Snt1 < Tnt1$, then the decision makers of the nth state will be motivated to adopt some policy initiative which is designed to increase Sn and/or decrease Tn at t2. (I.e., if the decision makers perceive that their government is only conditionally viable at t1, then the decision makers will be willing to increase their government's strengths or decrease the threat to its stability.)

Postulate 5: If and only if the decision makers of an nth state command the necessary capacity (or opportunity) to adopt some unilateral policy initiative and they are motivated (or willing) to do so, then the adoption of that initiative.[f]

4: UNIFIED ACTOR/GOVERNMENTAL STABILITY, FORMULATION D[b]

Axiom 1: The decision makers of an nth state are—or can be treated as—unified and value-maximizing actors who possess perfect information regarding all options and their consequences.

Axiom 2b: At any given point in time, the decision makers in an nth state perceive that their government has a certain degree of political strength (Snt) and is confronted by some degree of threat that it will be toppled by domestic forces (Tnt).[g]

Axiom 3d: The decision makers of an nth state are motivated or willing to establish the following inequality:[i]

$$[Snt/Tnt] \geq [Snt{-}1/Tnt{-}1]$$

Postulate 1: Only if the decision makers of an nth state command the necessary objective capability or opportunity (O) to adopt some unilateral policy initiative, then the adoption of that initiative.[e]

Postulate 2b: If the decision makers of an nth state perceive that their government's strength has been neglected or allowed to deteriorate between t0 and t1, they will perceive that $Snt0 > Snt1$.

Postulate 3b: If a given domestic opponent of the government increases its capacity between t0 and t1 and the decision makers in an nth state perceive that action as a threat to their government, they will perceive that $Tnt0 < Tnt1$.

Postulate 4d: If $[Snt1/Tnt1] < [Snt0/Tnt0]$, then the decision makers of the nth state will be motivated to adopt some policy initiative which is designed to increase Sn and/or decrease Tn at t2. (I.e., if the decision makers perceive that their government is worse off at t1 than at t0, then the decision makers will be willing to increase their government's strength or decrease the threat to its stability.)

Postulate 5: If and only if the decision makers of an nth state command the necessary capacity (or opportunity) to adopt some unilateral policy initiative and they are motivated (or willing) to do so, then the adoption of that initiative.

5: NATIONAL AND GOVERNMENTAL VIABILITY:
AN INTEGRATED FORMULATION[b,j]

Axiom 1: The decision makers of an nth state are—or can be treated as—unified and value-maximizing actors who possess perfect information regarding all options and their consequences.

Axiom 2: At any given point in time, the decision makers in an nth state perceive that:

a. They have a certain national defense capacity (Cnt) and are confronted by some degree of national risk or vulnerability (Rnt),[c] or

b. Their government has a certain degree of political strength (Snt) and is confronted by some degree of threat that it will be toppled by domestic forces (Tnt).[g]

Axiom 3: The decision makers of an nth state are motivated or willing to establish one or more of the following inequalities:

a. $\quad$ Cnt > Rnt
b. $\quad$ [Cnt/Rnt] $\geq$ [Cnt-1/Rnt-1]
c. $\quad$ Snt > Tnt
d. $\quad$ [Snt/Tnt] $\geq$ [Snt-1/Tnt-1]

Postulate 1: Only if the decision makers of an nth state command the necessary objective capability or opportunity (O) to adopt some unilateral policy initiative, then the adoption of that initiative.[c]

Postulate 2a: If the decision makers of an nth state perceive that their state's defense capacity has been neglected or allowed to deteriorate between $t0$ and $t1$, they will perceive that $Cnt0 > Cnt1$.

Postulate 2b: If the decision makers of an nth state perceive that their government's strength has been neglected or allowed to deteriorate between $t0$ and $t1$, they will perceive that $Snt0 > Snt1$.

Postulate 3a: If a given state increases its national defense capacity between $t0$ and $t1$ and the decision makers in an nth state perceive that action as a threat, they will perceive that $Rnt0 < Rnt1$.

Postulate 3b: If a given domestic opponent of the government increases its capacity between $t0$ and $t1$ and the decision makers in an nth state perceive that action as a threat to their government, they will perceive that $Tnt0 < Tnt1$.

Postulate 4: If

     a. $Cnt1 < Rnt1$,
     b. $[Cnt1/Rnt1] < [Cnt0/Rnt0]$,
     c. $Snt1 < Tnt1$, or
     d. $[Snt1/Tnt1] < [Snt0/Tnt0]$,

then the decision makers of the nth state will be motivated to adopt some policy initiative which is designed to increase Cn, decrease Rn, increase Sn or decrease Tn at $t2$.

Postulate 5: If and only if the decision makers of an nth state command the necessary capacity (or opportunity) to adopt some unilateral policy initiative and they are motivated (or willing) to do so, then the adoption of that initiative.[f]

CHAPTER 5 APPENDIXES NOTES

a. It is not important, given the purpose of the illustration, to consider how one might operationalize either Cnt or Rnt. Only three points need to be noted. First, it should be understood that both capacities (C) and risks (R) are conceptualized here in terms of decision makers' perceptions. Put simply, a nation's defense capacities and the risks it confronts are as they are recognized and understood by the decision makers. Consistent with this conceptualization, the capacities of "friendly" or distant nations may be discounted by an nth nation's decision-makers in their calculation of Rnt; similarly, the capacities of friendly, and especially allied, nations could be counted by the nth nation's decision makers as supplemental sources of Cnt. Finally, it should be clear that capacities (C) and risk (R) differ from what are referred to as the decision makers' objective capabilities or opportunities (see Postulate 1) which impact on policy initiatives regardless of whether or not they are (accurately) perceived by the decision makers.

b. With the possible exception of the first axiom, all of the axioms and postulates are consistent with Sprout and Sprout's arguments concerning environmental probabilism and environmental possiblism (1968, 1969).

c. It is not important, given the purpose of the illustration, to consider how one might operationalize either Cnt and Rnt. Only three points need to be noted. First, it should be understood that both capacities (C) and risks (R) are conceptualized here in terms of decision makers' perceptions. Put simply, a state's defense capacities and the risks it confronts are as they are recognized and understood by the decision makers. Consistent with this conceptualization, the capacities of "friendly" or distant states may be discounted by an nth state's decision makers in their calculation of Rnt; similarly, the capacities of friendly, and especially allied, states could be counted by the nth state's decision makers as supplemental sources of Cnt. Finally, it should be clear that capacities (C) and risk (R) differ from what are referred to as the decision makers' objective capabilities or opportunities (see postulate 1 below) which have an impact on policy initiatives regardless of whether or not they are (accurately) perceived by the decision makers.

d. The equation suggests that the leaders of any nth state believe that they face a security problem and that they want to be at least as secure at any point in time as they were at any prior point in time; it would be consistent with attempts to maintain at least the status quo.

e. The reader should recall that we argued in chapter 4 that attributes or characteristics of individual states cannot logically constitute sufficient conditions for the occurrence of phenomena which by definition must occur at least the dyadic level (e.g., wars, alliance formations, negotiations, and arms transfers as opposed to what we refer to here as unilateral foreign policy initiatives).

f. This postulate is drawn from Starr (1978) as refined in the preceding chapters: The opportunity (or capacity) to adopt a given unilateral foreign policy initiative and the willingness (motivation) to adopt it are jointly necessary and sufficient conditions for the measure's actual adoption.

g. Once again, it is not important, given the purpose of the illustration, to consider how one might operationalize either Snt or Tnt. Only three points need to be noted. First, it should be understood that both strength (S) and threats (T) are conceptualized here in terms of decision makers' perceptions. Put simply, a government's strengths and the domestic threats that it confronts are as they are recognized and understood by the decision makers.

Consistent with this conceptualization, the capacities of "friendly" or disinterested domestic forces may be discounted by an nth state's decision makers in their calculation of Tnt; similarly, the capacities of friendly, and especially allied, domestic actors should be counted by the nth state's decision makers as supplemental sources of Snt. Finally, it should be clear that strengths (S) and threats (R) differ from what are referred to as the decision makers' objective capabilities or opportunities (see postulate 1 below) which impact on policy initiatives regardless of whether or not they are (accurately) perceived by the decision makers.

h. The equation suggests that the leaders of any nth state believe that they face a governmental stability problem and that they want to be unconditionally viable (vis-á-vis domestic dissenters) or invulnerable to any domestic threat; it would be consistent with attempts to centralize power in the state.

i. The equation suggests that the leaders of any nth state believe that they face a governmental stability problem and that they want their government to be at least as secure at any point in time as it was at any prior point in time; it would be consistent with attempts to maintain at least the status quo.

j. The integrated argument shown here is perhaps illustrative of how one might proceed. Assuming that (*a*) an analyst has developed the "unified actor/security dilemma" formulation (figure 5.2) and found it useful in some set of cases and (*b*) that other researchers have had similar success in formulating and testing the arguments shown in appendixes 1–3, then (*c*) one could synthesize those islands of theory by developing a more general set of axioms or postulates such as is shown here. (The integration of the various arguments is facilitated, of course, by the fact that all of the formulations are developed within our general opportunity and willingness perspective.)

The advantage that the integrated formulation has over those shown in appendixes 1–4 is clear. *If* the original arguments apply to actual empirical domains of cases but each applies to at least a slightly different domain, then the integrated argument should apply to a larger set of cases. Put differently, the integrated argument would be expected to be more general. (It would still not necessarily be expected to be completely general, however, for the obvious reason that the axioms–particularly the first–are still rather restrictive.) That said, it should be stressed that this increase in generalizability would be achieved in this instance at the cost of a decrease in explanatory precision: Given a set of behaviors or acts that "fit" the expectations of the integrated formulation and perhaps a high Pearson's correlation coefficient or R^2, the analyst would be able to argue that the result is consistent with the overall or integrated process. There would be no way, however, to determine which of the various motive assumptions or what combination of them (if any) might in fact have effected that result. Any one of a variety of subprocesses are permitted by the integrated formulation and any one of them could have led to the action in question.

A more satisfactory statistical result might thus be obtained, but the analyst would be less able to explain just how and why—i.e., by what process(es)—the result came to be. Indeed, the researcher might not even be able to conclude authoritatively that the act indicates an attempt by the decision makers to alter their defense position (and hence, national viability) or change the position of their government. That this would be the case is easily seen by considering the equation that one might write in order to estimate the decision makers' degree of motivation or "willingness" to act. Because the concepts in postulate 4 might plausibly be expected to be operationalizable on the basis of exactly identical indicators, faithful expression of that postulate in a standard multiple regression equation, for example, would require the analyst the enter the *same indicators in each of several* of the terms on the right hand side. The alternative trigger problem would thus reappear; the only solution for those who would be interested in estimating the equation would be to delete terms, allowing each of those that remain to represent several possible motor cues.

6

THE LOGIC OF INTERNATIONAL STRUCTURE:
Power, War, and Micro-Macro Linkages

INTRODUCTION

We have, over the last several chapters, been working towards the argument that an understanding of interdependent and interactive international phenomena (such as the onset of violent conflict) requires a focus on micro-level decision processes. In looking at both the macro and micro levels of analysis, at both the environment and the environed entity, we have concluded by arguing that an understanding of international phenomena requires a focus on such micro-level processes. In the present chapter, however, we expand more fully on the macro/environment/opportunity level—and demonstrate that decision processes operate *within* structures that play an important role in the generation of international interactions such as war.

In this chapter we apply our arguments concerning logic to the questions regarding levels of analysis, and the applicability of systemic level theories and explanations to interdependent outcomes such as war. Again, using war and international conflict as illustrations, we carry our discussion of logic, theory and research design to questions of analysis at the systemic level, the application of power models, and a critical analysis of what our real abilities may be to test what only appear to be contradictory theories. The reader is asked to follow carefully our arguments, as we logically demonstrate that systemic models (such as those based on the polarity of the international system) and which have important willingness components, cannot explain phenomena based on interdependent outcomes. Similarly, we demonstrate the weaknesses of models based on the power capabilities (or attributes) of individual states, whether dressed up as systemic or even dyadic models. The results of these discussions are necessary for conclusions regarding logic, theory-testing, and the lack of utility of "critical tests" to be presented in the final chapter.

Focusing on the distribution of "power" at both the level of the international system (as for example, in research on the effects of polarity) and at the level of state dyads (as for example, in research on the so-called power preponderance and parity hypotheses), the present discussion demonstrates that such distributions are important components in the generation of international conflict, but that they also do not determine when, where or even the extent to which such conflict will occur. These arguments directly follow the critiques of Waltz and a reliance on system-level theory presented in chapter 5.

In sum, the nature of the role that international structures can play may not be what analysts typically appear to expect. Structures may be causally important for phenomena such as conflict even though they are neither logically nor statistically sufficient for its occurrence. In looking at polarity, power parity or preponderance, we see that structures may be important in the generation of conflict even though different structures and structural changes may not produce changes in the incidence, level, rate, or the intensity of international conflict. The effects of structures on interdependent outcomes such as conflict may not be detectable with standard techniques and approaches. All that aside, however, structures may nevertheless be important insofar as they delimit the ranges of behaviors that can be produced by decision makers—that is, structures delimit possible opportunities for behavior as part of the "menu for choice."

We also show specifically that the polarity of the international system and changes in system polarity could be important, but also that differences in system polarity *need not logically lead* to differences in the degrees of peace, war, or stability. At the dyadic level, it is demonstrated that neither of two contrasting distributions—preponderance and parity—is sufficient for conflict, that both types of distribution are consistent with peace, and that those distributions could nevertheless be logically seen as important for the occurrence of conflict. Thus, we use the preponderance/polarity debate as an example of the logical problems involved in the construction of opposing theories and the construction of critical tests for the evaluation (and disposal) of theories.

We should be careful to note that we do *not* present new empirical findings or reanalyses of previously collected data, but that we focus on the limits and possibilities that logically occur with preponderance or parity conditions. The state of our existing understanding of power is briefly reviewed in the first section below. A few stylized facts are then presented. A "first pass" at the power question is then undertaken by considering a series of hypothetical examples; a "second pass" is then made using simulated data.

Power

Few concepts seem to have captured the imagination of international relations scholars quite so much as "power." At both the system level, where the focus has been on the nature of the international system and power polarity, and at the state/dyadic level, where the concern has been with preponderance and parity, analyses of the role of power in the processes that lead to conflict pervade the literature.[1] Despite an almost uninterrupted barrage of criticism regarding the ambiguity and imprecision of the power concept, problems with its measurement and operationalizations,[2] and the logical consistency of power arguments,[3] the work goes on. It seems impossible to bring either theoretical or empirical closure to the issue.

As noted in chapter 2, we have tried to stay out of the morass of power, in part because much of what is conceptualized by that term can be easily handled by opportunity and willingness. Moving through the discussion in the present chapter we again see that as power is used by some scholars as an attribute, to mean military capability, we can translate it into opportunity. We also show that, because the psychologically-oriented influence dimension (willingness) of power is ignored in such models, they cannot work as proposed.

Our conclusion is that it is unclear that the work cited immediately above is leading toward unambiguous answers to analysts' questions. Waltz, Kaplan, and others debate which type of system—unipolar, bipolar, multipolar, bimultipolar, and so on—is more stable and less conducive to international conflict, and recent discussions of the impact of nuclear proliferation seem but an extension of that debate. There is continued disagreement over the meaning and measurement of polarity, stability, and even the most basic notion of what a system may be. Similarly, empirical analyses of the so-called "power parity" and "power preponderance" hypotheses, which are said to provide diametrically opposing predictions about the effects of dyadic power distributions on war, have both been supported in empirical research.[4]

To some extent, of course, the puzzling and contradictory findings are easily explained away by pointing out that different analysts use different research designs, analytical procedures, and data sets. Without doubting either the cogency of the existing methodological critiques or the genuine utility of the prescriptions for improved analyses that have been offered by others, however, one wonders if additional empirical studies—even if they are conducted in the prescribed ways—will ever be capable of yielding unambiguous answers to our questions. One wonders, to put the point more squarely, if improved logic and better theory, in addition to better empirical analysis, will not be needed to clarify the situation. Again, it should be clear that these comments apply to nature of the international system, and its relationship to state-level decision making and interdependent outcomes.

SOME MODEST BEGINNINGS: EXISTING EMPIRICAL EVIDENCE

In considering the roles that power, polarity, preponderance, and parity could play in generating international conflict, it is useful to begin with a few simple, extremely modest observations. Any argument that might be developed must be capable of dealing with existing empirical evidence—stylized facts. While these observations are simple and intentionally impressionistic, they may *not* be entirely trivial. They may provide useful insights on the roles that power, polarity, preponderance, and parity could play in generating conflict.

Although scholars clearly do not know all that they would like to know about the nature of the international system, they do in fact recognize and understand much more than they sometimes admit. A few of those points are worth mentioning:

1. In a decentralized or Westphalian self-help security system, such as supposedly exists in the world today, states are unable to entrust their national security to the good will of others. The leaders of some states appear to recognize this situation. They respond, at least ostensibly, by increasing their power so that others will be deterred from attacking; by and large, those states have managed to survive during

the post-World War II era. The leaders of other countries, in contrast, either do not recognize the situation or do not respond to it. They seem not to care at all that their militaries often do not deter others from attacking them; these states, too, have managed (so far) to survive during the post-World War II era.

2. Despite the attention that analysts pay to turmoil and conflict in the international system and the emphasis that they place on the Westphalian self-help security nature of that system, the world is remarkably "peaceful." There were only 9 interstate or extrasystemic wars underway with a total of 14 participating states in 1980. While that amount of warfare is dreadfully high in human terms, the fact remains, however, that in a world comprised of approximately 155 states there are 23,870 possible directed or asymmetric dyads (calculated as "dyads" in note 6), and hence statistical opportunities (in the Richardsonian sense) for dyadic war. While the real opportunities are far less, they are still quite large; yet the overwhelming majority of those dyads are at peace. They are at peace, moreover, *despite* the presumed nature of the system and *regardless* of whether or not power in a given pair is distributed in roughly equal or dramatically unequal fashion.

3. Despite the fact that the United States clearly held preponderant power vis-à-vis the USSR in 1945 and those two major powers appeared to be in approximate balance in 1982, overt military conflict erupted neither when power was unequally nor equally distributed. The United States attacked neither when it held sway nor when it lost its advantage; the USSR attacked neither when it was clearly only conditionally viable in Boulding's terms (1962) nor when it began to catch up and at least approach unconditional viability. Conflict erupted neither when the United States managed power in a system that was clearly unipolar nor when the system had evolved to at least a bipolar configuration.

4. The United States clearly holds a preponderance of power vis-à-vis both Canada and Mexico; Canada and Mexico, in turn, are apparently in roughly equal balance. Despite the fact that this North American regional subsystem (a geographically relevant triad) thus has two "preponderant" dyads and one that is "balanced", it is—and has been for some

time—totally at peace. Canada and Mexico are presumably deterred from attacking the United States because neither could hope to win. While the United States could attack either neighbor, it has not done so since the era of the Mexican Civil War.

5. Argentina and Brazil clearly hold a preponderance of power vis-à-vis Bolivia; they are themselves in apparently roughly equal balance. Despite the fact that this regionally geographic subsystem also has two "preponderant" dyads and one that is "balanced", it too is—and has been for some time—totally at peace. Whether its leaders have been deterred from doing so or because they have been occupied with other matters, Bolivia has not attacked its neighbors. Neither Argentina nor Brazil has attacked Bolivia.

A fairly substantial amount of systematic empirical evidence and data analysis might also be cited regarding patterns of violent conflict (see Small and Singer, 1982:chap. 7; and Beer, 1981:chap.2, for summaries of such research; see also Most and Starr, 1980 for a discussion of conflict data sets). For example, examining a number of indicators of the conflict which occurred between 1816 and 1980, Small and Singer conclude: "Whether we look at the number of wars, their severity, or their magnitude, there is no significant trend upward or down over the past 165 years" (1982:141). Analyses of post-1945 conflict appear to support that conclusion.

Despite the fact that it is generally accepted that the international system has evolved during the post-World War II era from a unipolar system, to a bipolar system, to a system which is variously viewed as tripolar, multipolar or bimultipolar and the fact that system membership (n) simultaneously expanded from some 66 nations in 1946 to 155 in 1980, for example, it is difficult to isolate systematic evidence that there has been a concomitant increase (or decrease) in the occurrence of international conflict.[5] On the basis of existing evidence (whether using COW, COPDAB, SIPRI, Wright or Richardson data—see Most and Starr, 1980), it does not appear that there has been a change in either the raw number of annual war initiations or the rate of initiations per state during the post-World War II period.

These empirical findings regarding the incidence of war also need to be considered within various dimensions of the changing context of the opportunity for war. As can be seen in figure 6.1 the post-

FIGURE 6.1.   Post–World War II Dyads

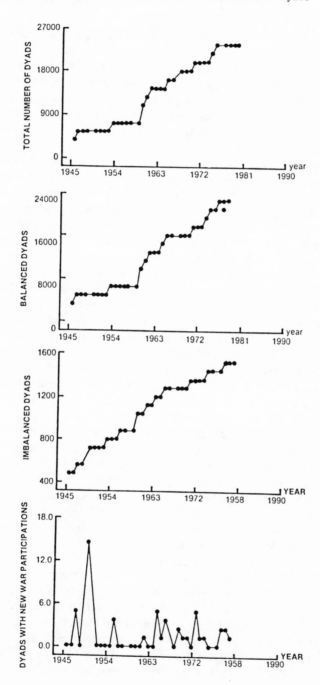

From Most and Starr (1987:212)

World War II international system has been characterized by an enormous expansion in the total number of dyads, the number of imbalanced dyads, and the number of balanced pairs of states. There has, however, been no concomitant increase in the numbers of dyads which have had new participations in interstate wars. *Despite* the increases in total, imbalanced, and balanced dyads, the rate of outbreaks of interstate war has remained roughly *constant* and *low.*

Whether it is dyadic power imbalance or balance which operates to structure the opportunity for conflict initiation, foreign policy decision makers tended *not* to take frequent advantage of the openings that at least theoretically can be said to have existed during the post-World War II period. For example, if one assumes that dyadic power imbalance creates the opportunity for initiation by the dominant member of the pair and divides the number of dyads that experienced new war participations in interstate wars in each year between 1946 and 1980 by $1/2$ the total number of imbalanced dyads in the system in the corresponding year an average of only 0.00427 is obtained; thus, if imbalance created the opportunity for all of those conflicts which were initiated, decision makers exercised that option only an average of 0.427% of the time it was available. If one makes the contrary assumption and posits that it is parity which creates the opportunity for conflict initiation and divides the number of dyads that experienced new war participations in interstate wars in each year by the number of balanced pairs in the corresponding year, an even smaller average of 0.000259 is obtained; if it was balance—and not imbalance—that created the opportunity for all of those conflicts initiated between 1946 and 1980, decision makers utilized that alternative only 0.0259% of the time that it was available. Again, whether it is dyadic power imbalance—a condition of power preponderance—or dyadic balance that creates the opportunities for conflict initiation, it seems clear that, during the post-World War II period at least, there were many more such chances for initiation than actual initiations.

We understand that the analyses noted above are based on the full set of possible interaction opportunities provided by the global system since the end of World War II. In this sense we have conveyed the vast range of *possibilities* afforded by an international system that almost tripled in size over a forty-year period. However, as in our studies of diffusion, we understand that it is more realistic to study groups of states that are relevant to each other through a variety of interaction opportunity mechanisms, such as borders, alliances, trading networks, etc. (see, for example, Russett, 1967). Even if we were to look at these relevant subsets and then sum the totals of dyads relevant to each other through any of these mechanisms, we still arrive at a very large number of "chances," which again greatly outnumber the actual initiation of conflicts.

The implication of all of these analyses and observations is *not* that post-World War II changes in system and polarity produced no changes whatsoever in the occurrence of conflict. The point instead is that *if* changes in system polarity during the post-World War II interval did, in fact, occur and those shifts produced changes in the rate of conflict (which could be detected in a forty-year period), evidence of those effects is *neither obvious nor easy to detect* when one looks at the stylized facts. Applications of standard methods to phenomena described above yield little evidence that system and polarity changes had any impact. Despite a number of dramatic increases in the size of the international system and a series of apparent shifts in system polarity, evidence from a variety of sources and on a variety of measures of occurrence suggests that conflict during the post-World War II period has been relatively stable, on the one hand, and rare on the other.

To return to a point made at the beginning of this section, the observations above constitute a potentially useful place to begin. Any theory or model of the roles that power, polarity, preponderance, and parity play in the generation of international conflict must begin with these bits of evidence. At the very leat, it should also be able to account for them. What we want are the outlines of a model that includes power, polarity, preponderance, and parity and that also accounts for what we already know by tracing a process that could have produced the facts described above.

So that our argument is not misunderstood, our logic follows that provided by Lave and March (1975) in their "model of the model-building process." The first step is to "observe some facts." The next step is to "look at the facts as though they were the end result of some unknown process (model)...and speculate about processes which might have produced such a result" (1975:19–20). We have completed the first step. It is to the latter stage that the discussion next turns. Specifically, it attempts to delineate a model—based at least partially in (supposedly systematic) concepts related to power, preponderance, parity, and polarity—that could have produced the existing impressionistic and empirical evidence.

A FIRST PASS

Initial Hypotheticals

In attempting to explain or account for the foregoing evidence, it is perhaps useful to begin with a consideration of the hypothetical systems shown in figures 6.2 and 6.3. Part A of figure 6.2 describes the numbers of imbalanced dyads that would exist in four systems (with varying numbers of actors, e.g., n = 3, 5, 10, 15) as the number of major powers (m) in each varies from 0 to n. Part B of the figure plots the numbers of balanced dyads.[6] Figure 6.3 traces the proportion of the total dyads that would be imbalanced in systems in which the number of states (n) ranges from 0 to 15 and the number of majors in each varies from 0 to 6.

Several aspects of those plots are important to note because scholars typically describe international systems in terms of their "polarity" or numbers of major powers and debate the stabilizing (or destabilizing) effects of unipolar, bipolar, tripolar, and various multipolar systems. Such analysts appear to be interested in the numbers of major powers—or poles—in different systems because they believe that such information provides insights on the distribution of power relationships at the dyadic level. Proponents of the general thesis that the power preponderance of some state i over a second state j leads to—or at least serves as a necessary condition for—conflict initiation would see systems with large numbers of such pairings as actually (or potentially) more dangerous than systems comprised primarily of balanced dyads; advocates of the power parity thesis would argue the reverse. In either case, it is important to recognize that the numbers of imbalanced and balanced dyads that comprise a given system are a function, *not* simply of the number of majors that are extant, but rather of both the number of majors and the total size of the system. For example:

—The shift of a 10 state system from unipolarity (m = 1) to bipolarity (m = 2) would raise the number of directed imbalanced dyads (calculated as "dyads" in note 6) from 18 to 32, while a similar shift in a 15 state system would raise the number of such pairings from 28 to 52. The implication that a shift from unipolarity to bipolarity would have for dyadic power distributions is affected by the size of the system in which the change occurred.

—If the types of dyads that comprise a system are important, then it is interesting to note that nearly identical numbers of

FIGURE 6.2.   Imbalanced and Balanced Dyads: Selected
Hypothetical Systems

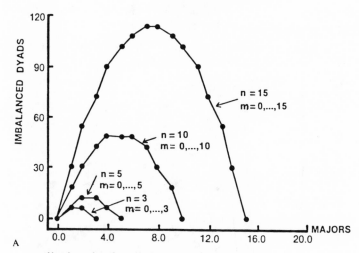

A

n = Number of nations in the system: n = 3,5,10,15
m = Number of 'major' powers in the system, n ≥ m

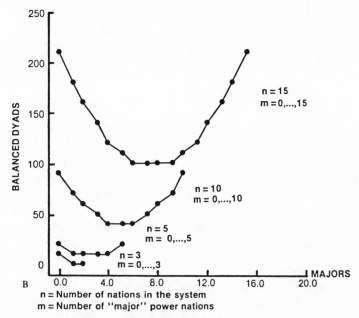

B

n = Number of nations in the system
m = Number of "major" power nations

Note: Dyads are counted asymmetrically; i-to-j and j-to-i
are counted as two separate relationships.

From Most and Starr (1987:215)

FIGURE 6.3.   Proportion of Imbalanced Dyads: Selected
                     Hypothetical Systems

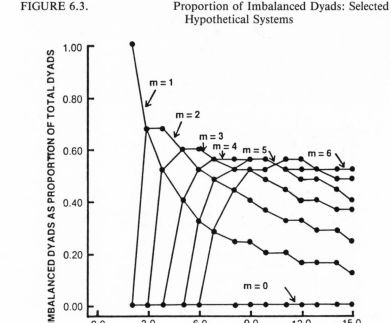

n = Number of nations in the system
m = Number of "major" powers, 0,....6; n ≥ m

From Most and Starr (1987:216)

imbalanced dyads would exist in a 15 state *uni*polar system
(m = 1), a 10 state *bi*polar system (m = 2), a 10 state *multi*polar
system (m = 8), and a 15 state (hyper-) *multi*polar system
(m = 14).

—Simple expansion of system size—in addition to changes in
the number of major powers—has a dramatic effect on the
numbers of imbalanced and balanced dyads. *Tri*polar systems
with 3, 5, 10 and 15 states would have 0, 12, 42, and 72 imbalanced dyads respectively.

—Regardless of whether power imbalance or power parity
leads more readily to conflict, the effects of expansions in the
numbers of majors, relative to the size of the total system, are
eventually reversed. Increases in the number of major powers
(m) anywhere in the range between 0 and $\frac{n}{2}$ imply both de-

creases in the number of balanced (mm) dyads and increases in the number of imbalanced (Mm) dyads; similar increases in the number of majors in the range between $\frac{n}{2}$ and n, however, lead to more balanced pairs (MM) and fewer imbalanced dyads. If dyadic-level power distributions are important for determining the rate of conflict in different systems, once again, it would appear that systems with both very small numbers of majors (m → 0) should be no more (or less) conflict prone than those with large numbers of majors (m → n).

—While one might intuitively expect 4 state systems with 1 and 3 major powers respectively to have very different conflict performances, those two systems would have identical numbers of imbalanced dyads as a proportion of total dyads. The same is true of 2 power and 6 power 7-state systems. Indeed, as the various points of intersection in figure 6.3 demonstrate, a number of systems that are commonly taken as being quite distinct in fact have *identical proportions* of imbalanced dyads.

Thus, the relationship between various types of systems and the numbers or proportions of balanced and imbalanced dyads that they contain is more complex than is customarily thought. Let us take an initial look at systems, *assuming* that (1) one can fruitfully dichotomize states as majors or minors, and (2) the power of any major state i does not degrade over distance to any minor state j or to any other existing major state k so that i truly dominates each minor and is roughly balanced with each of the other existing majors. It is, of course, possible to calculate the numbers of imbalanced and balanced dyads that will exist in any system of size n with the number of majors = 0, . . . , n.[7] Presumably, such work should yield deductions that have a bearing on conflict initiation.

As we will see in the next section, however, both the things that we have rehearsed about the post-World War II international system and a few simple logical illustrations suggest that those deductions *cannot* take the form which analysts typically expect. If we are to understand the implications that system structure has for conflict occurrence, it will be necessary to rethink the logical form that the structure/conflict linkages must take.

Systems at Peace and Logical Connectives

As a step toward delineating the types of connectives that might logically be expected to exist between systemic structures and conflict initiation, we consider two hypothetical situations. Suppose first that one has two systems which are in some sense structured differently so that they delimit the numbers of dyadic conflicts that can occur in a specified period of time, such as a calendar year, (that is, delimit systemic opportunities). Also suppose, however, that the ranges permitted by the two systems overlap in the following fashion:

System A   (------------)
System B   (-----------------------)

0   c   d   e

In other words the two systems have different maxima (d and e) but they both permit annual rates of occurrence in the 0–d range.

If one observed that exactly c conflicts occurred during the specified interval in System A ($0 < c < d$) and that an identical number occurred in system B, it might appear that systems and system types do not really matter very much: Differences in system types *do not* appear to be sufficient for differences in rates of occurrence.

System types are, however, important in this illustration. Insofar as annual rates of conflict occurrences are something in which one is interested and d and e are significantly different values, system types are important here, not because they determine what *does* occur or *has* occurred, but rather because they set ceilings on what *can* occur. The problem is that one might not recognize that fact. In looking at the empirical data, one would have observations or cases that might (or might not) reflect the full range of the rates of occurrence that are theoretically possible in the two systems. To that extent, moreover, it is obvious tht even though system B has not empirically been more conflict prone that system A, system A might be preferable to system B because the latter is potentially more dangerous.

The importance of our somewhat tedious review of postwar opportunities for conflict regarding the total number of possible dyads, the total number of balanced and unbalanced dyads, etc., as presented in figures 6.2 and 6.3, should now be clear. We needed to demonstrate empirically as well as logically the manner in which different systems create different ranges of possibilities; and that behavior taking place within overlapping ranges may be indistinguishable from system to system.

A more concrete example may be useful. Suppose we have two automobiles. One has a governor on its engine that limits maximum speed to 55 miles per hour, the other does not, and both are observed traveling down a city street at 35 miles per hour. The observation would not tell us anything about the importance of governed versus ungoverned engines. We would not conclude that governors are unimportant because both autos are traveling (at the moment) at only 35 miles per hour. Even though we would have difficulty demonstrating the point on the basis of the empirical observation at hand, common sense would tell us that the auto without the governor has a greater potential speed, and hence, is potentially more dangerous.

With that illustration in mind, let us reconsider the two triadic systems introduced as stylized facts.[8] These are examples of unipolar and bipolar systems (the United States-Canada-Mexico triad and the Argentina-Brazil-Bolivia triad respectively). We know that the so-called power parity hypothesis suggests that approximately equal power distributions at the dyadic level lead to peace while the preponderance postulate suggests that it is unequal dyadic power distributions that lead to peace. The two hypotheses seem to be antithetically opposed as Siverson and Sullivan (1983) suggest.

Consider, however, the relationships that would be holding when these systems are totally at peace, as both have been since World War II. Both the facts as we know them (and the hypotheticals in note 8) call attention to an important (if largely overlooked) problem: In any system that has greater than two members $(n > 2)$ and in which the number of major powers is at least one, but less than n $(1 < m < n)$, there will exist some dyads which are balanced and others which are imbalanced. To the extent that we know that such mixed systems exist and that they are at least sometimes totally at peace, it follows—initial appearances to the contrary notwithstanding—that *both* dyadic parity and preponderance must somehow be logically consistent with peace.

In considering how one might reconcile the hypotheses that link power preponderance and parity with war and peace, so that both could hold simultaneously, it is useful to recall that four types of linkages are commonly posited in the existing literature: (1) sufficiency, (2) necessity, (3) necessity and sufficiency, and (4) probability. Dichotomizing power distributions and conflict initiation, the implications of those linkages can be easily understood in the context of the following illustration (see also the Venn diagrams presented in chapter 3):

	Yes	(1)	(2)
Conflict			
Initiation	No	(3)	(4)
		E	-E

E: A balanced dyad in which both have approximately equal power

-E: An imbalanced dyad in which one has a preponderance of power

If the hypothesis that inequality or power preponderance is *sufficient* for conflict initiation is true, then (*a*) cases could fall in cells 3, 2, and 1, but (*b*) cell 4 should be null. Cell 1 could contain cases because inequality is sufficient but not necessary for conflict initiation; thus, conflicts could sometimes be initiated even when the dyad is balanced (E). Cell 4 should be empty, because each time the condition of inequality (-E) obtains, conflict initiations should follow. (See again the discussion in chapter 3.) In contrast, if the hypothesis that inequality is *necessary* for conflict initiation is true, then (*a*) cases could fall in cells 3, 2, and 4, but (*b*) cell 1 should be null. Cell 4 could contain cases because inequality is necessary but not sufficient for conflict initiation; thus, conflicts might not always be initiated even though the dyad is imbalanced (-E). Cell 1 should be empty because conflicts are never initiated unless the condition of inequality (-E) obtains. If, to take the third logical linkage, it is true that dyadic inequality is necessary and sufficient for conflict initiation, then (*a*) cases could fall in cells 3 and 2, but (*b*) cells 1 and 4 should be null. Conflicts are never initiated unless inequality obtains; they are always initiated whenever it does.

The predictions of the fourth type of linkage—probability—are a bit more complex. If inequality or imbalance increases the probability of conflict initiation, then (*a*) one would *not* expect that any of the cells should necessarily be null, but (*b*) one would expect the following inequalities to be satisified.[9]

$$\frac{(1)}{(1)+(3)} < \frac{(2)}{(2)+(4)} \quad \text{and} \quad \frac{(2)}{(1)+(2)} > \frac{(1)}{(1)+(2)}$$

With this as brief digression in mind, consider once again our two peaceful triadic systems. Recasting them, one can obtain the following crosstab tables in which the cell entries denote the numbers of dyads of each type:

		System 1 (with one major power)			System 2 (with two majors)	
	Yes	0	0	Yes	0	0
Conflict						
Initiation	No	1	2	No	1	2
		E	–E		E	–E

The immediate point should be clear: If it is plausible to imagine that the hypothetical systems are at least sometimes totally at peace, then it must follow that power distributions—whether preponderance or parity—cannot logically be sufficient for conflict initiation; because cases clearly do fall in the critical cell 4, both of the first (sufficiency) and third (necessity and sufficiency) linkages can be rejected immediately. It should be pointed out that this conclusion follows as a consequence of the stipulation of peace. It can be obtained *regardless* of whether one embraces the parity/conflict or preponderance/conflict postulates.

Insofar as one is willing to stipulate that peace can sometimes obtain in the two hypothetical systems, only the following necessity and probability linkages between dyadic power distributions and conflict initiation remain as viable possibilities:

— Only if dyadic power equality, then conflict initiation
— Only if dyadic power inequality, then conflict initiation
— If dyadic power equality, the increased probability of conflict initiation
— If dyadic power inequality, then increased probability of conflict initiation

Once one begins to think in terms of either necessity or probabilities, it becomes possible to see why the preponderance and parity hypotheses are not in fact logical opposites. Even if dyadic inequality is necessary for conflict initiation, to take just one example, such acts would not invariably occur whenever inequality obtains. Thus, both balanced and imbalanced dyads could be peaceful.

Seen in this light, one can begin to understand some of the things we know. It is no longer difficult to see how dyadic power distributions could be important even though the United States/Canada/Mexico and the Argentina/Brazil/Bolivia triads are at peace. It is no longer difficult to see why overt warfare has not erupted between the United States and the USSR even though the dyadic balance of power has undergone radical change in the post-World War II era. It even begins to become possible to see how a world in which power is tremendously important, at least in theory, could manage to remain so peaceful despite large numbers of balanced and unbalanced dyads.

INTEGRATING THE PREPONDERANCE AND PARITY HYPOTHESES: THE OPPORTUNITY AND WILLINGNESS FOR CONFLICT INITIATION

Having considered the type of logical connectives that might exist between structural factors and conflict, it becomes useful to outline the substantive arguments that one might find marshalled in the existing literature. First, peace in a balanced mm dyad (two minor powers) might be explained by pointing out that neither state has the capacity that would give it the opportunity to attack the other; peace in a balanced MM dyad (two major powers) however, would require a different explanation. Both have the opportunity to attack, but are apparently deterred from doing so (i.e., are made unwilling) by the other's power. Peace in imbalanced dyads could be explained by arguing that minor powers lack both the opportunity to attack a major power and are also presumably deterred from doing so while the major power has the capacity to attack a minor power but is—for some reason that has no apparent connection with deterrence (perhaps internal factors as developed in the previous chapter)—unwilling to do so.

Consider now the expansion of system size (especially as shown in sections C and D of note 8). Expansion of system size from three to five increases the number of dyadic relationships. Changes in the number of major powers alter the types of dyadic relationships that constitute the system. If power parity (at least among the majors) leads to peace as the standard balance of power theory suggests, the three state/bipolar system (number 2) should be less conflictual than the three state/unipolar system (number 1). In the same way, the five state/bipolar system (number 4) should be more tranquil than the five state/unipolar system (number 3). This is precisely the position that Waltz (1979), for example, adopts: The probability of conflict is low in a bipolar world. The expectations are quite different, however, if it is power preponderance, and not parity, that leads to peace as Organski (1958) has argued. If this assertion is valid, systems 1 and 3, which are both unipolar, should be more peaceful than systems 2 and 4 respectively.

Somewhat distinct implications appear to follow, however, if one focuses on power distributions at the dyadic level. *If* such distributions are important and it is also the case that dyadic parity leads to peace, for example, then the two triadic systems under discussion seem to have *identical* potentials for peace and war. Even though they differ in terms of the number of major powers, they both contain only one unique balanced dyad. The point to note in all of this is that efforts to account for why the various dyads (and hence the four systems, in note 8) are all peaceful involve two distinct uses of power. In some instances, power is taken to be an *objective* opportunity-related factor which is a function of states' military capabilities, in other instances power is entered as a *subjective* willingness-related concern which is a function of leaders' (psychological/cognitive) assessments of the costs and benefits of different policy options. Thus, peace in each dyad is said to obtain (i.e., no state initiates conflict) because both states in the pair are unable to attack (because they lack the necessary objective wherewithal) and/or are unwilling to do so (because they are deterred or are for other, unspecified reasons not interested in initiating hostilities).

The essential features of these arguments seem to be captured by the following conceptual equation:

$$(1) \ \text{Attack } ij = (Oij * Wij)$$

Where: Attack ij refers to an attack by the ith state on the jth; Oij denotes the opportunity or capacity of i to launch that attack on j; and Wij denotes the willingness of the leaders of i to do so (see also chapter 3).

Letting Oij and Wij be coded dichotomously as 1 or 0 to denote the presence or absence of opportunity and willingness respectively, it is obvious that a zero (0) value for either term would imply that an attack by i on j would not occur if the ith state is able, but its leaders are not willing ($Oij = 1$; $Wij = 0$), or if its leaders want to launch an attack, but they lack the necessary strike force ($Oij = 0$; $Wij = 1$; see chapter 4). Seen in these simple terms, explanations of peace in the various systemic combinations of major and minor powers, and perhaps indeed the debate between Waltz and Kaplan over the relative stability of different types of systems, seems to bear most directly on which terms—the Oijs and/or the Wijs for each dyad in each system—approach zero.

The more important point to be recognized here is that power distributions, whether they are preponderant or balanced, set structural limits insofar as they delimit the range of options that are objectively available to decision makers. Given certain power distributions it is impossible to attack; given other power distributions, however, attacks are possible. If this is true at the dyadic-level, it should also be true at the system level. If one knew what dyadic power configurations permit conflict initiation and also how many of those configurations existed in a given system, then one could calculate how many initiations are objectively possible in the system, and hence, just how conflictual that system could be.[10]

The *potential* for conflict is distinct from the *actual* occurrence of conflict, however. As the standard arguments seem to suggest, leaders' willingness to initiate conflict plays a role within the structurally-defined limits. If, for example, two systems have 6 and 4 dyads respectively in which conflict initiation is possible. And, if we also knew that leaders are always willing to avail themselves of the initiation option whenever it is present (i.e., that $W = 1$ whenever $O = 1$ in any given pair), it would be possible to deduce that the 6-dyad system would have more conflicts than the 4-dyad system.

The analytical problem, however, is that the existing evidence already tells us quite clearly that the international system since World War II has never performed at anything that has even approached its upper limit, in terms of total dyadic possibilities, or in terms of relevant groups of states. Regardless of whether it is parity or preponderance that creates the opportunity for conflict initiation, decision makers have not acted mechanistically to avail themselves of all of the opportunities that were presented (see again the plots shown in figure 6.1, and chapter 5). In some cases, they moved against their adversaries but substituted nonlethal, nonovertly conflictual means (see also, Greffenius, 1986). In other instances, leaders seemed not to move at all; they appeared to pursue other goals that had little or no connection with maintaining, protecting or enhancing their national security vis-à-vis the other state in the pair. Thus, the facts as we know them suggest that willingness has not invariably equaled 1 in all of those states that have had the opportunity to initiate conflict at any given point in time. Regardless of whether it is parity or preponderance that creates such options, too few states have gone to war.

At the same time, however, the evidence reviewed at the outset suggests that leaders' willingness to use force has at least sometimes equaled 1 in some states. While the rate of outbreaks in the international system is low in comparison with the opportunities that might be created by either power parity or preponderance, the full system has seldom been totally at peace. Some states *have* availed themselves of their opportunities to initiate conflict (one reason why the study of the diffusion of violent conflict is of concern to us). Certain distributions of willingess across the dyads in various systems lead one to observe identical rates of conflict occurrence. *Despite* the differences in their structures, both might have *identical rates of proneness* to conflict events.

As we will see in the next section, this situation creates certain logical problems that we will need to explore in some detail. For the moment, however, it may be useful to review some of the points that have been made thus far:

1. While system-level theorists have focused on the importance of system polarity or the number of major powers in their arguments regarding the relative conflict potential of different types of systems, *system size* is an equally important consideration. Changes in the numbers of major powers alter the types of dyads that constitute a system, but changes in the number of states (both of majors and minors) alter the numbers of pairs that exist.[11]
2. Even though the parity and preponderance hypotheses appear to be mutually exclusive, both relationships necessarily have to hold. Appearances notwithstanding, it must be logically possible to reconcile the two postulates.
3. Neither dyadic parity nor dyadic preponderance can logically be sufficient for conflict initiation.
4. "Power" is entered in the already existing arguments in two distinct ways when attempts are made to account for dyadic or system-level peace. It is considered once as an objective opportunity-related factor that is a function of states' military capacities. It is considered again as part of a subjective willingness-related concern that is a function of leaders' assessments of the desirability of launching an attack.
5. Systemic level phenomena—polarity, preponderance, and parity, in particular—appear logically to set limits, ceilings or constraints on the amount of dyadic conflict that is pos-

sible. Because systems have different sizes and numbers of major powers, different systems may set different ceilings.

6. Decision makers operate within those structurally-defined constraints. While leaders cannot execute options for which they lack the objective capability, the evidence suggests that they are also unwilling to utilize all of the conflict initiation opportunities with which they are presented. Put differently, micro-level decision processes operate within constraints that may be at least partially defined by systemic-level phenomena.

7. Even though certain systems or types of dyadic power distributions may have greater potential for conflict, those potentials may not be—and in the post-World War II period, were not—exploited. If opportunity and willingness are jointly necessary conditions for conflict initiation and decision makers typically defer from utilizing all of their opportunities for war initiation, then systems that are "inherently dangerous" (in terms of either their high ceilings for potential conflict or the large numbers of conflict initiation opportunities that they contain) may have no greater numbers of actual occurrences than much "safer" systems (with lower ceilings and fewer initiation opportunities).

A SECOND PASS

As we observed above, certain systems or types of dyadic power distributions may have greater *potentials* for overt conflict, but those potentials may not appear empirically. If conflict initiation is a multiplicative function of states' opportunities to attack and their willingness to do so, then a system in which large numbers of states have the necessary capability or opportunity to initiate conflict might in fact have no more actual initiations than a second system with fewer initiation opportunities. Leaders in the states in the first system would only need to be less willing to utilize their openings than the leaders in the second. Under this model, inherently "dangerous" systems or what Cioffi (1984) would call potentially "unreliable" systems—because they include large numbers of states that possess conflict initiation opportunities—might plausibly be expected to function peacefully for long durations and display overall rates of initiation which are in fact lower than those achieved by structurally "safer" systems. Thus, while power-related structural factors impose boundaries on ranges of behavior, it is also plausible that the ranges of behavior which are delimited by different structures tend to overlap considerably. To the extent that that is the case, different structures could, in any given trial, produce similar results. This should cause us to design system-level or system-structure analyses with great care, and to treat the results of previous systemic analyses similarly.

In this section we shall take a second pass at the problems of system-level analyses. To complement the logical analyses above (augmented with stylized facts and other empirical evidence) we have employed simulation approachs in this section as a means for more systematic investigation. To ease presentation, a more formal outline of the simulation procedures and results is set out in the Appendix to this chapter (chapter 6, appendix tables 6.1–6.5). Briefly, the dyadic power structure of a hypothetical 10 state system ($n = 10$) with the number of majors (m) equal to 1 was created for use in simulating possible outcomes. Thus formed, the system was described in what we labeled a power structure or opportunity vector which included an entry for each balanced dyad (coded as 0), for each ij pairing in which i was dominant over j (coded as 1), and for each ji dyad in which j was dominated by i (coded as -1). The overall number of dyads in the vector equaled 90—i.e., (n^2-n)—with the number of 0, 1, and -1 entries in each being a function of the number of major powers (see Appendix). The focus of interest was on how this system—and others with different numbers of states, numbers of major powers, and distinct dyadic structures—might be expected to perform.

The next step entailed the use of a Bernoulli trial routine to create 15 willingness vectors, each of which had 90 entries and consisted of 1's and 0's to denote the willingness or the lack of willingness to attack. In effect, the procedure entailed the tentative assumption that willingness can be thought of as a stochastic variable which occurs randomly across states. Because 15 such willingness vectors were generated, we in effect had 15 independent trials of how willingness and unwillingness might be distributed across the 10 nations and 90 dyads in the system. Finally, the opportunity vector for the 10 state/ 1 major system was multiplied by each of the 15 willingness vectors to produce 15 separate "conflict initiation" vectors.[12]

It is the make-up of the conflict initiation vectors that is of immediate interest. We are interested in the numbers of occasions in each that a positive (+ 1) occurs because such situations indicate the number dyads in which the opportunity to initiate existed *and* leaders were willing to exploit it.

Before turning to the results, however, one point needs to be reiterated. We have decided to present the illustrations below (and in the Appendix) on the basis of the preponderance or imbalance argument. Each + 1 coding in the opportunity vector for each system was treated as constituting a pair of states in which conflict could be initiated; that is, each ij coded as + 1 was taken as representing a situation in which the power of i dominated that of j and in which i could have launched an attack on its opposite. The key to observe, however, is that even though the simulations below are based on the preponderance/imbalance thesis, the conclusions that we draw are completely independent of the actual empirical soundness of that argument. Given our purposes, we could—with one minor modification of the simulation procedures—just have easily worked with the alternative parity/balance hypothesis. Identical theoretical and substantive conclusions would have followed.[13]

Necessity, Probability, and Micro-Macro Linkages

With these details in mind, let us look briefly at the types of results that could be obtained from simulations of the 10 state/5 major power systems when the probability of willingness [Pr(W)] was set equal to 0.02 (see appendix table 6.1).[14] Given the overall n of 10, there were 90 dyads. Twenty-five were positively imbalanced (i.e., power of i > power of j); by assumption under the imbalance/preponderance hypothesis, the ith state in each of those 25 dyads had the opportunity to initiate conflict. Of the remaining 65 dyads in the system, 25 were negatively imbalanced (i.e., power of j < power of i) while 40 were balanced (again by assumption under the imbalance/preponderance hypothesis, none of the states in these 40 pairs had the capacity to initiate conflict).

In trial 2 on this system, two states, 8% of the total that had the capability to do so, initiated conflicts; 92% of the states that had the opportunity to attack refrained from doing so. In trial 14, somewhat different results were obtained. All 25 of the states that had the capability to attack deferred. The point to note in considering these two illustrative examples should thus be clear: Even though everything was held constant (the number of states, the number of major powers, the numbers of the various types of dyads included in the system, and the willingness of decision makers to utilize force) *the structure permitted different rates of conflict performance.*

Even though the potential danger inherent in the system remained unchanged from one test to the next, the actual level of conflict varied. In some trials, conflicts occurred, while in others, the system remained totally at peace.[15]

Recall that these simulations are based on a model in which opportunity and willingness are jointly necessary and sufficient for conflict initiation:

(1) Attack ij = (Oij*Wij)

Each time in which the ith state has the opportunity to attack and its leaders are willing to exploit that opening, an attack actually occurs. Noting that this equation is, of course, a micro- or decision-level formulation, it is possible to imagine how one might operationalize all three concepts, collect data for each ij dyad, and proceed to conduct a *state-level analysis* of conflict initiations. Such a procedure would be analogous to each of the 15 trials conducted on the 10 state/5 major/Pr(W) system; each test was based on data representing opportunity, willingness and initiations for each ij pair in the system. Each time the ith state in a given ij pair had both opportunity and willingness, an initiation occurred; the total number of initiations in a given trial was a simple summation of the number of instances in which opportunity and willingness occurred concomitantly.

Given equation 1, however, it is also possible to imagine how one might proceed differently by *recasting it as a macro- or system-level equation:*

(2.1)	Attacks	= [Sum (Oij*Wij)]
		for all ij and ji pairs, i = 1, ..., n
(2.2)	Pr(Attack)	= [Pr(Oij)*Pr(Wij)]

Where Pr(Oij) is the probability that the ith state would have the opportunity to attack the jth in any given ij dyad chosen randomly, and Pr(Wij) is the probability that the leaders of the ith state would be willing to attack the jth in any given ij dyad chosen randomly:

(2.3)	Pr(Oij)	= [Sum (Oij)]/Total Number of Dyads
(2.4)	Pr(Wij)	= [Sum (Wij)]/Total Number of Dyads
(2.5)	Pr(Attack)	= [Attacks]/Total Number of Dyads

This formulation is identical to equation 1 except insofar as it entails a summation across all ij pairs and includes a system-level dependent variable rather than the state-level variable in equation 1.

Utilizing equation 2.2 and the values from the 10 state/5 major/ $Pr(W) = 0.02$ example, one obtains the following:

(3)   Pr(Attack) $= (25/90)*(0.02)$
$= (0.278)*(0.02)$
$= 0.00556$

Simple multiplication of this value (0.00556) by the Total Number of Dyads in the system (90) yields 0.5, which should equal the number of conflict initiations that one would expect to obtain in this system over repeated trials. (The result obtained from the simulations—0.60—is not markedly different.)

The point, then, is that it is possible to imagine two parallel models: one at the micro-level, the other at the macro. While each could be utilized independently, the two are also linked. In principle at least, one could begin with the micro-level formulation and aggregate (compose) to the macro-level. Alternatively, one could, again in principle, begin with the macro-level equations and disaggregate (decompose) to the micro-level.

The Effects of Changing System Structures

Given the possible linkages across levels we have now developed, what is the systemic effects of changes in willingness (clearly a decision/state level factor)? Consider, for example, the results that were obtained when the probability of willingness [Pr(W)] to attack was set in the Bernoulli trials at 0.02 and system size was held constant (appendix table 6.3). Increases in the number of major powers yield higher rates of conflict initiations. The "safest" 10 state system was the one with only 1 major power; the most dangerous 10 state-system had 5 majors. The "floors" and "ceilings" rose in the predicted direction as the number of major powers was increased from 1 to 5 $(1 - n/2)$. The critical point, however, is that changes in the number of majors did not make that great a difference. As the plots in the Appendix demonstrate, the systems had closely overlapping confidence intervals, with the mean rate of occurrence in all of the 10 state systems almost invariably falling within the confidence intervals of the other 10 state systems which had different numbers of majors.

In given trials, in other words, structurally distinct 10 state systems with different numbers of majors had identical actual performances. Structurally safe, 10 state systems with relatively few conflict initiation opportunities actually had greater numbers of conflict initiations in some trials than structurally more dangerous systems. Moreover, even though the 10 state systems were structured differently as a result of their distinct numbers of major powers, the difference of means test on the simulated conflict initiations failed to reject the null hypothesis of homogeneous rates of occurrence in the 75 independent trials (15 for each number of majors). While changing the number of majors in a 10 state system does make some visually apparent difference when Pr(W) is set in the trials at 0.02, and the nature of the difference is exactly as one would expect, the effect is *not* statistically significant.[16]

More Effects of Changing Willingness to Initiate

With these points in mind, consider the effects that develop when even a small change is made in the probability that decision makers will be willing to exercise their opportunities for conflict initiation. Analyses presented in the Appendix are based on changes in willingness (e.g., table 6.4 analyses are identical to those reported in table 6.3 except that a rather marginal increase has been made in the Pr(W)—from 0.02 to 0.05—used in the Bernoulli trials to generate the willingness vectors). One noteworthy substantive difference appears with a change from 0.02 to 0.05 probability. Even though decision makers have only a 0.05 probability of exploiting an opportunity to attack when such an option exists, that probability is sufficiently high that the importance of differing numbers of major powers becomes statistically significant in both the 10-state and 15-state analyses.

Only one somewhat more substantive point might be made. Even though there has been considerable debate about the effects of moving from unipolar to bipolar to tripolar and eventually to multipolar systems, there is still considerable overlap in these anlyses in the confidence intervals of consecutive systems. Even when the Pr(W) is set as high as 0.05, the performance of a unipolar system overlaps considerably with that of a bipolar system, a bipolar system has a range of performance which is not unlike that of a tripolar system, and so on.

There is one exception to this conclusion. Note the conflict initiations in a simulated 15-state/8-major power system, comparing the results obtained from trials conducted when the probability of willingness [Pr(W)] was set at 0.02 and 0.05 respectively (table 5). The situation might be analogous to the development of a "war mood" in a structurally unchanging system. The effects are fairly dramatic.

For the first time, *non*overlapping confidence intervals appear and statistically distinct differences in the mean rates of occurrence emerge. Even though a system is structurally unaltered, a marginal step increase in decision makers' willingness to use force *could* be expected to produce fairly sharp changes in the rate of conflict initiation. Our analyses suggest that surges (or declines) in Willingness can even override the effects of changing numbers of majors. Regardless of the number of majors (1, 2, . . . , 8) and hence the numbers of opportunities that were present, differences in decision makers' willingness to exploit extant openings resulted in significantly different mean rates of conflict initiation.

CONCLUSION

Many of our conclusions were reviewed at the end of the "First Pass" section. In the subsequent "Second Pass" we employed simulation techniques to confirm and reinforce those conclusions. The central point to be taken from these discussions is *not* that willingness is more important than opportuunity—is not that decision makers' willingness to utilize force is potentially more important than structurally engendered opportunities to initiate overt international conflict. Our argument is not based exclusively on either a so-called "reductionist" micro-level decision theory *or* a systemic approach. Factors at both levels are important. Structural factors appear to define opportunities and set the menu of available options. Insofar as decision makers are left with at least the minimal discretion of choosing whether or not they wish to exploit an option or to refrain from its execution, however, it follows both that those actors operate within structurally-defined parameters and also that how they act—the choices that they do or do not make—can be significant.[17]

Thus, when both opportunity and willingness are factored together we come to conclusions quite similar to those that were developed in regard to substitutability and nice laws and their effects on research design and theory. When the effects of both levels are put together, it follows quite readily that structurally very different systems could logically be expected to have rather similar rates of conflict. It follows also that structurally similar systems could perform rather distinctly, that structurally "dangerous" systems might be more peaceful than structurally "safe" systems, and that structurally "safe" systems might have higher rates of conflict than comparably more "dangerous" systems. We have come a long way in delineating the possible relationships between opportunity and willingness; one of the important results of the analyses in this chapter is the demonstration of the dynamic between opportunity and willingness. Recall that this was an issue raised and left unresolved in chapter 2.

In discussing substitutability we also argued that a foreign policy stimulus could produce many possible, and substitutable, foreign policy responses; or that many different stimuli could produce the same response. For that reason, nice laws, those which are clearly developed to apply to specific *sub-groups* of actors or situations or behaviors, are crucial. The same could be argued for the study of international systems and the opportunities they create.[18]

Indeed, if in fact the real world operates in the manner we describe, an explanation for our stylized facts begins to become clear. In particular, we can begin to understand why the rate of conflict since World War II has been so low overall and stable through time *in spite* of changing numbers of major powers and the expansion in system membership. If structure and process interplay in the fashion suggested and leaders were generally unwilling to initiate conflict, then the structurally different systems that have characterized the post-World War II era *should have* exhibited similar rates of conflict.

APPENDIX TO CHAPTER 6

TABLE 6.1 Outline of Simulation Procedures

Opportunity Vector*†		Willingness Vector BTrial #x‡		Conflict Initiation Vector Test #x§
1		1		1
0		1		0
−1		0		0
•		•		•
•		•		•
•		•		•
1	×	0	=	0
•		•		•
0		1		0
−1		1		−1
•		•		•
•		•		•
1		0		0

* Opportunity vectors—and the additional accompanying 15 willingness and conflict initiation vectors—were constructed for the following systems:

Nations	Majors	Nations	Majors
10	1	15	1
10	2	15	2
10	3	15	3
10	4	15	4
10	5	15	5
		15	6
		15	7
		15	8

† The number of rows or dyads represented in each vector is determined by the overall size of the system $= (n^2 - n)$. The number of 0s, 1s, and –1s in each opportunity vector is determined by the size of the system and the number of major powers in the manner described by the formulas in note 16. A 1 denotes an ij dyad in which i dominates j; a –1 denotes a ji dyad in which j is dominated by i; a 0 denotes a dyad in which the power is in balance.

‡ A value of 1 in this vector indicates a situation in which the leaders of a state are willing to initiate conflict against the second nation in the pair; a 0 indicates that they are unwilling to do so. The number of 0s and 1s in each willingness vector is determined by a Bernoulli generating procedure. A total of 15 such willingness vectors were generated for each system.

§ The values appearing in each conflict initiation vector are a function of simple multiplication of the opportunity vector and a given willingness vector. A –1 is interpretable as a situation in which a state is willing but unable to initiate. A 0 describes a situation in which a state is unable and/or unwilling to initiate. A + 1 describes a dyad in which a nation is has both the opportunity to initiate conflict and the willingness to do so. A total of 15 such conflict initiation vectors were constructed for each system.

TABLE 6.2   Illustrative Results: Simulations of Systems With 10 States and 5 Major Powers*

n   =   10
m   =   5
Pr(W) = 0.02

		Trial 2	
	Yes	0	2
Conflict Initiation	No	65	23
		No	Yes
		Opportunity	

n   =   10
m   =   5
Pr(W) = 0.02

		Trial 14	
	Yes	0	0
Conflict Initiation	No	65	25
		No	Yes
		Opportunity	

n   =   10
m   =   5
Pr(W) = 0.02

		Average Cell Entries Tests 1–15		**Sum Totals Cell Entries Tests 1–15**	
	Yes	0	0.6	0	9
Conflict Initiation	No	65	24.4	975	366
		No	Yes	No	Yes
		Opportunity		Opportunity	

*   As noted, the preponderance/imbalance hypothesis is assumed for the purpose of these analyses. Thus, "No" opportunity codings in these analyses include balanced ij dyads and negatively balanced ji dyads in which the jth nation is dominated by the ith. In a system with 10 states and 5 major powers, there are 40 and 25 such pairings respectively. An opportunity is said to exist in positively imbalanced ij dyads in which the ith nation dominates the jth. There are 25 such pairings in a 10 state/5 major system. The systems contain a total of 90 dyads.

TABLE 6.3. Simulated Conflict Initiations: Systems of 10 and 15 Nations with PR(W) = 0.02

Number of Majors (n = 10)	Tests (p = .02)	Mean Conflict Initiations	St. Dev.	Individual 95 pct CI's for Mean Based on pooled STDEV
1	15	0.1333	0.5164	
2	15	0.4000	0.8281	
3	15	0.4000	0.8281	
4	15	0.5333	0.7432	
5	15	0.6000	0.7368	

0.0   0.40   0.80

Pooled STDEV = 0.7394
F-Ratio = 0.88
Degrees of Freedom: 4, 70
Significance: NS

Number of Majors (n = 15)	Tests (p = .02)	Mean Conflict Initiations	St. Dev.	Individual 95 pct CI's for Mean Based on pooled STDEV
1	15	0.3333	0.7237	
2	15	0.6000	0.910	
3	15	0.8000	0.9411	
4	15	0.8667	1.1255	
5	15	0.9333	1.1629	
6	15	1.0667	1.1629	
7	15	1.0667	1.1629	
8	15	1.0667	1.1629	

0.00   0.50   1.00   1.50

Pooled STDEV = 1.0556
F-Ratio = 0.92
Degrees of Freedom: 7, 112
Significance: NS

TABLE 6.4. Simulated Conflict Initiations: Systems of 10 and 15 Nations with PR(W) = 0.05

Number of Majors (n = 10)	Tests (p = .05)	Mean Conflict Initiations	St. Dev.	Individual 95 pct CI's for Mean Based on pooled STDEV
1	15	0.4000	0.5071	
2	15	0.1333	0.0601	
3	15	0.2667	0.0328	
4	15	0.6000	0.2984	
5	15	0.6000	0.7368	

Pooled STDEV = 1.0529
F-Ratio = 3.11
Degrees of Freedom: 4, 70
Significance: .05

Number of Majors (n = 15)	Tests (p = .05)	Mean Conflict Initiations	St. Dev.	Individual 95 pct CI's for Mean Based on pooled STDEV
1	15	0.4667	0.8338	
2	15	1.2667	1.3345	
3	15	1.8000	1.6562	
4	15	2.6000	1.7238	
5	15	2.8000	1.4243	
6	15	2.6000	1.4541	
7	15	2.5333	1.1255	
8	15	2.6000	1.2984	

Pooled STDEV = 1.3823
F-Ratio = 5.47
Degrees of Freedom: 7, 112
Significance: .001

TABLE 6.5.   Simulated Conflict Initiations: Systems of 15 Nations with PR(W) = 0.02 and 0.05

Pr(W)	Tests [1]	Mean Conflict Initiations	St. Dev.	Individual 95 pct CI's for Mean Based on pooled STDEV
				----+---------+---------+---------+----
0.02	15	1.067	1.163	(------*-------)
0.05	15	2.600	1.298	(-------*-----)
				----+---------+---------+---------+----
				0.80 1.60 2.40 3.20

Pooled STDEV = 1.232
F-Ratio = 11.61
Degrees of Freedom: 4, 28
Significance: .001

Pr(W)	Tests [2]	Mean Conflict Initiations	St. Dev.	Individual 95 pct CI's for Mean Based on pooled STDEV
				----+---------+---------+---------+----
0.02	120	0.8417	1.0532	(---*----)
0.05	120	2.0833	1.5534	(----*---)
				----+---------+---------+---------+----
				1.00 1.5 2.00

Pooled STDEV = 1.3271
F-Ratio = 52.52
Degrees of Freedom: 7, 238
Significance: .001

1. The number of states = 15 and m = 8 in these tests.
2. The number of states = 15 and m = 1, 2, . . ., 8 in these tests. Fifteen trials were completed on each n/m combination.

7

CONCLUSION:
Closure, Cumulation, and International Relations Theory

OVERVIEW
In the opening chapter we introduced the three elements of the research triad—theory, method and logic. Using these elements, we have covered a great deal of ground in discussing the analysis and substance of international relations. We have looked at both micro and macro approaches, as well as the relationships between the two—especially as we have elaborated on the nature of, and interaction between, opportunity and willingness.

In the first chapter we noted that the ultimate end towards which we were working was a newer and more appropriate conceptualization of explanation in international relations and foreign policy. With that ultimate end in mind we developed a number of themes that comprise at least a partial reconceptualization of IR theory. One central theme that was developed argued for the superior utility of conceptualizing international relations phenomena such as war in terms of *process*. In the first chapter we presented a brief overview of what we mean by "process" and how the term would be employed throughout. A focus on process forces the investigator to deal with "how" questions—interactive "how" questions. That is, we have been concerned with phenomena that are the outcomes or resultants of interdependent interactions between states (or other international actors). The components of these outcomes are the results of a choice process *within* individual actors; the final resultant is the product of the interaction of actors.

Process has also denoted a concern with looking at the conditions of opportunity and willingness through time—the investigation of the changing sets of opportunities (system structures), and how they affect or change the incentive structures of decision makers that provide the willingness to take advantage of a set of opportunities. In several places this approach has been contrasted to deterministic theories or approaches—most fully in the discussion of the models of entity-environment relationships developed by the Sprouts specifically as alternatives to environmental determinism. In Ward's application of logical analysis to war, he notes that realist balance of power models as well as Marxist models developed at the system structure level are "decidedly deterministic" (Ward, 1987:1). Ward's conclusions, regarding what we have called process as contrasted to attribute and systemic structure approaches, buttress our arguments (Ward, 1987:2):

> If we examine the situation of a nation, set of nations, or the system as a whole, it may be said to be in one of the three states mentioned above: crisis, peace, or war. The thrust of the brief review. . . is to suggest that most current theory identifies structural factors (attributes broadly taken) to determine which of these three modes dominate world politics at any given point in time and space. I argue here that it would be useful to look at the transitions among these various system states for a different, and potentially more comprehensive and at the same time more context specific theory.

In the foregoing chapters we have argued (and demonstrated) that process models create a dynamic for the explanation of interdependent outcomes that is *logically precluded* by the use of static (often cross-national) attribute approaches. In the first chapter we noted that war has been employed in this book as an illustrative device; it does not require a special logic of its own. But, to study international relations we require a combination of logic and research design that will be able to handle phenomena—alliances, treaty making, etc.—which, like war, are the products of interdependent interaction. We have argued the logical requirements of going beyond the attributes or characteristics of any single state in the investigation of outcomes resulting from behavioral combinations—the behavioral outcomes of willingness in two or more states. To do this we have dealt with the logical elements of willingness (chapters 3 through 5); the logical elements of opportunity that affect, and help shape, the incentive structures of decision makers (especially developed in chapter 6); and the range of possible behavioral alternatives, their relationships to one another, and their relationships to willingness (especially developed in chapter 5 as substitutability).

However, the introduction of process, and the conception of international outcomes and behavior as a series of decisions and interactions, additionally forces the analyst to deal in probability models (of the sort Cioffi deals with as "political reliability"). With the logical introduction of probability concerns, the idea of looking for *which* processes occur under *what* conditions also follows. This combination of ideas then forms one basis for our attention to "nice laws," and a mode of research design to be discussed below.

Thus, the theme of process eventually brings us to the consideration of nice laws. A second theme that was developed (and which also leads to nice laws) concerned the reintroduction of "grand theory" to our thinking about international relations. We developed arguments (culminating in chapter 5) that broader, grand theoretical conceptualizations were required by scholars. We argued that too narrow theorizing would hinder our thinking about each of the three elements noted directly above—opportunity, willingness, the set of behavioral alternatives—as well as thinking about the relationships among them. Our call for a broader set of conceptualizations was both to promote the development of "better" theory, and in order to develop more useful and rigorous research design. These broader conceptualizations were to be especially important in the problemation cluster of research design activities. They were needed by the researcher to help understand exactly *what* phenomena and concepts were of interest, and *why*. They were needed to help guard against the isolation (and even reification) of international phenomena, and the design of meaningless research projects. We concluded that the use of broad theory to inform the purpose and context of our questions—more truly "puzzles" in the Rosenauian sense—will lead us to ask which processes work under what conditions. Thus, once again, we are back to a concern with nice laws.

While the concern with theory called for broader conceptualizations, the concern with logic and method demonstrated that once grand theory was employed to help generate more meaningful questions of greater utility to cumulation, research design demanded the rigor necessary to ensure that the questions were properly investigated. The application of logic to method and research design forces us to distinguish among necessary, sufficient, and necessary and sufficient factors and processes, and understand the utility of searching for subgeneral laws. Thus, grand theory, while clarifying our thought *does not* call for general laws. The combination of fuller conceptualization and greater research design rigor also moves us toward the fuller explanation of subsets through nice laws.

In this chapter we want to synthesize and elaborate on (some of) our previous discussions. We introduced the concept and intellectual goal of cumulation in the first chapter. The question "why doesn't international relations research add up?" can be addressed to numerous areas and subfields—for example, international conflict, the relationship between internal and external politics/ behavior, or the comparative study of foreign policy. Our response in this book is twofold: (1) We haven't been asking the questions correctly (2) our research design has often been logically flawed. Critical reviews of the comparative study of foreign policy have raised approximately similar questions (see Papadakis and Starr, 1987; Starr, 1988). A recent overview of the comparative study of foreign policy reviews continuing problems such as ad hoc hypothesis testing, the absence of theory, and the need to move beyond "monadic state-centered attributes" (Caporaso, et al., 1988).

The call for broader, grand theory to inform our concepts and problemation leads to stronger research design. The use of logic to match analysis to the question also leads to stronger design. We then enter the theory/research design/research/theory loop, presented in chapter one, with a greater probability that our research will improve theory and "add up."

CUMULATION: THEORY AND EXPLANATION

In addressing the first broad response noted above (not asking questions correctly) we presented several ideas that ultimately lead us to an argument for grand theory as developed in chapter 5. Clearly theory, and "good" theory is required for integrative cumulation. Theory should be broad enough to set concepts and phenomena within a meaningful intellectual context. These conclusions are in line with Abraham Kaplan's (1964) "paradox of conceptualization," which notes that while the proper concepts are required for the development of good theory, we require good theory to help us develop the proper concepts.

Theory will also be facilitated if we focus on true puzzles or anomalies, and concern ourselves with attempts to rationalize or synthesize apparently contradictory pieces of evidence. This argues for the use of stylized facts as we have done throughout this book. It also argues for a willingness to accept that several possible processes (or hypotheses or models) are working at the same time, but for different subsets of the units of analysis under consideration within different circumstances.[1] At the same time this reinforces our need to ask "how" phenomena occur and therefore to focus on process questions (which in turn indicates a need to increase the development and application of interactive/interplay models).

The various themes and arguments presented in this book also work towards changing the meaning of explanation (along with a rather eclectic view of "theory"). The standard approach to explanation, put rather simply, is to place some particular event or action within the context of some general covering law. However, if there *is* *no* general covering law, a different mode of inquiry is needed. As we have demonstrated in a number of questions concerning the nature of international conflict at both the micro- and macro-level, there are logical as well as empirical impediments to general covering laws. That is, it will be difficult to generalize the behavior, or outcomes, of foreign policy making and interactive processes. However, the processes themselves may certainly be "stable"—in the sense that they are recurring patterns of behavior which are theoretically isolatable in terms of regularity and "rulefulness" (the core of Eckstein's conception of theory; 1975:88). This aspect of stability was demonstrated in chapter 6 in discussing the effects of systemic polarity on the occurrence of violent international conflict. The arguments concerning nice laws and substitutability presented in chapter 5 also pointed to the possibility of understandable and regular (stable) processes leading to different empirical results.

We are dealing with a changing meaning of explanation if the ultimate end of our research is *not* empirical universals, but rather the *prior conditions* by which processes will generate certain types of results for certain types of behavioral units (as most fully developed in chapter 5). Returning to opportunity and willingness, the sorts of empirical universals expected under general covering laws will not appear if we conceive the environment as providing a complex range of overlapping opportunities for choice. We then have decision making (or choice making or policymaking) as a complex process within certain types of environments. These environments, of course could be governmental, bureaucratic, societal/domestic, or international. Thus, the analyses presented here could be, and should be, extended to any decision making entity within any set of environments, especially if the phenomena under investigation is an interdependent outcome of interaction between the decision making entities.

The ultimate end is now to understand the processes, and to understand how processes may generate different results under different conditions. The different conditions include both the environment that provides opportunities and the characteristics of the decision making units. The processes also require close attention to the interactive/interdependent behavior to be explained. In our terms there may also be different processes that lead to policy decisions, and each of those processes might operate under different conditions or have its own domain of validity.

These conclusions clearly rest upon a *probabilistic* conception of theory and explanation. We have consciously avoided becoming involved in the complex and contentious debate over what exactly *is* "theory." Our usage has meant to be broad and inclusive, rather than highly formal and narrow. Following the more relaxed set of assumptions for theory that many philosophers of science present for the social sciences (e.g., see Rapoport, 1958; Nagel, 1961; Meehan, 1965), we have used theory in terms of being a guide to research, and as a logical instrument for organizing and ordering experiences and phenomena. Eckstein (1975:88) provides a straightforward statement mirroring our views on, and use of, theory:

> The quintessential end of theorizing is to arrive at *statements of regularity* about the structure, behavior, and interaction of phenomena. "Regularity" here means, literally, "rulefulness": the discovery of rules that phenomena observe in the concrete world....Such regularity can exist in many senses. The rules may describe simple relations among variables without specification of their exact nature; or they may describe sequences like causal paths or historical and genetic patterns; or they may be statements of the conditions of persistence or efficacy of structures. The rules may also be less "ruleful." They may be "probability statements" that permit no inferences about individual cases but only more or less confident ones about sets of them (emphasis in original).

Evaluation of Theory: Logic and Process

Concern with the "rulefulness" of phenomena is another way of expressing our concern with process, especially in terms of specifying sequences of activity, and the logical rules by which phenomena combine and interact. But, as Eckstein's comments indicate, we do not simply equate theory with process. Instead, we are arguing that looking at theory in certain ways, looking at research design in certain ways, and employing logic in certain ways, will facilitate the development of theory and the cumulation of knowledge in international relations.

We have also argued the need to shift the orientation of research away from the search for general patterns, and thus to alter the analytical and statistical procedures we use (as demonstrated by our research on diffusion). We will need to look closely at the standard criteria for evaluating a theory, which include characteristics such as broad scope and generalizability, parsimony, and causality (e.g., see Przeworski and Teune, 1970). If all of this is true (and we think so, based on the logical analyses presented throughout the book, the simulation in chapter 5, and our empirical analyses of the positive spatial diffusion of violent conflict), we need to change procedures for (or the bases on which) we evaluate theories and models. If all of this is true then we should not expect our models to be very general, but closer to nice laws. Therefore, our efforts need to be directed at looking at subsets of phenomena, at investigating the specific sets of conditions under which specific models work. By looking at the combination of environmental conditions (i.e., opportunity) and how those relate to choice and action (i.e., willingness), and how those choices interact with the choices of others to produce outcomes, we are back to our concept of process.

Our efforts need to go into the delineation and evaluation of processes, rather than *events* as most international relations research has done. This redirection may be found in the current debate over the future of the comparative study of foreign policy, and the place of event data in the definition and direction of that movement. The call for the use of detailed "scripts" of historical situations, rather than simply the final "event" which may have occurred, recognizes that, events are, at best, "traces"; or "residues" of the processes under consideration.[2] Recall that we have also noted how problems with research design can create poor data selection and focus attention on the "wrong" sorts of events for answering the research question.

Clearly we have not made things easier for the systematic analyst of international relations. The general problem of locating and agreeing on a/the dependent variable found in the study of foreign policy (e.g., see Papadakis and Starr, 1987)—does one study the foreign policy process? the governmental decision? the actual events that occur? or the consequences of those events?—now needs to be addressed across most of international relations. What we are saying also has implications for both cross-sectional designs (different polities might not be characterized by the same process at any given time t) and time series designs (the nature of the process which gives rise to a phenomenon in any given polity could change through time).

One response is to increase the use of *theoretically-guided* comparative case-study designs (see especially, Eckstein, 1975; George, 1979). Examples of such work may be found. Mancur Olson (1982) has presented a theoretically sophisticated process linking the logic of collective action to the rise and decline of states—one that can differentiate between states at any one time, but also indicates different processes at work in any one state at different points in time. Olson's theoretical sections are followed by a series of (admittedly controversial) case studies. Bueno de Mesquita's theory of expected utility is another example, having been made more complex to handle different policy areas across states and within states across time (Bueno de Mesquita, Newman and Rabuska, 1985). The data collection and analyses in this work are essentially highly structured, comparative case studies.

Saying that we need to develop process models is easy. More difficult is discovering whether there are *different types* of process models (e.g., those in physics that focus on the interplay of objects and forces, and those which deal with animate actors and their relationships). It is also more difficult to demonstrate that process models will *always* be superior to nonprocess models (as they were in the examples presented here and in the research on war diffusion). As shown here, they certainly will do better in cases where we want to explain the outcomes of interaction and interdependent relationships.

If, however, we reject the standard advice given by Przeworski and Teune that "good" theories provide broad scope and generality, and if following nice laws we also abandon a Popperian refutationist/rejectionist position (perhaps in favor of a Lakatosian view based on excess empirical content), then, what criteria are left that could be used to evaluate a good theory? We have indicated throughout that one should assess theories or models in terms of their internal logical consistency and completeness. That is, a theory is "better" if it specifies more of the sequentially-occurring linkages (or perhaps better seen as "rules"), and does so in logically consistent fashion. Given two models, M1 and M2, with M1 being the more consistent and complete, we could argue that it should be assessed as the more valuable even if it had a narrower scope, less generality and lower postdictive capacity than M2 (this may, however, also run counter to Lakatos). For example, consider the following two models:

Model 1	Model 2
If A, then B	If A, then Y
If B, then C	
If C, then Y	

Both yield identical predictions on the basis of an identical first factor. Let us assume that the predictions are well-supported by the existing empirical evidence. Given our position above, M1 is preferred over M2, even though it is less parsimonious and no more general than M2.

Our position thus argues that our challenges or problems are primarily theoretical in the sense of being logical/mathematical rather than empirical (although our discussion in chapter 1 indicates that we need to keep all the clusters of research design going to be successful, including the empirical data analysis). The centrality of logic and theory also helps us in dealing with the various micro/decisional/willingness black boxes that will confront us, and which might not be as amenable to unpacking as M1 above. Such boxes are "black" (unpackable) only at the empirical or observable level. That is, variables B and C (or...N) might not be measurable or operationalizable. However, the processes can be mapped theoretically. To the extent that they are theoretically mapped, it is then possible to specify (again theoretically) each sequential step. Once done, there is no need to unpack the boxes empirically; knowing A—a presumed observable and measurable condition or factor—one could logically deduce Y.

This sort of logical approach to investigation has been applied in the sciences (e.g., Kaufman, Urbain, and Thomas, 1985), and can be used as a model for social science analyses. Ward (1987:9-10) summarizes his research in terms directly related to our conclusions above: "Building on the pioneering approach of the so-called *Bruxelles école* I have shown how simple box and arrow diagrams, such as those that populate social science articles, can be easily be turned into logical (state transition) equations, and how those logical equations can in turn be simply transformed into moderately complex nonlinear differential equation systems."

Various work across the sciences, and a few social science investigators such as Ward, have begun to demonstrate the utility in investigating the logical structure of theory, research design, political argumentation, and the relationships among real-world phenomena.[3] The application of logical equations and representations is especially beneficial to international relations (and interactive outcomes such as war) because many of the social science theories dealing with such topics are really couched in logical rather than covariational language. That is, the language of the theory or model often looks at some phenomena as expected only in the absence of some factors and the presence of others. We have demonstrated this point elsewhere in the discussion of the relationship between internal and external conflict (see, for example, Starr and Most, 1985b). A relationship that requires us to look at different logical forms, and at the logical structure of conditions, has often been translated into regression equations that have failed to reveal much (e.g., see Stohl's 1980 review of the literature).

The use of quite simple Boolean logic as a starting place for theory construction seems relatively straightforward as it thus captures the manner in which our natural language conceptualizes cause and effect—this and this go together; either this or that; and, never in the presence of this will you see that. Many of the theories found in international relations (or the social sciences in general) are phrased in exactly this way. In addition, such logical approaches have been successsful in the sciences dealing with natural and physical settings characterized by great variability; they have been important in the cumulation of knowledge in these areas (e.g., biology, immunology, neural sciences, genetics, and climatology). As argued throughout this book, and particularly highlighted in this chapter, logical approaches force the investigator to start at the conceptual level and constrains one to some simple assertions, assertions from which one may derive a better understanding of both the processes (dynamics) and the structures generating them. This can be done clearly and economically with a logical approach. In addition, this approach allows one to entertain simple on/off thresholds (as we have done throughout using the presence and absence of opportunity and willingness), without precluding the investigation of more complicated thresholds (e.g., multivalued logic).

The payoffs from the use of logical approaches can be quite valuable; indeed, the entire field is growing rapidly, especially in disciplines that focus on the interstitial areas of natural, physical, and social sciences. This emerging approach is gaining great popularity as a "first step" to modeling in many fields, and is often called the "conceptual modeling" approach. This is exactly the type of modeling process we have demonstrated in this book, and have illustrated with our own research on the diffusion of conflict. In our efforts to model the process of positive spatial diffusion we have employed a similar modeling procedure, continually asking what the world would "look like" if the diffusion process worked this way, or that way, etc. The reader should recognize that such an approach also follows Lave and March's (1975:19-20) procedure for the development of disciplined speculation. Let us note once more the steps set out in this procedure:

1. Observe some facts.
2. Look at the facts as though they were the end result of some unknown process (model). Then speculate about processes that might have produced such a result.
3. Then deduce other results (implications/consequences/predictions) from the model.
4. Then ask yourself whether these other implications are true and produce new models if necessary.

With an understanding of conceptual modeling it should be clear why our search for a new and more appropriate conceptualization of explanation in international relations led us to the logical approach: we need to be able to start with simple, uncomplicated assumptions about the phenomena under consideration and glean what we can by way of deduction from them. This is illustrated by our use of stylized facts, and our particular ways of "getting started" with such facts, and the "what would the world look like" approach.

One significant general result of using such approaches is described in the writings of Prigogine (1980; Prigogine and Stengers, 1984)—that most systems are in disequilibrium and rarely does a single unique equilibrium exist. Rather, many systems studied with a logical approach reveal the existence of multiple equilibria. This type of phenomena has been the concern of chapter 5, with its emphasis on substitutability and nice laws. Such findings have not, in general, characterized the findings in international relations, primarily because of conceptual blinders of the sort we have identified in earlier chapters.

Thus, if we are correct in arguing that there are processes (as opposed to a single process) or that there may be puzzles (as opposed to a single puzzle) connected with the occurrence of a given phenomenon, then we may again conclude that our tasks are becoming more logical and theoretical and less empirical. For example, given two process models, M3 and M4, each of which is accepted as having some (real or potential) domain of validity, the task becomes one of learning how to predict the conditions under which one or the other (or some additional M5...Mn) model will explain how the phenomenon in question occurred. Again, the predictions, then, are theoretical and not empirical—and that seems to be a departure from what we usually do. As we shall see in the following section, a combination of such logic/theory along with empirical factors, brings the whole notion of critical or crucial tests for international relations models into question.

EVALUATION OF THEORY: CLOSURE, DEAD ENDS AND CRITICAL TESTS

The question of why our efforts do not add up cannot be addressed solely in terms of how we generate questions, but must also include how we design the research to study them and how we think about them. Similarly, we are concerned with the evaluation of theory to assist in the development of integrative cumulation. In part this can be done by the development of approaches and methods to analysis which have a greater chance of avoiding dead ends and promoting theoretical and conceptual movement in productive directions. With the proper questions, and the use of logic along with method and theory, we will also be able to come more quickly to closure in the evaluation of theory, concepts and hypotheses.

It is obvious that the creative scholar can generate many postdictive explanations for any phenomenon; indeed there are too many "plausible"/intuitive hypotheses and postulates for almost any area of international relations. We have already discussed one possible reason for this condition, the problem of inchoate linkages between theory and empirical analysis; i.e., that the theory and linkages are not sufficiently deductive. We have also noted what we see as the problem of the goal of empirical generalization: The search for general covering laws creates a situation in which analysts feel compelled to ask (reach) the same questions (or only slightly different questions) on new data sets (new cases and/or time periods), using new measures/indicators and/or methods.

The result, as we see it, is little cumulation due in part from the difficulty in: (*a*) closing off/down unproductive research questions; (*b*) opening new research questions; (*c*) asking 2nd/3rd/4th...nth questions which follow on (build from) the first question.[4] We find individual scholars continually returning to first principles or questions, unable (or unwilling) to judge theoretical dead ends from promising ones. We have tried to demonstrate that the inability to discriminate derives in large part from the failure to deal with the broad theoretical context, and from asking narrow questions that do not (and cannot) stand alone, as well as the inability to work through the logic and consistency of the theory and design.

In chapter 6 we use the example of the literature on the relationship between the structure of the international system (including polarity, stability, the distribution of military capabilities, alliances, etc.) and conflict. We know there are logical flaws in the theory, and that there is little or no empirical support for the various proposals and theoretical positions. Yet, despite critical analyses of the flaws in the logic of the theory, as well as a lack of empirical support, some students still try to find some (empirical) way to make it work. Others move on to different concerns but fail to use the information/knowledge that has been gained through critical analyses of system structure-conflict hypotheses. For cumulation to occur, we must instead conclude that there is little to found in this research area, at least in ways that are currently specified, and then *use* this knowledge. These problems have occurred in other areas of international relations research. The question of whether states interact, especially in terms of arms races is one such area, and one of the major puzzles identified by Zinnes (1980). Arms races were also discussed by Russett (1983) in his review of the debates over international interactions and processes, as was the internal-external linkage area of study.

Returning to the idea of changing the meaning of explanation, closure here means better ways of moving down the branches of logical trees, and quicker ways to prune the branches of those trees—and *not* the use of "critical" tests. For Popper, one could devise critical or crucial tests to refute or falsify whole theories, in turn pointing to another theory (Popper, 1962:112): "For to say that without the theory in question we should have expected a different result implies that our expectation was the result of some other (perhaps older) theory, however dimly we may have been aware of this fact." This standard usage may be found in Job and Ostrom's (1976:60) critique of the Correlates of War Project where they indicate that critical tests between models means pitting models against each other to see which performs better and whether there is logical incompatibility between models (see also Hempel, 1966).

The ideas of nice laws and substitutability, the distinction between necessary and sufficient conditions, and the subsequent introduction of process and probability all argue *against* borrowing the concept of the crucial or critical test into international relations to distinguish between contending approaches or hypotheses. Such tests are confounded by nice laws, in that some theory may not work in one region but may be quite useful in another; the refutation of whole theories (and the possible acceptance of other whole theories) will miss the subsets or conditions under which the theory might apply. We hope that this was clearly demonstrated in our approach to the debates in the literature concerning the effects of power preponderance and parity, and polarity, on the incidence of international conflict in chapter 6.

Our discussion in that chapter indicated that by clarifying the (empirical) conditions, or sets of expectations,[5] required by necessity, sufficiency, necessity and sufficiency, and probability, we could demonstrate the impossibility of distinguishing between power polarity and power parity in terms of either being sufficient or necessary and sufficient. These conditions, however, are just those that are required for a "critical" test between the two hypotheses. As noted in chapter 6, "Once one begins to think in terms of either necessity or probabilities, it becomes possible to see why the preponderance and parity hypotheses *are not in fact logical opposites.*" The combined use of nice laws and the application of logic as developed in this book, indicate the difficulty of finding theories that are fully logically incompatible with each other. Instead of the critical test perspective, which asks "which model/theory is better?" we want to ask "under what conditions does each model/theory work?"

Stylized Facts and Getting Started in Research

Informed by logic, our approach to research design has been clearly set out at various points above—an approach that understands the difficulty of designing critical tests. Indeed, we rarely begin with the standard descriptive approaches that wish to "look at" or "write about" some general topic. Nor do we start with the standard questions: "How do I (or could one) 'explain' y?"; "who is 'right'?" in regard to some issue; "what would the results look like if we take another look using new indicators, new measures, new analytical techniques, etc.?"

Much more commonly our interest has been directed to situations where it initially appears that y and –y are, in some sense, both "true." While other analysts may be equally intrigued by the same question, they are inclined to sort out the y/–y problem by conducting some sort of crucial or critical test to see which is "right." Our response is different. If theory, empirical research (note that this is where the empirical component again returns to importance), crude interpretations of reality (the beginning of a Lave and March theory-building process), or any combination of these considerations suggest that y and –y are both "true," that is to be simply accepted. The focus is then shifted not to which is right, but rather on *how both* could be right.

This is the approach demonstrated most fully in chapter 6. In reconstructing the process used to develop those analyses it appears two things were done differently (see Most, 1986). First, we tried to think through "what the world would look like if" one or another of the power hypotheses held. This was done rather quickly, generating rather crude and impressionistic predictions or derivations. Given these directional indicators, a second step was taken—a "quick and dirty," intentionally nonsystematic consideration of some stylized facts and a simple hypothetical case were developed. This type of procedure fits quite closely with Eckstein's (1975:118) typology of case studies, especially his notion of "must fit" cases. Our version of stylized facts indicates how case studies can be used to help delineate nice laws, or the conditions under which different models/theories might be expected to work.

Again, in chapter 6 the stylized facts and hypothetical cases were developed rather quickly in terms of an experiment that would produce conditions and conclusions regarding the logical properties of the hypotheses. One great advantage of presenting and considering several stylized facts (e.g., in chapter 6 the use of the peaceful United States/Canada/Mexico triad; the Bolivia/Argentina/Brazil subsystem; and the shifting power relationship between the United States and USSR in the postwar era), is the ability to delineate what could or could not be sufficient (or necessary) conditions.

As demonstrated in chapter 6 and noted above, both hypotheses could be true *sometimes*. Given that presumptive conclusion from the impressionistic, quick and dirty, and logical considerations, the next step was to move to an attempt to figure out what the additional conditions—prior to conditional—might be that influence which outcome will pertain (and to ignore the question of which was right). Thus, we concluded with an exercise in the development of nice laws.[6]

In effect, these activities were directed primarily towards the second step in the procedures suggested by Lave and March—speculating about what conditions, linkages, and processes could have brought about the results observed in the world. Along with the application of logic and stylized facts, two analogies were helpful in this speculation. The first of these—the set of concepts provided by opportunity and willingness—was described in detail in chapters 1 and 2. This analogy facilitated the analysis of necessity or sufficiency, and forced us (or any analyst) to deal with the nature of the entities involved, the environments or contexts in which they were embedded, and with the relationships between the entity and environment. As noted at the beginning of this book, opportunity and willingness provided a framework for the organization of any of the factors that could be related to the phenomena under consideration—as simple mechanisms underlying complex behavior (see note 18 in chapter 6).

A second analogy of great utility, but not developed at any length above, is the simple computer program flowchart or logical tree. A flowchart or tree may facilitate the analyst's conception of a process in terms of how it begins and then operates over some period. Eventually, a branch point is reached; processes then go different ways—into different subroutines, if you will—and come out *differently*. This analogy thus helps one think (speculate) about the various possible outcomes of processes. By its nature it also facilitates thinking in terms of nice laws as well as substitutability (especially the mapping of one to many). The logical tree analogy also naturally leads us away from critical test dichotomies where one model is held to be "true" and another "false," and toward the question of under what conditions a process holds. Recall the discussion in chapter 5 on moving beyond the simple truth or falsity of a model, and the conceptualization of axioms as dichotomous variables which can play a partitioning role. The branches of a flowchart or logical tree suggest a series of such partitions.

The key point is that the flowchart procedure indicates, from yet another perspective, that critical tests are not required for theoretical closure. The movement down the branches of a flowchart/ logical tree can help us to identify promising theoretical paths while weeding out the unpromising ones. The whole process set out in this book, and summarized in the present discussion, has been used in other disciplines. As noted elsewhere (Most, 1986) this style of inquiry has been successful in generating theory and research results in physics, biophysics, chemistry, and biochemistry among others. It is obvious that there are different styles or ways of *beginning* to do research, and certainly no one best way for all analysts studying all problems (a nice law infinite loop?). Nonetheless, *how* one begins does appear to affect the quality of the work; many of the most successful researchers have learned to reason and research in ways that are particularly efficient.

Using approaches similar to the procedures outlined here, some of our most noted scientists appear to have had ways of increasing the odds that they would "get lucky" in the intuitive, creative "art" of theoretical insight. This disciplined creativity is noted in John Platt's (1964:351) discussion of Pasteur's methods of discovery and his use of experiments to build up a logical tree of exclusions. Platt sees Pasteur's work as exemplary of the drama of discovery based on "strong inference." Even if it is the case that creativity, inspiration, intuitive leaps, and so on are important components of successful research, it seems clear that some analysts and teams of researchers have some sort of creative knack for getting the job done.

Such methods have been found in a highly successful "mentor chain" of pharmacologists, whose procedures have been passed along through six "generations" of extraordinarily successful researchers.[7] According to Kanigel (1981), each member of the chain has earned great distinction in the field; taken together, the group's performance has been outstanding. As described by Kanigel each senior analyst had apprentice Ph.D. candidates and post-doctoral researchers. Each of the older, more seasoned researchers proceeded in his or her turn to pass along knowledge and technique to their apprentices. Each senior scientist did more than that, however. As Kanigel puts it, each one also passed along "an approach, a style, a taste in the mouth or a feel in the gut for just what makes 'good science.'" The scientific legacy, which began with Dr. Bernard Brodie, has been summarized this way (Kanigel, 1981:8):

Don't bother with the routine problems; leave them to others. Don't bother, either, with big, fundamental problems that are simply not approachable with available techniques and knowledge; why beat your head against the wall? Half the battle is asking the right question at the right time—when it's neither premature to tackle it, nor invites too obvious an answer; when the right methodology is available; when enthusiasm is at its peak.... And then just do it. Don't spend all year in the library getting ready to do it. Don't wait until you've gotten all the boring little preparatory experiments out of the way. Don't worry about scientific control, at least for now. Just go with your hunch, your scientific intuition, and isolate that simple, elegant, pointed experiment that will tell you in a flash *whether you're on the right track* (emphasis added).

The combination of broad, grand theory to help generate puzzles, and the use of stylized facts and logical trees as approaches to getting started and to generating designs to facilitate finding answers, as developed in this book, is clearly reflected in this description of the "Brodie legacy." It is also reflected in the comments of William N. Lipscomb, 1976 Nobel Prize Winner in chemistry:

...people tend to think that scientists work by adding one fact to another. That is a misconception. A scientist proceeds in making discoveries in very much the same way an artist goes about working. You have to master a large discipline, and your discoveries are not necessarily made by planning them. They arise intuitively. You suddenly perceive brand-new connections that you were unaware of before. Material somehow reorganizes itself in your mind, and that leads to the spawning of a new group of ideas.

One of the major problems in this process is not the lack of information but rather the abundance of contradictory material. You somehow have to see through the contradictions and fit the material together in a new way. Then, all of a sudden, things click. You begin to think, 'Well, maybe there is something to it.' The scientific method comes into play only after you make your intuitive jump. You use it to test your ideas— but not in the generation of new ideas. (*U.S. News and World Report,* April 21, 1981, p. 85 interview).

OPPORTUNITY, WILLINGNESS, AND LEVELS OF ANALYSIS

Before concluding, we must return to our other central analogy, the key substantive component of the material presented in the preceding chapters. The use of opportunity and willingness has forced us to look at all three elements of the Sprouts' ecological triad, especially the interactive effects of the environment and the decision-making process of the entities. Particularly as developed in chapters 5 and 6, we argue against various forms of system-based determinism (or system-centric theorizing). Despite the need for both opportunity and willingness, we have answered questions raised in chapter 2 about the relationship of the two concepts by focusing on the *more* dynamic nature of the willingness/choice process.

We have reached similar conclusions in our research on the diffusion of conflict (see especially Most and Starr, 1981). Diffusion can be, and has been, conceived as a systemic phenomenon and studied on a macro-level. However, using approaches similar to those employed in chapters 5 and 6 (though preceding them in part), we demonstrate logically that diffusion must be *mapped through* decision makers. In brief, there is a need to take decision makers and their perceptions into account *even if* the relevant world and decision makers' perceptions of it are identical. The issue hinges on the logical or theoretical completeness of the environmental arguments.

Consider the following syllogism:
If some environmental factor, then certain decision-maker calculations.
If certain decision-maker calculations, then a certain policy decision.

Assuming the validity of the two initial statements, the observation of the environmental factor would allow the analyst to deduce the occurrence of the policy. The environmental factor and the decision makers' calculations are respectively the remote and proximate conditions in the causal sequence that leads to the policy.

The perceptions and calculations of decision makers may thus serve as what McGaw and Watson (1976:50) refer to as "contributory conditions" such that: If certain decision-maker perceptions, then if some environmental factor, then the policy. Reformulated, this implies the interactive relationship between perceptions and the environment. As one could derive from Richardson's study of arms races, the relationship between environment and policy decisions does not hold automatically.[8] Rather, it exists because certain decision maker perceptions and calculations are also (assumed to be) present. The decision makers' perceptions are initial conditions whose specification is necessary for theoretical completeness. In the study of diffusion, this leads to the conclusion that we should "reserve the diffusion/contagion concepts for situations in which local policy makers decide and cue their decisions on similar behaviors in other polities" (Most and Starr, 1981:12).

The discussion in chapters 5 and 6 lead us to focus on decision makers, and how their goals and perceptions of the environment affect the willingness to make certain choices. Interestingly enough, these observations, and those concerning willingness and a state's capacity-to-risk ratio (C/R ratio) help us get a handle on system change, learning and evolution. Thus, analyses that lead us to focus on the micro-level may also lead us back to important linkages and observations about the macro-level.

Decision makers in each state operate in an environment that is partially defined at any time (t) on the basis of their own capacities and the distribution of capacities across other states in the system, (i.e., the systemic quality of polarity). These factors set a state's C/R ratio at any initial t. Decision makers in some initially dominant state may be satisfied (e.g., Ci may be > Ri), but those in some other, initially weak state may not be content. Working under the general condition of the security dilemma through the search for security, the decision makers of the latter state seek C > R. To do this they would pursue some combination of increasing capacities and decreasing risks. They might not succeed in doing either but if they do, the other state's C/R state would be altered and it, too, would act and react (assuming again the goal of security and also following the security dilemma, and the possibly dangerous opportunity and willingness loops described in chapter 2).

If the initially weak state succeeds and/or the initially dominant state fails to react, a new power emerges and the system is transformed from unipolarity to bipolarity. If the initially weak state keeps going (now pursuing the goal of unconditional viability and system dominance), it could actually subjugate the initially dominant state and return the system to unipolarity. This scenario should not be unfamiliar to the student of international politics. It contains the classic security dilemma and conflict spiral. It also models the process of system change and cycles of hegemonic change offered by Robert Gilpin (1981). Gilpin's model (or those presented by proponents of long-cycles such as Modelski and

Thompson) is presented as a macro-model of systemic structure, yet it is based on the expected utility calculations of challengers to the system hegemon as captured by our discussion of the C/R ratio. Hence, there is a clear linkage between macro-level system change models to micro-level models of choice, such as those presented by Bueno de Mesquita.

In sum, we can show that the type of system as discussed by Waltz and others, sets initial conditions and may have an impact on both the *probability* of system transformation (what decision makers are willing to do), and the *possibility* of such changes (what they are capable of actually doing). That said, micro-level decision processes could be posited to have generative effects—if decision makers pursue certain goals and are successful in their pursuits, systems should be expected to transform in intelligible ways.[9]

In addition, we can say something about various types of system change. Although Gilpin (1981:39–44) sets out different forms of change—systems change, systemic change, interaction change—most students of change in the international system focus on systems change. These scholars, looking at long-cycles or the rise and fall of system hegemons, are concerned with world wars or "general" wars involving most or all of the great powers, which lead to a major reorientation of the nature of the actors involved in terms of the political and military structure of the system.[10] Yet, given our presentations both in the present chapter and chapter five, it is clear that there may be many routes to changes in states' C/R ratios. As a consequence of the substitutability phenomenon, system transformations could occur with or without the occurrence of war (see chapters 4 and 5 especially). And again, following on the conclusions of chapter 6 we can challenge assertions that certain types of systems would be more or less war prone. Certain types of systems may affect the probabilities that some states will want to change the political hierarchy and the possibilities that they will succeed. But such systems do not seem likely to determine the *means* by which states will act.

While this is important in terms of war and change in the international arena, it might be useful to emphasize a broader theoretical and epistemological point. Despite admonitions that such arguments cannot and should not be developed, we are suggesting that it is indeed possible to develop logical and systematic relationships between phenomena at different levels of analysis. In this book we have only begun to think about how we might develop laws of *com-*

position and *decomposition* which will allow analysts to "go up" from the individual or nation-state levels and "get down" from the system level.

To do this, however, we *do not* have to assume that decision makers are homogeneous or homogeneously seek any particular goal or objective—the security dilemma/security goals posited above were simply illustrative.[11] Our arguments do not require the assertion of an empirically questionable motive force, as does, for example Waltz's *Theory of International Politics*. As in chapter 6 (where we could have used either power preponderance *or* power parity in the demonstration of our points) we do not need a specific single condition to hold. As such, our comments about levels of analysis and approaches to composition/decomposition provide another perspective on the importance of domain specific laws. We do not have to expect any particular deduction or initial condition to hold universally.

SOME FINAL COMMENTS

Let us briefly summarize the positions taken in the chapters above. We must start with the grand theories of broad conceptualizations to help us identify genuine puzzles. At that point the application of logic to research design will help us deal with those puzzles as rigorously as possible. We should employ flowcharts or logical trees in order to ask the crucial "what would the world look like if" questions. We should use stylized facts both to help form the trees, and for the initial run-through of the logic presented by the trees. At this point middle-range theories and concepts may be brought into play to help deal with the domain specific nice laws. Middle-range (and perhaps narrower) theories can then be investigated with empirical techniques.

We have argued that analysts, by *starting* with such middle-range theories (rather than getting to them through the process developed throughout this book, and outlined in this chapter) have created untestable situations. We have concepts that float free of theoretical moorings, and hypotheses that do not move us along the logical trees to exclude branches and help bring about closure on the least promising ones.

If we have been at least partially successful in communicating the complexity and excitement of both theorizing and analysis, then we can count this enterprise as a success. If we have prompted the reader to discover new puzzles in the study of international relations we have also been successful. If the analyst of international relations finds the phenomena of the field more amenable to study through the use of opportunity and willingness we have succeeded. As Ben Most once noted (1986:15) it may be very "useful to think from time to time about how we work. While there's probably not too much that any one of us can do to make ourselves more intelligent, we certainly can learn to reason and research more efficiently or with greater effectiveness."

NOTES

NOTES TO CHAPTER 1

1. In her impressive review and analysis of such systematic approaches to the study of international relations, Zinnes (1976b) referred to the enterprise as the "scientific study of international politics" (SSIP). A number of early reviews of SSIP were discussed in Starr (1974). In addition to the work noted above, Hoole and Zinnes (1976) also present an in-depth critique and analysis of the four major SSIP projects of the 1960s-early 1970s—what Deutsch (or Starr) would call the "third wave." At the same time, Rosenau (1976a) collected a number of autobiographical statements as well as discussions of cumulation, theory, and the comparative study of foreign policy. All of these works began a decade of self-conscious review and stock-taking in the study of war, the comparative study of foreign policy, events data, and other areas (a process continued by such exchanges as the June 1985 symposium on methodological considerations in the study of international relations and conflict which appeared in *International Studies Quarterly*, or the recent volume on the comparative study of foreign policy edited by Hermann, Kegley and Rosenau [1987]).

2. See Bueno de Mesquita (1985a) for an overview of the possible components of such a research triad, as well as a strong statement on the need to deal, fully and explicitly, with the research component devoted to logic. We return to this theme in chapter 7.

3. Elinor Ostrom (1982b:81) similarly notes: "The lack of coherence in our discipline may partially result from the domination of the languages of data analysis over the languages of theory construction." See Boynton (1982a) for a discussion on the use of formal languages.

4. In Most and Starr (1981), for example, the application of logic to the phenomenon of diffusion—to its several possible forms including reinforcement as well as spatial diffusion—helped to clarify *what exactly* was of concern and to be studied. It became clear that five different types of diffusion explanations were possible, and even more importantly, that several of those forms were logically similar to, and could be "usefully seen as a specialized subfield of linkage politics." It was found that, "diffusion/contagion concerns can be readily reformulated in terms which are congruent with the more general linkage models" (Most and Starr, 1981:15).

5. See also Most and Starr (1983), as well as analyses of war that draw heavily from the Most and Starr commentary, such as Bulkeley (1983).

6. In a review of the study of arms races, Bulkeley (1983) also takes care to sort the various arguments and models of arms races and war in terms of those dealing with necessary conditions and those dealing with sufficient conditions.

7. John Dryzek (1986:301) argues that "progress" in science implies rationality: "Rationality in this context is choice between competing theories or theoretical frameworks based on good cognitive reasons." Here, we will be reconceptualizing the meaning of Dryzek's notion of "choice."

8. Dryzek (1986:302) uses progress in three ways: "The progress of a discipline is referred to as global progress. Progress inside a research tradition, itself within a discipline, is called internal progress. And the reinterpretation of progress as a capacity to cope with contingency is termed lateral progress." See also Ostrom (1982b:14).

9. Rosenau (1980b:233) initially notes that a "genuine puzzle" is "founded more on awe than confusion," and that the paradigmatic context needed for cumulation may not come "*until* we become genuinely puzzled" (emphasis in original). Puzzles are more than the general, open-ended questions of "what" and "why." Zinnes (1980:316) notes that a puzzle consists of "pieces of information, the belief that the pieces fit together into a meaningful picture—but the inability to fit the pieces together initially." Rosenau (1980b:235) similarly notes that, "A genuine puzzle, however, must stem from curiosity, since one must be perplexed about an effect before one can raise questions about causation...they come out of repeated observations and they compel us to sort out from all the phenomena we observe those that are both patterned and intriguing." It may now be clearer how the "puzzle" is one version of Lave and March's (1975) dynamic model building process.

10. According to Snidal (1985:32–33) a model "can be tailored precisely to the problem under investigation. Its key distinguishing characteristic is a formal logic that is both deductive and internal..." while theory "contains a deductive structure plus an interpretation of fundamental assumptions and theoretical constructs. This richer interpretive structure...provides for greater richness of explanation" (1985:34–35).

NOTES TO CHAPTER 2

1. The first published version of Starr's discussion of opportunity and willingness (Starr, 1978) reflected several years of revision and input from colleagues. This chapter is a revised version of Starr (1978).

2. One of the first was Gray, et al. (1968). This lengthy key word bibliography was followed by one of the most well known of peace research bibliographies, Pickus and Woito (1970). A slightly earlier but less well-known annotated bibliography was Newcombe and Newcombe (1969). In 1974 two bibliographies appeared, both products of university institutes: Aggarawal (1974); and Boulding and Passmore (1974). Other reviews, overviews, and books with extensive citations included, Alcock (1972); Pruitt and Snyder (1969); M. Haas (1974); and Dedring (1976). While the trend to bibliography has tailed off (with the major exception of Woito, 1982), the summary of research findings and the review of

major works in the field continues (see particularly Singer, 1980, 1981; Rummel, 1979; Gurr, 1980; Wilkinson, 1980; Beer, 1981; Sullivan and Siverson, 1981; Intriligator, 1982; North and Willard, 1983; Luterbacher, 1984).

3. Additionally, one of the earliest sources of our thinking along the lines of opportunity and willingness was Denton and Phillips (1968).

4. The work of Snyder, Bruck and Sapin (e.g., 1962) developing the idea of the "definition of the situation" was an important precursor to the Sprouts' work on perception. Snyder, et al. were also early exponents of models based on an internal-external factor dichotomy, and how those factors affected decision makers.

5. This "strong" cognitive behaviorism view may be somewhat misleading. The reader should be aware that one can go beyond the contention of the Sprouts that environmental factors can have an impact on policy decisions only to the extent that they are "perceived, reacted to, and taken into account" by decision makers. *Un*perceived environmental factors can affect decisions insofar as they have an impact on: (1) actors' opportunities and power, and thereby affect who participates in the policy making arena, and hence, what interests, goals and preferences are represented therein (see Bachrach and Baratz, 1962 and 1963); (2) the knowledge available to the actors and/or the ways in which they examine and evaluate options; and (3) actors' capacities to execute preferred options. Indeed, the Sprouts recognize this critique in part, when they note:

> ...the relation of environmental factors to performance and accomplishment (that is, to the operational outcomes or results of decisions and undertakings) may present an *additional* dimension. In the latter context, environmental factors may be conceived as a sort of a matrix, or encompassing channel, metaphorically speaking, which limits the execution of undertakings. Such limitations on performance, accomplishment, outcome or operational result *may not—often do not*—derive from or depend upon the environed individual's perception or other psychological behavior. In many instances, environmental limitations on outcome or performance may be effective even though the limiting factors were not perceived and reacted to in the process of reaching a decision and initiating a course of action (1965:11, emphasis added).

6. The literature indicates that proximity—economic, political, cultural as well as geographic—contributes to a higher level of interactions, including conflictual interactions. See, for example, Zipf (1949); Gleditsch (1969); Richardson (1960a:176–183); and Midlarsky (1974). Reviews of this literature, and the related diffusion literature can be found in Starr and Most (1976, 1978); Most and Starr (1980, 1981). See also the useful review by O'Loughlin (1984), for a geographer's overview and analysis.

7. The most important work in this area is being done by Bruce Bueno de Mesquita and associates in the development and refinement of expected utility theory. As applied to war, see especially Bueno de Mesquita (1981a, 1983, 1985b); and Bueno de Mesquita and Lalman (1986). For a general review of expected utility theory on the study of international conflict, see Bueno de Mesquita (1986). For an extension of expected utility theory to the policy analysis and policy prediction, see Bueno de Mesquita, Newman and Rabushka (1985).

8. There is an extensive literature on the relationship between cognitive/perceptual/psychological factors and foreign policy behavior. See Jervis (1976) for the most complete single treatment of the application of psychological concerns to the study of international politics and foreign policy. See also: Rapoport (1960:part III); Holsti (1976a, 1976b); Holsti and George (1975); Shapiro and Bonham (1973); Axelrod (1976); Steinbruner (1974); Heradstveit and Narvesen (1978); M. Hermann (1977); Falkowski (1979); and Starr (1984).

9. The literature on periodicity or cycles in international conflict, indicating the continued presence of war in the international system, also implies that the opportunity of war is constant and that the key focus should be on willingness. See: Denton and Phillips (1968:194). See also Denton (1966); Richardson (1960a:chap. 3); Moyal (1949); Small and Singer (1982:chaps. 6–8). Similar arguments may be made concerning the arguments for "long cycles" of international interactions, see: Goldstein (1985, 1988); Levy (1983, 1985); Gilpin (1981); and Modelski (1978).

10. On the mobilization of resources and the "conversion process" from resource potential to actual capabilities, see, for example, Organski and Kugler (1981); Baldwin (1979) and Hart (1976). On the willingness to suffer, see, for example, Rosen (1972); and Mack (1975).

11. See M. Haas (1965; 1974:chaps. 6–8) for reviews of societal and domestic factors as correlates of war. The work that discusses the impact of the form of government on the occurrence of war is also relevant here. See, for example: Wilkenfeld (1968, 1972); Waltz (1954:chaps. 4, 5); Babst (1970); Small and Singer (1976); Chan (1984); Weede (1984).

12. One possible application of the ethology literature is to help us understand somewhat more clearly *how* people came to be "cultural animals," and the relationships between the individual and the group, between the love/friendship bond and aggression. See, for example, Corning (1971); Fox (1971); Tinbergen (1968); Nelson (1974).

13. Somewhat related is the Galtungian view that many units will inevitably form a hierarchy of "topdogs" and "underdogs," and that rank disequilibrium in the units of this system provides constant opportunity for aggression. See, Galtung (1964, 1968, 1971).

14. See, for example, the literature on the relationships between internal and external conflict, relating the willingness to war externally to domestic unrest or dissension, (e.g., Gurr, 1980:chaps. 3–7; Wilkenfeld, 1973; Zinnes, 1976b: chap. 8).

15. The extensive literature on arms races, much of which follows from the pioneering work of Richardson (1960b), is connected to willingness in a number of ways. Axelrod (1984:28) explicitly notes that, "Richardson's model of the arms race is based on an interaction which is essentially a Prisoner's Dilemma, played once a year with the budgets of competing nations." A decision maker, seeing others acquire arms, and given past grievances and present perceptions of threat, may then become willing to acquire arms and use them. See, for example: Richardson (1960b); Busch (1970); Zinnes (1976b: chaps. 14, 15); Intriligator (1982); Russett (1983).

16. A useful example in regard to the work of an individual scholar is Robert North. The Stanford Studies of the 1914 pre-World War I period were directly concerned with the effects of crisis conditions on perceptions of willingness

(e.g., see Holsti, 1972; and Hoole and Zinnes, 1976: chaps. 17–21, for overviews of the project). It is interesting to note how North moved from the study of willingness to the study of opportunity. In a personal communication, North noted that the 1914 studies alone were not satisfying in explaining the conflict processes that led to World War I. Subsequently, he engaged in research that studied the structural and systemic environment (based on the relationships among technology, resources and population and driven by lateral pressure) that brought the European decision makers to the point where there had to make the choice between war and no-war (see Choucri and North, 1975).

17. In another study of the transition from peace to war using logical analyses, Ward (1987:7) describes the use of "state variables" and thresholds: "Let us assume that these various state variables may be either *on* or *off*—setting aside for the moment the question of where the thresholds are." This is essentially the position we are taking at this time regarding opportunity and willingness.

18. Such fear may explain the difference in outcomes of the 1914 crisis and the Cuban missile crisis—lack of willingness in the latter situation based on nuclear fear. See, Holsti, Brody and North (1965).

NOTES TO CHAPTER 3

1. The important analogs between events data analysis and work on the outbreak of international conflict should be apparent in discussions covering definitional, methodological and other issues, by Burgess and Lawton (1972); Azar and Ben-Dak (1975); and Kegley, Raymond, Rood, and Skinner (1975). While conflict analysts might object that they are not analyzing events data when they focus on factors such as the number of battle deaths in wars, their durations, and so on, the position here is that such factors do (or perhaps better put, are intended to) reflect the size, magnitude, or intensity of war occurrences (i.e., events). The implications of indicators of this type are explored below. See also, Most and Starr (1981).

2. See, for example, Starr (1976); Duvall (1976) for comments on the validity and reliability of the Correlates of War data set, along with a response from J. David Singer (1976). For other issues in coding data from historical sources, see the exchanges between Schroeder (1977) and Small (1977) and between Schroeder and Alexandroff, Rosecrance, and Stein (1977); see also Small (1976). Specific discussions of war data lists can be found in Most and Starr (1976, 1977); Eckhardt and Azar (1978a).

3. Figure 3.1 does not, of course, exhaust the full range of ways in which X may contribute to the occurrence of Y. In addition to serving as a necessary and/or sufficient condition for Y, X could also act as a contributory condition, one of several alternative conditions, a contingent condition, a proximate condition, a remote condition, or as part of a pattern of plural causation. See McGaw and Watson (1976). For a further explication of the relationships shown in figure 3.1, see note 10.

4. It should go without saying that the analyst in this situation will not be able to assert that the hypothesis is somehow "proven" by the analysis. To do so, of course, would force the researcher to commit the fallacy of affirming the consequent.

Note: The reader should note the special character of many of the figures and tables in this book. Perhaps it would have been more accurate to label them as exercises, as they resemble the exercises highlighted in statistics and methodology texts. As in table 3.1 many of the tables and figures *do not* simply summarize results or arguments, but are presented so that the reader may *work through* the arguments presented verbally in the text—to follow the arguments by working through the examples given, and working through others at the reader's own pace.

5. It should perhaps be noted, however, that much of the early work on the Correlates of War Project dealt with through time or across space aggregations of the dependent war variable. It should also be said that much of the more recent work of COW researchers (e.g., articles in the section, "Accounting for the Onset of War," in Singer, 1980, and the Behavioral Correlates of War research), avoid these traps in various ways.

6. Despite Bueno de Mesquita's disclaimers, and the arguments set out above, it seems to us that some critics are not satisfied. That is, their arguments appear to suggest that providing insight only into necessary conditions is not enough. Apparently they want Bueno de Mesquita's expected utility model to deal with sufficient conditions, and critique the model because it does not (just a few years ago standard logic texts were saying that it was in principle impossible to identify necessary conditions). This critique becomes another version of wanting a researcher to answer different questions from those the researcher has decided to address.

However, even if we are interested in sufficiency (as we are in certain instances), we are confronted with a problem which is as difficult to solve as it is overlooked. If we return to the cross-tab type table above, we are faced with a difficult, but technically feasible problem. Unfortunately, we are overlooking a critical issue: we *really do not have* the table set out in the text. Instead, we have the following:

		Expected Utility	
		≤ 0	>0
Conflict			
Initiation	Yes	(1)	(2)

This is a table in which we have no "cases" of *non*Conflict Initiation. Such "cases" occur of course, but we do not include them in our data because we do not know how to count them; how do we count the literally hundreds of non-Conflict Initiations going on every minute.

As we will develop in later chapters, we need to be concerned with nonevents, or the problem of limited variance. When confronted with such a nonevent/lack of variance situation we may *want* to ask about sufficiency, but we cannot. Sufficiency hypotheses predict an empty cell 4 (as necessity predicted an empty cell 1)—but we no longer have such a cell to look at to see if cases occur or not. In contrast, even though we may not (really) want to ask about necessity, we can at least do that through the necessity prediction of an empty cell 1.

7. One could, of course, test for the sufficient conditions of battle deaths greater than zero or operationalize the dependent variable in terms of some through-time or across-space aggregation. As has been argued elsewhere, however, the first strategy suggests a very different question—very possibly with a

very different explanation—from why wars begin in the first place. See Richardson (1960a); Voevodsky (1969); and Starr (1976). The second strategy entails the abandonment of the state or the nation year as the unit of analysis.

8. For arguments concerning the existence of a continuum between "peace" and "war" or between "conflict" and "cooperation," see Boulding (1962:chap. 13); Bloomfield and Leiss (1969); Galtung (1969); and Rummel (1979:chaps. 13 and 18 especially).

9. See, for example, Bloomfield and Leiss (1969); Barringer (1972); and Zinnes, Hill, Jones and Majeski (1982); research on the "Behavioral Correlates of War" such as that of Leng and Goodsell (1979); efforts by Newcombe and Wert (1972) on the inter-nation tensionmeter; and the Azar-Sloan scale of inter-nation events used in the Cooperation and Peace Data Bank Project. For additional examples in which both war and peace are used as independent variables in studying the consequences of war for war, see the authors' work on war diffusion (Most and Starr, 1976, 1977, 1980).

10. If one lets X_1, X_2 and Y denote sets of elements with x_{1i}, x_{2i} and y_i denoting individual cases of elements in those sets, it is of course possible to translate hypotheses a–h in figures 3.1 and 3.2 in the following fashion:

a. If X_1, then Y: X_1 is equivalent to and implies Y (all x_{1i} are y_i); Y is not equivalent to and does not imply X_1 (all y_i are not x_{1i}).

b. Only if X_1, then Y: Y is equivalent to and implies X_1 (all y_i are x_{1i}); X_1 is not equivalent to and does not imply Y (all x_{1i} are not y_i).

c. If and only if X_1, then Y: X_1 and Y are equivalent; X implies Y and vice versa (all x_{1i} are y_i; all y_i are x_{1i}).

d. If X_1 and X_2, then Y: The intersection of X_1 and X_2 is equivalent to and implies Y (all cases that are both x_{1i} and x_{2i} are also y_i); Y is not equivalent to and does not imply the intersection of X_1 and X_2 (all y_i are not x_{1i} and x_{2i}).

Note: Elements included in the intersection of two sets are elements that are included in both of those sets. The hypothesis thus posits that X_1 and X_2 have an interactive (multiplicative)/sufficient relationship with Y.

e. If X_1 or X_2, then Y: The union of X_1 and X_2 is equivalent to and implies Y (all cases that are x_{1i} and/or x_{2i} are y_i); Y is not equivalent to and does not imply the union of X_1 and X_2 (all y_i are not x_{1i} and/or x_{2i}).

Note: Elements included in the union of two sets are elements that are included in one or both (either/or) of those sets. The hypothesis thus posits that X_1 and X_2 have an additive/sufficient relationship with Y.

f. Only if X_1 and X_2, then Y: Y is equivalent to and implies the intersection of X_1 and X_2 (all y_i are both x_{1i} and x_{2i}); the intersection of X_1 and X_2 is not equivalent to and does not imply Y (all cases that are both x_{1i} and x_{2i} are not also y_i).

Note: Elements included in the intersection of two sets are elements that are included in both of those sets. The hypothesis thus posits that X_1 and X_2 have an interactive (multiplicative)/necessary relationship with Y.

g. Only if X_1 or X_2, then Y: Y is equivalent to and implies the union of X_1 and X_2 (all y_i are x_{1i} and/or x_{2i}); the union of X_1 and X_2 is not equivalent to and does not imply Y (all x_{1i} and/or x_{2i} are not also y_i).

Note: Elements included in the union of two sets are elements that are included in one or both (either/or) of those sets. The hypothesis thus posits that X_1 and X_2 have an additive/necessary relationship with Y.

h. If and only if X_1 and X_2, then Y: The intersection of X_1 and X_2 is equivalent to and implies Y (all cases that are x_{1i} and x_{2i} are y_i); Y is equivalent to and implies the union of X_1 and X_2 (all y_i are x_{1i} and x_{2i}).

Note: Elements included in the intersection of two sets are elements that are included in both of those sets. The hypothesis thus posits that X_1 and X_2 have an interactive (multiplicative)/sufficient/necessary relationship with Y.

NOTES TO CHAPTER 4

1. To the extent that international war is understood to be a form of the more general concept of social conflict, the thesis that wars are at least dyadic is apparent in North's (1968:226) observation that:

Conflicts take place between individuals, between individuals and organizations or groups, between distinct organizations or groups, between an organization and one or more of its components, or between component parts of a single organization or group. A conflict emerges whenever two or more persons (or groups) seek to possess the same object, occupy the same space or the same exclusive position, play incompatible roles, maintain incompatible goals, or undertake mutually incompatible means for achieving their purposes.

The point is made even more forcefully by Midlarsky (1975:4);

. . . intergroup conflict in general and international warfare in particular require the existence of at least two conflicting protagonists. A declaration of war is always against an adversary; it cannot exist without the presence of some antagonist. For this antagonism to exist, there must be some mutual interaction between the conflicting parties that eventually leads to the outbreak of war.

2. Boulding (1962:4) argues that the parties must have incompatible or mutually exclusive goals such that "the realization of either one makes impossible the realization of the other." While such zero-sum objectives may indeed be important, a somewhat less constraining notion of conflicting goals is suggested in much of the literature.

3. Notions of just what thresholds would be utilized in defining "immediate" defeat and the minimal numbers of casualties incurred or caused vary across different researchers.

4. A complete influence structure need not be present, of course, in situations characterized by Galtung's concept of structural violence.

5. It should be said that Zinnes does not explicitly hypothesize—and probably does not mean to imply—that there must necessarily be a linear statistical relationship between any given $X_i(s)$ and war. Midlarsky (1975), whose analyses she cites for example, reports correlations between the log of the number of borders and the frequencies of states' war involvements.

6. Przeworski and Teune (1970:20–22) argue that these characteristics serve as useful criteria for evaluating theories.

7. In singling out Zinnes in this fashion, we by no means wish to find particular fault with her work. We note Zinnes here only because her argument in the two cited papers appears to typify the work of scholars who have attempted to isolate state-level correlates of international war. For a general review of work on the linkages between national attributes and war participation, see McGowan and Shapiro (1973:98).

8. See Coser's (1956) distinctions between realistic and nonrealistic violence.

9. In saying that opportunity and willingness could be conceptualized as requisite conditions for both attacking and attacked countries, we do not mean to imply that the two require equal amounts or levels of either.

10. It should be noted that Kende (1971) does classify the United States intervention in the Dominican Republic in 1965 as a war.

11. The first possibility is strongly supported by Bueno de Mesquita (1981a:chap. 5). In an analysis of war and calculations of the expected utility of war (based on probability, uncertainty, risk taking and congruence of interests), he demonstrates that his expected utility model provides better explanations than simple balance of power models. Both possibilities have been discussed in work on the balance of power and the power preponderance hypothesis (see Siverson and Sullivan, 1982, for a useful summary).

12. This logic explains why Bueno de Mesquita calls his extensive study of "willingness" (our term, not his) a study of necessary but not sufficient conditions for war.

13. Readers who had difficulty in accepting the delineation of the second problem above and who would like an additional example of the conditions under which different relationships might hold in different states should perhaps take special note of this point. Seeing states' decisions to go to war in a broader foreign policy context is important because a number of comparative foreign policy analysts have been theorizing for some time that different relationships may hold between one's predictor and the dependent foreign policy variables in different nations. A more in-depth discussion of the need to begin our research inquiries with such general concepts will be presented in the next chapter.

14. Both Moul (1973); and Midlarsky (1975:3) argue that this is in fact one of Singer's basic points in the article in question. They may be only partially correct. Singer quite clearly does recognize that one's choice of a level of analysis has important implications for the development of what he refers to as "causal statements" (i.e., "If..., then..." relationships). While the systemic level "may be an inadequate foundation upon which to base any *causal* statements," he observes that "it offers a reasonably adequate basis for *correlative* statements" (1969:23, emphasis in the original). In dealing with the subsystemic or national actor, in contrast, "we are enabled to go beyond the limitations imposed by the system level and to replace mere correlation with more significant causation" (1969:28). The possibility that a focus on some aggregate level above that of the nation-state will yield even correlational understanding, moreover, is clearly recognized by Singer to be predicated on an assumption of national homogeneity. The systemic level of analysis "almost certainly requires that we postulate a high degree of uniformity in the foreign policy operational codes of our national actors. By definition, we allow little room for divergence in the behavior of our parts when we focus upon the whole" (1969:23). Seen in these

terms, it seems clear that Singer understands at least the outlines of both of the problems under discussion here.

NOTES TO CHAPTER 5

1. For two analysts who have argued differently, see: Kenneth Waltz (1979); and J. David Singer (1981). Waltz (1979:18–19) states his position rather clearly: "Theories of international politics that concentrate causes at the individual or national level are reductionist.... With a reductionist approach, the whole is understood by knowing the attributes and the interactions of its parts.... Many have tried to explain international-political events in terms of psychological factors or social-psychological phenomena or national political and economic characteristics.... In no case, however, are those nonpolitical theories strong enough to provide reliable explanations or predictions."

2. Exceptions could readily be cited. Our contention is only that the practices outlined below are typical of much of what is done, and that they seem to reflect how scholars tend to approach their research problems.

3. Analysts who work with the WEIS, CREON and COPDAB events data sets adopt a different approach, of course. Rosenau's "pre-theory" of foreign policy and its various extensions and tests also quite clearly depart from the pattern by hypothesizing that different explanations may hold in different types of nations. See for example, Rosenau (1966); Rosenau and Hoggard (1974); East (1973). Our contention is only that such researchers tend to be the exception rather than the rule. It should also be said that a number of analysts report nongeneral findings, e.g., results that hold in the nineteenth century but not the twentieth or that apply to major powers but not to minors. The point to note, however, is that the majority of these analysts initially look for—and apparently expect to find—general relationships. They have no *initial* theoretical expectation that their model *should* be applicable to some limited domain or that it should be useful only under certain conditions.

4. For research that adopts a narrow focus on war, see Most and Starr (1980); and Starr and Most (1983). For a study that deals exclusively with alliances, see Job (1976). For a study focusing exclusively on arms races, see Schrodt (1976). Research dealing exclusively with international arms transfers is reported by Peleg (1980). For an analysis that focuses exclusively on international negotiations, see Snyder and Diesing (1977). Analysts who have written about "islands of theory" in international relations include Guetzkow (1950); and Forward (1971).

5. See for example, East (1972); and Wallace (1973).

6. We are referring here to standard uses of the so-called "general covering law" or "refutationist" approach developed by scholars such as Hempel and Popper. For a brief rehearsal see Raymond (1974). The reasoning underlying this approach can be crudely reconstructed in syllogistic form: *If* a "true" (i.e., universal) law exists between some concepts X and Y, then that law should *always* hold in the empirical world and should be evidenced by whatever are the appropriate associations between the respective operational indicators of the concepts, x_i and y_i. Empirical analyses are conducted to test for such associations between the occurrences of the x_i and y_i in the expectation that those results will inform us about whether or not a law actually exists between the X and Y. The

absence of the association between the x_i and y_i allows us—if the reasoning is sound—to reject the X/Y law, while the appearance of the anticipated x_i/y_i relationship allows us to say that the data are consistent with or support the existence of the X/Y law.

7. If $y_1, y_2, \ldots, y_n$ are all potential means for attaining an assumed foreign policy goal, then each y_i is a potentially valid indicator of Y (e.g., the initiation of an overt military strike or an increase in defense spending are complementary indicators of the concept "efforts to maintain or enhance security" or "foreign policy means.") Once this is recognized, the problem is easily understood: A focus on any given y_i fails to provide full coverage of the range of possible behaviors in the "means" concept. Analysts who focus on a given y_i—but on only one y_i—are thus focusing on only "successful" occurrences and we are again faced with the logical conclusion derived in chapter 3, that an examination of the possible sufficiency relationship between any presumed causal factor (x_i) and the y_i is precluded.

8. The reader may think that researchers could readily resolve this problem by constructing some composite scale of the various y_i. In the past, the standard operating procedure would have been to factor analyze the y_i. Such a strategy would work, however, only if it is reasonable to assume that a given phenomenon y_i invariably indicates the concept Y. As the discussion in the next section suggests, such a postulate might not be plausible. While the initiation of conflict may sometimes reflect decision makers' desires to establish (or reestablish) their country's external security or viability, for example, the same behavior could reflect a desire to increase their government's viability in the face of domestic pressures.

9. The need to reverse the tendency to attack international and foreign policy phenomena in fragmented, piece-meal fashion can be defended on other grounds. The point has been made in excellent fashion by Ostrom (1982b) and Boynton (1982a), as partially presented in the opening chapter. Perhaps Bronowski (1965:13–15), puts the point most clearly:

All science is the search for unity in hidden likenesses.... The scientist looks for order in appearances of nature by exploring such likenesses. For order does not display itself; if it can be said to be there at all, it is not there for the mere looking. There is no way of pointing a finger or a camera at it; order must be discovered and, in a deep sense, it must be created. What we see, as we see it, is mere disorder.... [Full grown] science grows from a comparison. It has seized a likeness between two unlike appearances.... The progress of science is the discovery at each step of a new order which gives unity to what seemed unlikely.

10. See, Morgenthau (1973); Jervis (1978); and Keohane (1983). It should be added that we depart from Sprout and Sprout insofar as we see policy initiations as "outcomes" of the interplay between what decision makers want to do and see capable of doing.

11. For example, see Zinnes, et al. (1985), for an empirical example of this phenomenon in which "neutral" war behavior plays the key role in model structure and evaluation. Dealing with empty cells, neutral, or other nonbehaviors is also important if willingness is as central to theory as we have claimed—as we

are faced with the difficult research problem of knowing when decision makers are or are not willing.

12. Even though a universal or "true" relationship may exist, for example, difficulties with indicator validity and reliability could mask that association at the empirical level. In chapter 3 we suggested that additional complications may develop as a result of faulty case selection procedures or the failure to specify the correct logical linkages among the concepts and indicators. Those problems are critical. They raise doubts about the standard approach. To the extent that such difficulties exist—or at least cannot be ruled out—the results of the tests become ambiguous. The lack of empirical support in a given analysis could indeed imply that a supposed law is not true, but it could also mean that operation of a true law is obscured by the procedures adopted by the researcher conducting the test.

13. Bueno de Mesquita (1981a:4–5) appears to have exactly this problem in mind when he considers research on the outbreak of war and observes that:

> ...the set of conditions sufficient for war may be so large that its specification is virtually impossible....Most efforts to find the cause or causes of war focus on environmental circumstances that compel policymakers to wage war, but if we attempt to show causal relationships between environments and war, we are forced to ignore the role of national leaders and to act as though nations were no more than automatically reacting mechanisms.

It is this line of argument—combined with his contention that decision makers are not mechanistically compelled—which leads Bueno de Mesquita to conclude that the search for the sufficient conditions for war should be abandoned in favor of a search for necessary conditions. A similar position is suggested by Singer (1981). Other related points are contributed by: Kurth (1971:373–404); and von Bertalanffy (1968).

14. It is perhaps worth noting that this case structure entails an important simplifying assumption that states have the opportunity to act whenever they are willing to do so. Under the unified actor/national security dilemma formulation outlined in figure 5.2, one would expect either increasing external risks or decreasing defense capacity to contribute to leaders' willingness to resolve the security problem if the change in either factor is sufficient to reverse previously positive capacity-to-risk inequalities. Whether or not the decision makers would act on that disposition, however, would be affected by their objective opportunities to act.

15. Technically of course, it is not necessary to use words and phrases such as "domain specific" or "nice" in connection with "laws." They are used here only to emphasize our point that analysts may err if they necessarily equate "laws" with "universals."

16. Because the points depart so sharply from accepted arguments and assumptions, it may be worthwhile to consider the following observations from scholars who use somewhat different terms but nevertheless come to identical conclusions:

> There is a widespread misconception that theories are either "true" or "false." A number of examples in physical science stand in direct contradiction to this....Each of these theories or models is tautologically true, *when*

their postulates are fulfilled....They are not theories to be confirmed or disconfirmed in general, but only confirmed or disconfirmed in specific applications. As a result, they are not theories which explain "how people behave"; they are theories or models which describe how people behave in this or that circumstance....One fruitful line of development...will be not to ask what is *the* theory of a certain kind of behavior, or what are *the* postulates which correctly describe a general area of behavior. The tactic proposed here is to set about developing and applying a number of sometimes-true theories which relate consequences to postulates, and which may adequately describe behavior in a given situation. Coleman (1964: 516–518; emphasis in the original).

The laws of mathematics were invented too. The only demand made on them is that of consistency in a given context. *But in different contexts, different laws may operate.* Therefore, any statement of mathematics is valid or invalid not because certain relations are true or not true in the real world, but because these statements are or are not consequences of certain definitions and assumptions, which we are free to choose. The ambiguity of a mathematical statement results from a failure to specify with sufficient precision the exact context in which the statement is made. Rapoport (1960:297–298 emphasis added).

Laws of nature...are different: to them the words "true", "probable" and the like seem to have no application....[We could] adopt Snell's formula tentatively, hypothetically, as a guide to further experiments to see whether the phenomena always happen so. On this level, we might ask "is Snell's *hypothesis* true or false?", meaning, "have any limitations been found to the application of his formula?" But very soon—indeed as soon as its fruitfulness has been established—the formula in our hypothesis comes to be treated as a *law*, i.e. as something of which we ask not "is it true?" but "when does it hold?" When this happens, it becomes part of the framework of optical theory, and is treated as a standard. Departures from the law and limitations on its scope...come to be spoken of as anomalies and thought of as things in need of explanation. Toulmin (1953:78–79).

17. Singer, himself a long-time proponent of the systemic-level approach and the view that foreign policy decision makers may at least initially be presumed to be rather homogeneous, comes close to this point in reviewing the realpolitik, arms race, power transition, economic development and imperialism models (1981:14–15):

...at rock bottom the most important difference amongst the contending causes of war models is that of the foreign policy decision process. That is, each model assumes—often implicitly—a different class of decision makers in power and each postulates a different set of decision rules....Note that we have assumed, to this juncture, a high degree of homogeneity in decision makers and the rules they employ, but *to move closer to a full explanation that assumption would have to be relaxed* (emphasis added).

18. However, our analyses in chapter 6 suggest strong limitations in theorizing at the level of the international system.

19. The micro-level model that appears to underlie Waltz's systemic theory has recently been summarized in the following way by Ruggie (1983:267):

> From the principle of self-help...one can infer that states will try to put themselves in a position that will enable them to take care of themselves. They have two means at their disposal: 'internal efforts (moves to increase economic capability, to increase military strength, to develop clever strategies) and external efforts (moves to strengthen one's own alliance or to weaken and shrink an opposing one)'.... As one or more states successfully undertake any such measure, however, 'others will emulate them or fall by the wayside'.... As other states emulate them, power-balancing ensues. Thus the international security order is governed by balance-of-power politics.

20. On this point, Waltz (1979:72) seems quite clear:

> Systems theories, whether political or economic, are theories that explain how the organization of a realm acts as a constraining and disposing force on the interacting units within it. Such theories tell us about the forces the units are subject to. From them, we can infer some things about the expected behavior and fate of the units; namely, how they will have to compete with and adjust to one another if they are to survive and flourish.... Systems theories explain why different units behave similarly and, despite their variations, produce outcomes that fall within expected ranges. Conversely, theories at the unit level tell us why different units behave differently despite their similar placement in a system. A theory about foreign policy is a theory at the national level. It leads to expectations about the responses that dissimilar polities will make to external pressures. A theory of international politics bears on the foreign policies of nations while claiming to explain only certain aspects of them. It can tell us what international conditions national polities have to cope with. To think that a theory of international politics can in itself say how the coping is likely to be done is the opposite of the reductionist error.

The differences that Waltz sees between foreign policy (i.e., analytic or reductionist) theories and theories of international politics (i.e., systemic formulations) are explored throughout Waltz, chapter 4 (and also on pages 122–123). The two types of theories begin differently and have the potential for yielding different sorts of insights, according to Waltz.

21. Ruggie (1983:285) argues that Waltz himself has no similar generative component in his formulation and that that is a critically important shortcoming of his argument. Lacking a generative component, Ruggie argues, Waltz cannot explain changes in system structure: "The problem with Waltz's posture is that, in any social system, structural change itself ultimately has no source *other than* unit-level processes. By banishing these from the domain of systemic theory, Waltz also exogenizes the ultimate source of systemic change."

NOTES TO CHAPTER 6

1. A short bibliography of the literature on international systems would include: Kaplan (1957, 1969); Rosecrance (1963, 1966); Waltz (1964, 1969, 1979); Deutsch and Singer (1964); Deutsch (1967); Singer and Small (1968); and Bueno de Mesquita (1975, 1978). Especially useful summaries may be found in Sullivan (1976:chap. 5) and Dougherty and Pfaltzgraff (1981:chaps. 3, 4). For reviews of the role of power at the dyadic level, see Garnham (1976); Weede (1976); Baldwin (1979); Bueno de Mesquita (1981b); and Siverson and Sullivan (1983).

2. See the discussions in Sullivan (1976); Dougherty and Pfaltzgraff (1981); Bueno de Mesquita (1980b, 1981b); and Hart (1976), respectively.

3. Logical critiques of the power and balance of power arguments are now common in the literature; see for example: Claude (1962); Riker (1962); and Bueno de Mesquita (1980b).

4. The "Power Parity" hypothesis suggests that "the relatively equal distribution of power among major actors in the international system brings about an equilibrium in which war is relatively unlikely" (Siverson and Sullivan, 1983:474). The "Power Preponderance" postulate, in contrast, argues that "equality of power (or power parity) is likely to bring about war" (Siverson and Sullivan, 1983:474). Because Siverson and Sullivan see the two hypotheses as contradictory, they are puzzled about how both could be supported. The thrust of their discussion centers on this issue:

> The two theories [*sic*]...make completely opposite predictions about the effect of the equality of power in the international system. Although this position is *most often stated in terms of the international system,* it has clearly been generalized to the dyadic relationship existing between two nations through the operation of deterrence....While some might caution against combining theoretical propositions, as well as findings, from both systemic and dyadic levels, the underlying rationale for the hypotheses at both levels is similar enough—at least in terms of general theory building—that it would be disadvantageous not to compare them (Siverson and Sullivan, 1983:474; emphasis added).

5. Regressing interstate and extrasystemic wars begun in each year between 1946 and 1980 against time yields an adjusted R^2 of .026, an insignificant t-statistic, and no indication of positive first order autocorrelation. Regressing the numbers of outbreaks on time is a standard, exploratory first step for discovering whether or not the data have time dependent patterns.

Efforts to control for changes in system size by dividing the number of wars begun in each year by the number of states then in existence produced similar results. Force loading dummy variables designed to account for possible system changes in 1955/56 (a shift from unipolarity to bipolarity) and 1970/71 (a shift from bipolarity to multi- or bimultipolarity) were similarly unproductive. No evidence of either slope or intercept changes was isolated. Finally, with the exception of one comparison involving the 1946–70 and 1971–80 periods, difference of means tests on the average rates of war initiations in different periods failed to detect any evidence of statistically distinct rates of occurrence.

6. A dyad is imbalanced here if it involves a major and a minor (Mn) or a minor and a major (mM). A dyad is balanced if it included two minors (mm) or

two majors (MM). The former (mm) dyads might be thought of as "low" balanced dyads or as pairings among two weak states; the latter (MM) dyads are, in contrast, "high" balanced dyads. The following simple formulas can be used to calculate the number of dyads, unique dyads, balanced and imbalanced dyads:

Let: $n = m + p =$ number of actors in the system
         $m =$ number of "major" actors
         $p =$ number of "minor" actors

Dyads	$= D = (n^2 - n)$
Unique Dyads	$= UD = .5(D) = .5(n^2 - n)$
Balanced Dyads	$= BD = D - [(2m)(p)]$
	$= D - (2mp)$
	$= (n^2 - n) - (2mp)$
Imbalanced Dyads	$= ID = D - BD$
	$= (n^2 - n) - (m^2 - m) - (p^2 - p)$
High Balanced Dyads	$= HD = (m^2 - m)$
Low Balanced Dyads	$= LD = (p^2 - p)$

7. We will review these assumptions below. One major confounding factor in regard to the second assumption is the possibility of the diffusion of conflict (see Most and Starr, 1980; Starr and Most, 1983, 1985b). If some major power i attacks a second state j in a given system and a state i expends (or at least commits) a significant proportion of its power to the war, for example, the world is altered for other states (k, p,. . . , n) in the system. To the extent that they had in the past been conditionally viable vis-à-vis state i, they may now become unconditionally viable; to the extent they were previously in rough balance with i, they may now find themselves in a dominant position. In either case, the onset of one conflict could alter structural relationships. Again, a restructured range of opportunities for conflict initiation would result. To the extent the decision makers act to avail themselves of those new opportunities, the initial conflict may diffuse.

8. The effects of different system sizes, with different numbers of major powers, and thus different numbers of balanced and unbalanced dyads can be demonstrated by the following four hypothetical systems:

     A. A three state *unipolar* system comprised of states i, j, and k in which i is a "major" power and j and k are "minors."

Number of Unique Dyads	$= 3$ (ij, ik, jk)
Number of Imbalanced Dyads	$= 2$ (ij, ik)
Number of Balanced Dyads	$= 1$ (jk)

     B. A three state *bipolar* system comprised of states i, j, and k in which i and j are "major" powers and k is a "minor."

Number of Unique Dyads	$= 3$ (ij, ik, jk)
Number of Imbalanced Dyads	$= 2$ (ij, jk)
Number of Balanced Dyads	$= 1$ (ik)

C. A *five* state unipolar system comprised of states i, j, k, p, and q in which i is a "major" power and j, k, p, and q are "minors."

Number of Unique Dyads	= 10 (ij, ik, ip, iq, jk, jp, jq, kp, kq, pq)
Number of Imbalanced Dyads	= 4 (ij, ik, ip, iq)
Number of Balanced Dyads	= 6 (jk, jp, jq, kp, kq, pq)

D. A *five* state bipolar system comprised of states i, j, k, p, and q in which i and j are "major" powers and k, p, and q are "minors."

Number of Unique Dyads	= 10 (ij, ik, ip, iq, jk, jp, jq, kp, kq, pq)
Number of Imbalanced Dyads	= 6 (ik, ip, iq, jk, jp, jq)
Number of Balanced Dyads	= 4 (ij, kp, kq, pq)

9. Preliminary explanations of these predictions, as it turns out, appear in the empirical analyses of diffusion in Most and Starr (1980); the rows and columns are simply reversed here to maintain continuity with the foregoing illustrations. Several additional points seem worth noting in connection with the probabilistic hypotheses. First, as has been said, their predictions are considerably more complex than those for the hypotheses noted. Second, while they permit the possibility that some cells will be empty or null, they entail no predictions that there necessarily will be empty cells. Third, they permit an overwhelming number of cases to fall in cells 3 and 4 (i.e., no conflict initiation); more to the point, *they permit one to make progress even though the data have very little variance.* This is one way to deal with the "empty cell" problem noted in previous chapters.

Fourth, even though the (hypothetical) data here are consistent, as has been said, with the proposition that inequality increases the probability of initiation, that pattern is not at all like the ones that are associated (both correctly and incorrectly) with (*a*) sufficiency, (*b*) necessity, or (*c*) necessity and sufficiency. Fifth, it is questionable whether or not analysts' standard techniques would detect the relationship.

10. The systems in note 8 illustrate the possibility. Suppose, simply for the purpose of argument, that it is imbalance—or the preponderance of the ith state over the jth in any given dyad—that constitutes the opportunity for the ith to attack. Recasting the two five state systems in note 8 in terms of equation 1 and writing an equation for each ij and ji pairing, we obtain the following:

	System 3		System 4	
	$n = 5$	$m = 1$	$n = 5$	$m = 2$
Low Balanced Dyads:				
	Attack jk $= f(0 \times Wjk)$			
	Attack jp $= f(0 \times Wjp)$			
	Attack jp $= f(0 \times Wjq)$			
	Attack kp $= f(0 \times Wkp)$		Attack kp $= f(0 \times Wkp)$	
	Attack kq $= f(0 \times Wkq)$		Attack kq $= f(0 \times Wkq)$	
	Attack pq $= f(0 \times Wpq)$		Attack pq $= f(0 \times Wpq)$	
	Attack kj $= f(0 \times Wkj)$			
	Attack pj $= f(0 \times Wpj)$			
	Attack qj $= f(0 \times Wqj)$			

Attack pk = f(0 × Wpk)   Attack pk = f(0 × Wpk)
Attack qk = f(0 × Wqk)   Attack qk = f(0 × Wqk)
Attack qp = f(0 × Wqp)   Attack qp = f(0 × Wqp)

Imbalanced Dyads:
First State Dominant Over the Second
Attack ij = f(1 × Wij)
Attack ik = f(1 × Wik)   Attack ik = f(1 × Wik)
Attack ip = f(1 × Wip)   Attack ip = F(1 × Wip)
Attack iq = f(1 × Wiq)   Attack iq = f(1 × Wiq)
Attack jk = f(1 × Wjk)
Attack jp = f(1 × Wjp)
Attack jq = f(1 × Wjq)

Second State Dominated by the First
Attack ji = f(0 × Wji)
Attack ki = f(0 × Wki)   Attack ki = f(0 × Wki)
Attack pi = f(0 × Wpi)   Attack pi = f(0 × Wpi)
Attack qi = f(0 × Wqi)   Attack qi = f(0 × Wqi)
Attack kj = f(0 × Wkj)
Attack pj = f(0 × Wpj)
Attack qj = f(0 × Wqj)

High Balanced Dyads:
Attack ij = f(0 × Wij)
Attack ji = f(0 × Wji)

Seen in this fashion, it is clear that in system 4 (n = 5; m = 2) there are 6 opportunities for conflict initiation in comparison with the 4 that exist in system 3 (n = 5; m = 1). *If* it is in fact valid to assume that it is preponderance or imbalance that creates conflict initiation opportunities, we can deduce which system is potentially more volatile, and indeed, which dyads are the most likely to erupt in conflict.

11. Alliance formations and dissolutions may effect de facto changes in the size and composition of international systems. The five nation unipolar system in note 8 in which i is a major power and j, k, p, and q are minors, for example, would be radically transformed were alliances to form between j and k and between p and q. Assuming that the jk and pq alliances were tight, and that each alliance dominated the power of the ith state alone, the five state unipolar system would become a structurally very different three unit system in which there were two major actors and a restructured range of opportunities for conflict initiation. To the extent that alliances do restructure systems in such a fashion, however, it should be obvious that those shifts should not be expected to translate directly into altered rates of conflict or stability.

12. Note that opportunity vectors were created for a total of five 10-state systems. The number of major powers (m) was varied from 1–5 (i.e., from 1 to $\frac{n}{2}$) across those systems so that we had a 10 state system with three majors, and so on. Because each of those vectors was created on the assumption of a distinct number of majors, it followed that each was comprised of slightly different numbers of + 1's, –1's, and 0's. A parallel set of eight 15-state systems (n = 15) was also created, with m varying across those system from 1–8. Fifteen separate willingness vectors were created *for each* of the five 10-state and eight 15-state

systems. In the manner described above, fifteen separate Conflict Initiation vectors were then created for each system.

13. A related issue concerns the values over which the number of major powers was allowed to vary (1–5 in the 10 state systems and 1–8 in the 15 state systems). It will be recalled from figure 6.2 that, when system size (n) is held constant, the number of imbalanced dyads in a given system increases as the number of extant major powers (m) is increased from 1 to ($\frac{n}{2}$). When $m = 0$, all existing dyads are balanced; once the number of majors passes the ($\frac{n}{2}$) threshold and begins to approach n, the system becomes increasingly characterized by balanced dyads. Thus, the decision to vary the number of majors between 1 and 5 in the 10 state systems and between 1 and 8 in the 15 state trials is directly connected to the preponderance/imbalance hypothesis. *If* it is in fact the case that imbalance is linked in some fashion to conflict occurrence, then systems should be potentially the most dangerous—or at least have the maximum numbers of conflict initiation opportunities—when the number of majors powers (m) is in the range between 1 and ($\frac{n}{2}$). A system with 10 states and 1 major should be structurally more dangerous than a similar system with 0 majors. The 10 state/2 major system, in turn, should be more dangerous than a 10 state/1 major system. A 10 state/5 major system, however, should be more—not less—dangerous than a 10 state/6 major system.

14. Readers who are familiar with Bernoulli trials will know that the procedure entails the generation of a series of 0's and 1's with the probability (p) of the occurrence of a 1 being set by the analyst. In the procedure used here, that probability is equivalent to the probability that the leaders of a given state will be willing to use force, or in our notation, $p = \Pr(W)$. If $\Pr(W) = 1.00$ in a given trial, only 1's will be generated. In effect, leaders in every dyad will be willing to initiate; multiplication of such a willingness vector by an opportunity vector would create a conflict initiation vector that would be identical to the opportunity vector. The system would be operating at its ceiling. Leaders would always be willing to initiate; the number of initiations would equal the number of opportunities existing in the system. If, on the other hand, $\Pr(W) = 0.00$ only 0's would appear in the willingness vector. Leaders would never be willing to initiate; multiplication of that vector by an opportunity column would yield zero outbreaks in the conflict initiation vector. Because leaders are not willing to use force, the system—despite whatever opportunities are present—would be operating at its floor. It would be totally at peace.

The value chosen for the probability of willingness $\Pr(W)$ in the Bernoulli trials is thus of potentially critical importance. Depending upon the desired results, one could produce simulated findings that demonstrate either that systemically-determined structural parameters are either very important or totally trivial factors in the process that leads to the outbreak of international conflict. That said, it should be understood that our purposes require a "plausible," rather than empirically accurate estimate of $\Pr(W)$. If setting $\Pr(W)$ at either 0.02 or 0.05 is an error, moreover, it is an error that would favor the conclusion that structural factors are important. As has been noted, the existing evidence suggests that leaders failed to exploit initiation opportunities during the post-World War II era (see the above discussion concerning figure 6.1). Finally, it might be said that a few simple calculations suggest quite persuasively that $\Pr(W)$ settings of 0.02 or 0.05 are too high. If one looks at the international system as it existed in 1980 with 155 states and 5 major powers, one can quickly calculate that it included 23,870 dyads. Of those, 22,370 were balanced, 750 were positively imbalanced, and 750 negatively imbalanced. If one focuses first on the preponderance/imbalance proposition, takes the number of positively imbalanced dyads as constituting initiation opportunities, and calculates how many conflicts should have been initiated in 1980 if willingness were a randomly distributed variable with a probability of occurrence equaling 0.02 or 0.05, one would obtain values of 10 and 32 respectively. If one focuses instead on the balanced pairs and takes them as constituting initiation opportunities, one would obtain predictions of 453 and 1147 initiations respectively when Pr(W) is set at 0.02 and 0.05. As the plot in figure 6.1 shows, the system was not characterized in 1980 by anything even approaching those levels of conflict occurrence.

15. The third matrix in Appendix Table 6.1 presents the average cell entries which were obtained over all 15 trials of the 10 state/5 major/ Pr(W) = 0.02 system. On average, only 0.6 conflicts were initiated in each (a total of 9 initiations over the 15 trials). Several points should be observed in connection with those results. First, when one looks at the table, the lack of variance in the data is striking. Regardless of whether or not they had the opportunity to attack, most states remained at peace. Second, even though the average simulated rate of conflict is low in the 15 trials, the inequalities outlined in the foregoing section quite clearly reflect the danger inherent in positive imbalance:

$$\frac{\text{cell } 1}{\text{cell } 1 + \text{cell } 3} = \frac{0}{65} < \frac{0.6}{25} = \frac{\text{cell } 2}{\text{cell } 2 + \text{cell } 4}$$

$$\frac{\text{cell } 2}{\text{cell } 1 + \text{cell } 2} = \frac{0.6}{0.6} > \frac{0}{0.6} = \frac{\text{cell } 1}{\text{cell } 1 + \text{cell } 2}$$

In light of the fact that analysis of the parent matrix from these trials (data not shown) yields a Pearson correlation between opportunity (i.e., imbalance or preponderance in this illustration) and conflict initiation of only 0.132, the clarity of these inequalities seems to compare favorably.

16. Identical results were obtained in the analyses of the 15-state systems (table 6.2). Once again, floors and ceilings rose as one moved from 1 major power systems to those with 8. Also once again, however, the confidence intervals overlapped and the difference of means test on initiations failed to reject the null hypothesis of homogeneous means. Similar results were obtained from analyses of the effects of simple differences in system size (n) when the number of majors (m) and Pr(W) were held constant in each test. Recalling figure 6.2 in which it was shown that the number of imbalanced dyads—and hence, the number of hypothesized initiation opportunities—increases as one holds the number of major powers constant but moves to larger and larger systems, it was expected that 10 state systems would tend to have fewer outbreaks than systems with 15 states. In general, such results were obtained when Pr(W) = 0.02 and m = 1, 2, 3, 4, or 5, and n = 10 or 15 (data not shown). Once again, however, the intervals overlapped. No statistically significant differences of means were found.

17. Axelrod and Keohane, investigating the creation and impact of regimes within the "anarchic" structure of the international system, come to an analo-

gous conclusion (1986:228): "Analysis of the context of games leads us to regard context as malleable: not only can actors in world politics pursue different strategies within an established context of interaction, they may also seek to alter that context through building institutions embodying particular principles, norms, rules, or procedures for the conduct of international relations."

18. It has been suggested that one lesson of this discussion is similar to arguments by Herbert Simon—that apparently complex behavior can be the product of a relatively few underlying mechanisms.

NOTES TO CHAPTER 7

1. The use of "stylized" facts in the manner presented may help us get around the argument that there are no "facts" apart from theories.

2. The concept of an international event, and the event data movement have been subjected to close scrutiny and critique in recent years. Events data, as related to the comparative study of foreign policy, is discussed in Hermann, Kegley and Rosenau (1987). See also the reports and the newsletters of the Data Development for International Research (*DDIR-Update*). The DDIR has devoted considerable time to the review of event data. The first DDIR conference on event data, held in May 1987 at Columbus, Ohio was directed towards assessing the role of event data in future international relations research. A second conference in November 1987 at Cambridge, Massachusetts, was directed at new technological possibilities for conceptualizing, storing, associating, retrieving and analyzing event data.

3. The following material discussing the application of logic to inquiry in the sciences and the social sciences is based on commentary supplied by Michael Ward. We wish to acknowledge his generous and useful assistance on this topic. See especially, Ward (1987) and the expanded and revised version in Ward (1988).

4. The development of follow-up questions tends to happen only *within* projects or programs of individual scholars, and not across projects. Again, this is a sign of the lack of integrative cumulation.

5. The structuring of a research design to derive empirical expectations from a theory-based logic was followed in the research on war diffusion; see especially Most and Starr (1976; 1980).

6. This is similar to the process followed in the diffusion research, where we moved to distinguish positive diffusion or reinforcement from negative diffusion or reinforcement, and then to distinguish positive diffusion from positive reinforcement.

7. Most (1986) draws on the material from Kanigel (1981) to demonstrate the "mentor chain" that existed in terms of each student, in turn, learning a style of inquiry from his or her mentor.

Julius Axelrod, 1970 Nobel Prize Winner in Physiology and Medicine on his mentor Bernard Brodie: "He made every experiment seem earth-shattering and encouraged the kind of 'quick and dirty' experiment that might suggest whether an approach was worth pursuing more deliberately.... Do an apparently simple experiment that gives you an important bit of information.... Ask the important question at the right time. If you ask it later, then it's obvious."

Solomon H. Snyder, professor of pharmacology at Johns Hopkins Medical Center, on his mentor, Julius Axelrod: "He'd talk of theories that were beautiful ...symmetrical...the kind of things you get excited about....A student will say, 'But it's good science, isn't it?' And I'll say, 'Yes, but it's boring. I think we can do something more exciting."

Gavril Pasternak, assistant professor of neurology and pharmacology at Memorial Sloan-Kettering, New York, on what he learned from his mentor, Solomon H. Snyder: "To perceive when a question is not right to ask...the ability to say what is the essential question that holds the machine together."

Candace Pert, National Institutes of Health, on her mentor, Solomon H. Snyder: "He had a pragmatic, handyman approach to science. He was always sidestepping the grey muck of scientific tedium, always reaching for the heady scientific heights—the more fundamental, more exciting problems that sneered at routine."

Terry Moody, assistant professor of biochemistry at the George Washington Medical Center, on his mentor, Candace Pert: "She's always willing to take the longshot."

8. Richardson's (1960b) approach to the relationship of perception to environment should also be noted. Richardson posits that ecological or environmental factors, from the point of view of decision makers in each ith polity, explain the defense spending decisions of those actors. Richardson argues that (1960b:12):

> The equations are merely a description of what people would do if they did not stop to think. Why are so many nations reluctantly but steadily increasing their armaments as if they were mechanically compelled to do so? Because, I say, they follow their traditions, which are fixtures, and their instincts, which are mechanical and because they have not yet made a sufficiently strenuous intellectual and moral effort to control the situation. The process described by the...equations is not to be thought of as inevitable. It is what *would occur if instinct and tradition were allowed to act uncontrolled* (emphasis in original).

While Richardson thus does appear to posit direct efforts between certain environmental factors and any ith country's defense spending, that relationship is expected to hold because decision makers in the ith nation think in particular ways and cue on particular extra- and intra-societal phenomena.

9. Review Ruggie's (1983) comments on Waltz; see also note 21, chap. 5.

10. See, for example, Levy (1985); Modelski (1978); Modelski and Morgan (1985); Gilpin (1981); and Thompson (1986; 1983).

11. For an interesting discussion of the assumptions undergirding unitary actor models of foreign policy making, see McGinnis (1988).

REFERENCES

Aggarawaral, L. K. 1974. *Peace Research: A Bibliography.* Philadelphia: Department of Peace Science, University of Pennsylvania.

Alcock, Norman Z. 1972. *The War Disease.* Oakville, Ont.: Canadian Peace Research Institute Press.

Alexandroff, Alan, Richard Rosecrance, and Arthur Stein. 1977. "History, quantitative analysis, and the balance of power." *Journal of Conflict Resolution* 21: 35–56.

Alker, Hayward R. 1976. "Individual achievements rarely sum to collective progress," pp. 38–57 in J. N. Rosenau, ed., *In Search of Global Patterns.* New York: Free Press.

Allison, Graham T. 1971. *Essence of Decision.* Boston: Little, Brown.

Altfeld, Michael F. and Bruce Bueno de Mesquita. 1979. "Choosing sides in wars." *International Studies Quarterly* 23: 87–112.

Ashley, Richard K. 1976. "Noticing pre-paradigmatic progress," pp. 150–157 in J. N. Rosenau, ed., *In Search of Global Patterns.* New York: Free Press.

———. 1980. *The Political Economy of War and Peace.* London: Frances Pinter.

Axelrod, Robert, ed. 1976. *The Structure of Decision.* Princeton: Princeton University Press.

———. 1984. *The Evolution of Cooperation.* New York: Basic Books.

Axelrod, Robert and R. O. Keohane. 1986. "Achieving cooperation under anarchy: strategies and institutions," pp. 226–254 in K. A. Oye,. ed., *Cooperation under Anarchy.* Princeton: Princeton University Press.

Azar, Edward and Joseph Ben-Dak, eds. 1975. *Theory and Practice of Events Research.* New York: Gordon and Breach.

Babst, Dean. 1972. "A force for peace." *Industrial Research* April: 55–58.

Bachrach, Peter and Morton S. Baratz. 1962. "Two faces of power." *American Political Science Review* 56: 947–952.

———. 1963. "Decisions and non-decisions: an analytical framework." *American Political Science Review* 57: 632–642.

Baldwin, David A. 1979. "Power analysis and world politics: new trends versus old tendencies." *World Politics* 31: 161–194.

Barringer, Richard E. 1972. *War: Patterns of Conflict.* Cambridge, Mass.: MIT Press.

Beer, Francis A. 1981. *Peace Against War.* San Francisco: W. H. Freeman.

Blainey, Geoffrey. 1973. *The Causes of War.* New York: Free Press.

Bloomfield, Lincoln P. and A. Leiss. 1969. *Controlling Small Wars.* New York: Knopf.

Boulding, Elise and J. R. Passmore. 1974. *Bibliography on World Conflict and Peace.* Boulder, Colo.: Institute of Behavioral Science, University of Colorado.

Boulding, Kenneth E. 1962. *Conflict and Defense.* New York: Harper and Row.

Boyd, James M. 1971. *United Nations Peace Keeping Operations: A Military and Political Appraisal.* New York: Praeger.

Boynton, G. R. 1976. "Cumulativeness in international relations," pp. 145-149 in J. N. Rosenau, ed., *In Search of Global Patterns.* New York: Free Press.

────── . 1982a. "Linking problem definition and research activities: using formal languages," pp. 43-60 in J. A. Gillespie and D. A. Zinnes, eds., *Missing Elements in Political Inquiry.* Beverly Hills: Sage.

────── . 1982b. "On getting from here to there: reflections on two paragraphs and other things," pp. 29-68 in E. Ostrom, ed., *Strategies of Political Inquiry.* Beverly Hills: Sage.

Bronowski, J. 1965. *Science and Human Values.* New York: Harper.

Bueno de Mesquita, Bruce. 1975. "Measuring systemic polarity." *Journal of Conflict Resolution* 19: 187-216.

────── . 1978. "Systemic polarization and the occurrence and duration of war." *Journal of Conflict Resolution* 22: 241-268.

────── . 1980. "An expected utility theory of international conflict." *American Political Science Review* 74: 917-931.

────── . 1981. *The War Trap.* New Haven: Yale University Press.

────── . 1983. "The costs of war: a rational expectations approach." *American Political Science Review* 77: 347-357.

────── . 1985a. "Toward a scientific understanding of international conflict: a personal view." *International Studies Quarterly* 29 (June): 121-136.

────── . 1985b. "The war trap revisited." *American Political Science Review* 79: 157-176.

────── . 1986. "The contribution of expected utility theory to the study of international conflict." Paper presented at the Annual Meeting of the American Political Science Association, Washington, D.C.

Bueno de Mesquita, Bruce and D. Lalman. 1986. "Reason and war." *American Political Science Review* 80: 1113-1128.

Bueno de Mesquita, Bruce, D. Newman and A. Rabushka. 1985. *Forecasting Political Events: The Future of Hong Kong.* New Haven: Yale University Press.

Bulkeley, R. I. P. 1983. "Vegetius vindicatus? giving an old hypothesis a fair break." *Current Research on Peace and Violence* 6: 233-257.

Burgess, Phillip M. and Raymond W. Lawton. 1972. *Indicators of International Behavior: An Assessment of Events Data Research.* Beverly Hills: Sage.

Busch, Peter A. 1970. "Appendix: mathematical models of arms races," pp. 193-234 in B.M. Russett, *What Price Vigilance: The Burdens of National Defense.* New Haven: Yale University Press.

Campbell, Donald T. and Julian Stanley. 1963. *Experimental and Quasi-Experimental Research.* Chicago: Rand McNally.

Caporaso, James A., et al. 1988. "The comparative study of foreign policy: perspectives on the future." *"International Studies Notes* 13: 32-46.

Chan, Steven. 1984. "Mirror, mirror on the wall...: are the free countries more pacific?" *Journal of Conflict Resolution* 28: 617–648.

Choucri, Nazli and R. C. North. 1975. *Nations in Conflict.* San Francisco: W. H. Freeman.

Cioffi-Revilla, Claudio (N. D.) "More (final?) observations on the study of complex political systems." Presented at the Illinois-Indiana-Iowa Seminar on the Study of Complex Systems, Urbana, Illinois.

———. 1981. "Fuzzy sets and models of international relations." *American Journal of Political Science* 25: 129–159.

———. 1984. "Political reliability in international relations," pp. 11–45 in D. A. Zinnes, ed., *Conflict Processes and the Breakdown of International Systems.* Denver: University of Denver Monograph Series in World Affairs.

Claude, Inis. 1962. *Power and International Relations.* New York: Random House.

Coleman, James S. 1964. *Introduction to Mathematical Sociology.* Glencoe: The Free Press of Glencoe.

Copson, Raymond W. 1973. "Foreign policy conflict among African states," pp. 189–217 in P. J. McGowan, ed., *Sage International Yearbook of Foreign Policy Studies,* vol. 1. Beverly Hills: Sage.

Corning, Peter A. 1971. "The biological bases of behavior and some implications for political science." *World Politics* 23: 321–370.

Coser, Lewis A. 1956. *The Functions of Social Conflict.* New York: Free Press.

Dedring, Jurgen. 1976. *Recent Advances in Peace and Conflict Research.* Beverly Hills: Sage.

Denton, Frank H. 1966. "Some regularities in international conflict, 1820–1949." *Background* 9: 283–296.

Denton, Frank H. and W. Phillips. 1968. "Some patterns in the history of violence." *Journal of Conflict Resolution* 12: 182–195.

Deutsch, Karl W. 1967. "On the concepts of politics and power." *Journal of International Affairs* 21: 332–341.

———. 1969. "The point of no return in the progression toward war," pp. 60–61 in D. G. Pruitt and R. C. Snyder, eds., *Theory and Research on the Causes of War.* Englewood Cliffs, N.J.: Prentice-Hall.

Deutsch, Karl W. and J. D. Singer. 1964. "Multipolar power systems and international stability." *World Politics* 16: 390–406.

Deutsch, Morton. 1973. *The Resolution of Conflict.* New Haven: Yale University Press.

Dougherty, James E. and Robert Pfaltzgraff. 1981. *Contending Theories of International Relations,* 2nd ed. New York: Harper and Row.

Dryzek, John S. 1986. "The progress of political science." *Journal of Politics* 48: 301–320.

Duvall, Raymond. 1976. "An appraisal of the methodological and statistical procedures of the Correlates of War project," pp. 67–98 in F. W. Hoole and D. A. Zinnes, eds., *Quantitative International Politics: An Appraisal.* New York: Praeger.

East, Maurice A. 1972. "Status discrepancy and violence in the international system:

an empirical analysis," pp. 299–319 in J. N. Rosenau, V. Davis and M. A. East, eds., *The Analysis of International Politics*. New York: Free Press.

————. 1973. "Size and foreign policy behavior." *World Politics* 25: 556–576.

Eckhardt, William and Edward Azar. 1978a. "Major world conflicts and interventions." *International Interactions* 5: 75–110.

————. 1978b. "Major world cooperation events, 1945–1975." *International Interactions* 5: 203–239.

Eckstein, Harry. 1975. "Case study and theory in political science," pp. 79–137 in F. I. Greenstein and N. W. Polsby eds., *Handbook of Political Science*, vol. 7, *Strategies of Inquiry*. Reading, Mass.: Addison-Wesley.

Falk, Richard A. 1975. *A Study of Future Worlds*. New York: Free Press.

Falkowski, Lawrence S., ed. 1979. *Psychological Models in International Politics*. Boulder, Colo.: Westview Press.

Feraru, Anne T. 1974. *International Conflict*. Consortium for International Studies Education of the International Studies Association, Learning Package No. 5.

Forward, Nigel. 1971. *The Field of Nations*. Boston: Little, Brown.

Fox, Robin. 1971. "The cultural animal," pp. 275–296 in J.F. Eisenberg and W.S. Dillon, eds., *Man and Beast: Comparative Social Behavior*. Washington, D.C.: Smithsonian Institution Press.

Galtung, Johan. 1964. "A structural theory of aggression." *Journal of Peace Research* 1: 95–119.

————. 1968. "A structural theory of integration." *Journal of Peace Research* 5: 375–395.

————. 1969. "Violence, peace, and peace research." *Journal of Peace Research* 6: 167–192.

————. 1971. "A structural theory of imperialism." *Journal of Peace Research* 8: 81–117.

Garnham, David. 1976. "Power parity and lethal international violence, 1969–1973." *Journal of Conflict Resolution* 20: 379–394.

George, Alexander L. 1979. "Case studies and theory development: the method of structured, focused comparison," pp. 43–68 in Paul G. Lauren, ed., *Diplomacy*. New York: Free Press.

Gillespie, Judith A. 1982. "Introduction: some basic puzzles in political inquiry," pp. 11–34 in J. A. Gillespie and D. A. Zinnes, eds., *Missing Elements in Political Inquiry*. Beverly Hills: Sage.

Gilpin, Robert. 1981. *War and Change in World Politics*. Cambridge, Eng.: Cambridge University Press.

Gladstone, Arthur L. 1959. "The concept of the enemy." *Journal of Conflict Resolution* 3: 132–137.

Gleditsch, Nils P. 1969. "The international airline network: a test of the Zipf and Stouffer hypotheses." *Peace Research Society, Papers* 11: 123–153.

Gochman, Charles. 1976. "Studies of international violence: five easy pieces?" *Journal of Conflict Resolution* 20: 539–560.

Goldstein, Joshua S. 1985. "Kondratieff waves as war cycles." *International Studies Quarterly* 29: 411–444.

————. 1988. *Long Cycles: Prosperity and War in the Modern Age.* New Haven: Yale University Press.

Gray, C. H. et al. 1968. *A Bibliography of Peace Research, Indexed by Key Words.* Eugene, Oreg.: General Research Analysis Methods.

Greffenius, Steven. 1986. "Foreign policy substitution in the Arab-Israeli conflict." *International Interactions* 13: 1–21.

Guetzkow, Harold. 1950. "Long range research in international relations." *American Perspective* 4: 421–440.

————. 1976. "Sizing up a study in simulated international processes," pp. 91–104 in J. N. Rosenau, ed., *In Search of Global Patterns.* New York: Free Press.

Gurr, Ted R. 1972. *Politimetrics.* Englewood Cliffs, N.J.: Prentice-Hall.

————, ed. 1980. *Handbook of Political Conflict.* New York: Free Press.

Haas, Ernst B. 1983. "Regime decay: conflict management and international organizations, 1954–1981." *International Organization* 37: 189–256.

Haas, Ernst B., et al. 1972. *Conflict Management by International Organizations.* Morristown, N. J.: General Learning Press.

Haas, Michael. 1965. "Societal approaches to the study of war." *Journal of Peace Research* 2: 307–323.

————. 1972. "Sources of international conflict," pp. 252–277 in J. N. Rosenau, V. Davis, and M. A. East, eds., *The Analysis of International Conflict.* New York: Free Press.

————. 1974. *International Conflict.* Indianapolis: Bobbs-Merrill.

Harrison, Robert. 1973. *Warfare.* Minneapolis: Burgess Publishing.

Hart, Jeffrey. 1976. "Three approaches to the measurement of power in international relations." *International Organization* 30: 289–308.

Hempel, Carl G. 1966. *Philosophy of Natural Science.* Englewood Cliffs, N.J.: Prentice-Hall.

Heradstveit, Daniel and O. Narvesen. 1978. "Psychological constraints on decision making. A discussion of cognitive approaches: operational code and cognitive maps." *Cooperation and Conflict* 13: 77–92.

Hermann, Charles F., Charles W. Kegley, and James N. Rosenau, eds. 1987. *New Directions in the Study of Foreign Policy.* Boston: Allen and Unwin.

Hermann, Margaret G., ed. 1977. *A Psychological Examination of Political Leaders.* New York: Free Press.

Holsti, K. J. 1972. *International Politics: A Framework for Analysis.* Englewood Cliffs, N.J.: Prentice-Hall.

Holsti, Ole R. 1972. *Crisis, Escalation, War.* Montreal: McGill-Queen's University Press.

————. 1976a. "Foreign policy decision makers viewed psychologically: 'cognitive process' approaches," pp. 120–144 in J. N. Rosenau, ed., *In Search of Global Patterns.* New York: Free Press.

————. 1976b. "Foreign policy formation viewed cognitively," pp. 18–54 in R. Axelrod, ed., *Structure of Decision.* Princeton: Princeton University Press.

Holsti, Ole R., R. Brody and R. C. North. 1965. "Measuring affect and action in international reaction models: empirical materials from the 1962 Cuban crisis." *Peace Research Society, Papers* 2: 170–190.

Holsti, Ole R. and A. L. George. 1975. "The effects of stress on the performance of foreign policy makers," pp. 255–319 in C. P. Cotter, ed., *Political Science Annual*, vol. 6. Indianapolis: Bobbs-Merrill.

Hoole, Francis W. and D. A. Zinnes, eds. 1976. *Quantitative International Politics: An Appraisal*. New York: Praeger.

Hopmann, P. Terrence, D. A. Zinnes, and J. D. Singer, eds. 1981. *Cumulation in International Relations Research*. Denver: University of Denver Monograph Series in World Affairs.

Huth, Paul and B. Russett. 1984. "What makes deterrence work? cases from 1900 to 1980." *World Politics* 36: 496–526.

Intriligator, Michael D. 1982. "Research on conflict theory: analytic approaches and areas of application." *Journal of Conflict Resolution* 26: 307–327.

Janis, Irving L. 1982. *Groupthink*. Boston: Houghton-Mifflin.

Jervis, Robert. 1976. *Perception and Misperception in International Politics*. Princeton: Princeton University Press.

———. 1978. "Cooperation under the security dilemma." *World Politics* 30: 167–214.

Job, Brian L. 1976. "Membership in inter-nation alliances, 1815–1965: an exploration utilizing mathematical models," pp. 74–109 in D. A. Zinnes and J. V. Gillespie, eds., *Mathematical Models in International Relations*. New York: Praeger.

———. 1981. "Grins without cats: in pursuit of knowledge of international alliances," pp. 39–63 in P. T. Hopmann, D. A. Zinnes, and J. D. Singer, eds., *Cumulation in International Relations Research*. Denver: University of Denver Monograph Series in World Affairs.

Job, Brian L. and Charles W. Ostrom. 1976. "An appraisal of the research design and philosophy of science of the correlates of war project," pp. 43–66 in F. W. Hoole and D. A. Zinnes, eds., *Quantitative International Politics: An Appraisal*. New York: Praeger.

Kanigel, Robert. 1981. "The mentor chain." *F&M Today* 10: 1–8.

Kaplan, Abraham. 1964. *The Conduct of Inquiry*. San Francisco: Chandler.

Kaplan, Morton A. 1957. *System and Process in International Politics*. New York: Wiley.

———. 1969. "Variants on six models of the international system," pp. 291–303 in J. N. Rosenau, ed., *International Politics and Foreign Policy*, revised ed. New York: Free Press.

Kaufman, M., J. Urbain, and R. Thomas. 1985. "Towards a logical analysis of the immune response." *Journal of Theoretical Biology* 114: 527–561.

Kegley, Charles W., Gregory Raymond, Robert Rood, and Richard Skinner, eds. 1975. *International Events and the Comparative Analysis of Foreign Policy*. Columbia, S.C.: University of South Carolina Press.

Kende, Istvan. 1971. "Twenty-five years of local wars." *Journal of Peace Research* 8: 5–22.

———. 1978. "Wars of ten years (1967–1976)." *Journal of Peace Research* 15: 227–241.

Keohane, Robert O. 1984. *After Hegemony: Cooperation and Discord in the World Political Economy*. Princeton: Princeton University Press.

————. 1983. "Theory of world politics: structural realism and beyond," pp. 503–540 in Ada Finifter, ed., *Political Science: The State of the Discipline*. Washington, D.C.: American Political Science Association.

Krasner, Stephen, ed. 1983. *International Regimes*. Ithaca: Cornell University Press.

Kuhn, Thomas S. 1962. *The Structure of Scientific Revolutions*. Chicago: University of Chicago Press.

Kurth, James R. 1971. "A widening gyre: the logic of American weapons procurement." *Public Policy* 19: 373–404.

Lakatos, Imre 1970. "Falsification and the methodology of scientific research programmes," pp. 91–196 in I. Lakatos and A. Musgrave, eds., *Criticism and the Growth of Knowledge*. Cambridge, Eng.: Cambridge University Press.

————. 1978. *The Methodology of Scientific Research Programmes*, vol. 1. London: Cambridge University Press.

Lave, Charles A. and J. G. March, eds. 1975. *An Introduction to Models in the Social Sciences*. New York: Harper and Row.

Leng, Russell J. and Robert Goodsell. 1979. "Behaviorial indicators of war proneness in bilateral conflicts," pp. 208–239 in J. D. Singer, ed., *Explaining War*. Beverly Hills: Sage.

Levy, Jack S. 1983. *War in the Modern Great Power System*. Lexington: University Press of Kentucky.

————. 1985. "Theories of general war." *World Politics* 37: 344–374.

————. 1987. "Declining power and preventive motivation for war." *World Politics* 40: 82–107.

Lipson, Charles. 1984. "International cooperation in economic and security affairs." *World Politics* 37: 1–23.

Liska, George. 1962. *Nations in Alliance*. Baltimore: Johns Hopkins Press.

Luterbacher, Urs. 1984. "Last words about war? a review article." *Journal of Conflict Resolution* 28: 165–182.

Mack, Andrew. 1975. "Why big nations lose small wars: the politics of asymmetric conflict." *World Politics* 27: 175–200.

McClelland, Charles A. and G. D. Hoggard. 1969. "Conflict patterns in the interactions among nations," pp. 711–724 in J. N. Rosenau, ed., *International Politics and Foreign Policy*. New York: Free Press.

McGaw, Dickinson and George Watson. 1976. *Political and Social Inquiry*. New York: Wiley.

McGinnis, Michael. 1988. "Domestic political competition and the unitary rational actor assumption: models of security rivalries." Paper presented at the International Studies Association Annual Meeting, St. Louis.

McGowan, Patrick J. and Howard B. Shapiro. 1973. *The Comparative Study of Foreign Policy*. Beverly Hills: Sage.

Meehan, Eugene J. 1965. *The Theory and Method of Political Analysis*. Homewood, Ill.: Dorsey Press.

Mendlovitz, Saul H., ed. 1975. *On the Creation of a Just World Order*. New York: Free Press.

Midlarsky, Manus. 1974. "Power, uncertainty and the onset of international violence." *Journal of Conflict Resolution* 18: 395–431.

————. 1975. *On War*. New York: Free Press.

Milgram, Stanley. 1974. *Obedience to Authority*. New York: Harper and Row.

Modelski, George. 1972. "War and the great powers." *Peace Research Society, Papers* 18: 45–59.

————. 1978. "The long cycle of global politics and the nation-state." *Comparative Studies in Society and History* 20: 214–223.

Modelski, George and P. M. Morgan. 1985. "Understanding global war." *Journal of Conflict Resolution* 29: 391–417.

Morgan, Patrick M. 1983. *Deterrence, A Conceptual Analysis*. Beverly Hills: Sage.

Morgan, T. Clifton and J. S. Levy. 1986. "The structure of the international system and the relationship between the frequency and seriousness of war," pp. 75–98 in M. P. Karns, ed., *Persistent Patterns and Emergent Structures in a Waning Century*. New York: Praeger.

Morgenthau, Hans J. 1973. *Politics Among Nations*, 5th ed. New York: Knopf.

Most, Benjamin A. 1979. *Changing Authoritarian Political Systems: An Assessment of Their Impact on Argentine Public Policy, 1930–1970*. Ph.D. diss., Indiana University.

————. 1986. "Getting started on political research." Paper presented at the Midwest Political Science Association Annual Meeting, Chicago.

Most, Benjamin A., P. Schrodt, R. A. Siverson, and Harvey Starr. 1987. "Border and alliance effects in the diffusion of major power conflict, 1815–1965." Paper presented at the International Studies Association Annual Meeting, Washington, D.C.

Most, Benjamin A. and H. Starr. 1975. "The consequences of war for war: a design for the study of contagion/diffusion effects." Paper presented at the Annual Meeting of the Peace Science Society (International), Midwest Section, Chicago.

————. 1976. "Techniques for the detection of diffusion: geopolitical considerations in the spread of war." Paper presented at the Annual Meeting of the International Studies Association, Toronto.

————. 1977. "The spread of war: an empirical critique of the Poisson/modified Poisson approach to the study of diffusion. Center for International Policy Studies, Indiana University, Report No. F77-01.

————. 1980. "Diffusion, reinforcement, geo-politics and the spread of war." *American Political Science Review* 74 (December): 932–946.

————. 1981. "Theoretical and methodological issues in the study of diffusion and contagion: examples from the research on war." Paper presented at the Annual Meeting of the International Studies Association, Philadelphia.

————. 1983. "Conceptualizing 'war': consequences for theory and research." *Journal of Conflict Resolution* 27 (March): 137–159.

————. 1984. "International relations theory, foreign policy substitutability, and 'nice' laws." *World Politics* 36 (April): 383–406.

————. 1985. "Geopolitics and war: the study of the diffusion of international conflict." Paper presented at the Annual Meeting of the Association of American Geographers, Detroit.

Moul, W. B. 1973. "The level of analysis problem revisited." *Canadian Journal of Political Science* 6: 494–513.

Moyal, J. G. 1949. "Distribution of wars in time." *Journal of the Royal Statistical Society* 112: 446–458.

Nagel, Ernest. 1961. *The Structure of Science.* New York: Harcourt Brace and World.

Naroll, Raoul. 1969. "Deterrence in history," pp. 150–164 in D. G. Pruitt and R. C. Snyder, eds., *Theory and Research on the Causes of War.* Englewood Cliffs, N.J.: Prentice-Hall.

Nelson, Steven D. 1974. "Nature/nuture revisited I: a review of the biological bases of conflict." *Journal of Conflict Resolution* 18: 285–335.

Newcombe, Alan and James Wert. 1972. *An Inter-nation Tensionmeter for the Prediction of War.* Oakville, Ont.: Canadian Peace Research Institute Press.

Newcombe, Hannah and Alan Newcombe. 1969. *Peace Research Around the World.* Oakville, Ont.: Canadian Peace Research Institute Press.

North, Robert C. 1968. "Conflict," in the *International Encyclopedia of the Social Sciences,* vol. 3. New York: Crowell & Collier.

North, Robert C., R. A. Brody, and O. R. Holsti, 1964. "Some empirical data on the conflict spiral." *Peace Research Society, Papers* 9: 125–137.

North, Robert C. and N. Choucri. 1983. "Economic and political factors in international conflict and integration." *International Studies Quarterly* 27: 443–461.

North, Robert C. and M. Willard. 1983. "The convergence effect: challenge to parsimony." *International Organization* 37: 339–358.

O'Loughlin, John. 1984. "Geographic models of international conflicts," pp. 202–226 in P. J. Taylor and J. House, eds., *Political Geography: Recent Advances and Future Directions.* London: Croom Helm.

Olson, Mancur. 1982. *The Rise and Decline of Nations.* New Haven: Yale University Press.

Organski, A. F. K. 1958. *World Politics.* New York: Alfred A. Knopf.

Organski, A. F. K. and J. Kugler. 1981. *The War Ledger.* Chicago: University of Chicago Press.

Ostrom, Elinor, ed. 1982a. *Strategies of Political Inquiry.* Beverly Hills: Sage.

———. 1982b. "Beyond positivism: an introduction to this volume," pp. 11–28 in E. Ostrom, ed., *Strategies of Political Inquiry.* Beverly Hills: Sage.

Oye, Kenneth A., ed. 1986. *Cooperation under Anarchy.* Princeton: Princeton University Press.

Papadakis, Maria and H. Starr. 1987. "Opportunity, willingness and small states: the relationship between environment and foreign policy," pp. 409–432 in Charles F. Hermann, Charles W. Kegley, and James N. Rosenau, eds., *New Directions in the Study of Foreign Policy.* Boston: George Allen and Unwin.

Pearson, Frederick S. 1974. "Geographic proximity and foreign military intervention." *Journal of Conflict Resolution* 18: 432–460.

Peleg, Ilan. 1980. "Military production in Third World countries," pp. 209–230 in P. McGowan and C. W. Kegley, eds., *Threats, Weapons and Foreign Policy.* Beverly Hills: Sage.

Phillips, Warren R. 1974. "Where have all the theories gone?" *World Politics* 26: 155–188.

Pickus, R. and R. Woito. 1970. *To End War: An Introduction to the Ideas, Books, Organizations and Works.* Chicago: World Without War Publications.

Platt, John R. 1964. "Strong inference." *Science* 146: 347–353.

Popper, Karl R. 1962. *Conjectures and Refutations.* New York: Basic Books.

Prigogine, Ilya. 1980. *From Being to Becoming: Time and Complexity in the Physical Sciences.* San Francisco: W. H. Freeman.

Prigogine, Ilya and I. Stengers. 1984. *Order Out of Chaos: Man's New Dialogue with Nature.* New York: Bantam Books.

Pruitt, Dean G. and R. C. Snyder, eds. 1969. *Theory and Research on the Causes of War.* Englewood Cliffs, N.J.: Prentice-Hall.

Przeworski, Adam and Henry Teune. 1970. *The Logic of Comparative Social Inquiry.* New York: Wiley-Interscience.

Rapoport, Anatol. 1958. "Various meanings of theory." *American Political Science Review* 52: 972–988.

———. 1960. *Fights, Games and Debates.* Ann Arbor: University of Michigan Press.

Raymond, Gregory A. 1975. "Introduction: comparative analysis and nomological explanation," pp. 41–51 in C. W. Kegley, et al., eds., *International Events and the Comparative Analysis of Foreign Policy.* Columbia, S.C.: University of South Carolina Press.

Richardson, Lewis F. 1960a. *The Statistics of Deadly Quarrels.* Chicago: Quadrangle Books.

———. 1960b. *Arms and Insecurity.* Chicago: Quandrangle Books.

Riker, William. 1962. *The Theory of Political Coalitions.* New Haven: Yale University Press.

Rosecrance, Richard. 1963. *Action and Reaction in World Politics.* Boston: Little, Brown.

———. 1966. "Bipolarity, multipolarity, and the future." *Journal of Conflict Resolution* 10: 314–337.

Rosen, Steven. 1972. "War power and the willingness to suffer," pp. 167–184 in B. M. Russett, ed., *Peace, War, and Numbers.* Beverly Hills: Sage.

Rosenau, James N. 1966. "Pre-theories and theories of foreign policy," pp. 27–92 in R.B. Farrell, ed., *Approaches to Comparative and International Politics.* Evanston: Northwestern University Press.

———, ed. 1969. *International Politics and Foreign Policy.* New York: Free Press.

———, ed. 1976a. *In Search of Global Patterns.* New York: Free Press.

———. 1976b. "The restless quest," pp. 1–9 in J. N. Rosenau, ed., *In Search of Global Patterns.* New York: Free Press.

———. 1980a. "Thinking theory thoroughly," pp. 19–331 in J. N. Rosenau, *The Scientific Study of Foreign Policy,* rev. ed. London: Frances Pinter.

———. 1980b. "Puzzlement in foreign policy," pp. 321–39 in J. N. Rosenau, *The Scientific Study of Foreign Policy,* rev. ed. London: Frances Pinter.

Rosenau, James N. and Gary Hoggard. 1974. "Foreign policy behavior in dyadic relationships: testing a pre-theoretical extension," pp. 117–149 in J. N. Rosenau, ed. *Comparing Foreign Policies.* New York: John Wiley and Son.

Ruggie, John G. 1983. "Continuity and transformation in the world polity: toward a neorealist synthesis." *World Politics* 35: 261–285.

Rummel, R. J. 1979. *Understanding Conflict and War,* vol. 4, *War, Power, Peace.* Beverly Hills: Sage.

Russett, Bruce M. 1967. *International Regions and the International System.* Chicago: Rand McNally.

———. 1972. "A macroscopic view of international politics," pp. 109–124 in J. N. Rosenau, V. Davis, M. A. East, eds., *The Analysis of International Politics*. New York: Free Press.

———. 1983. "International interactions and processes: the internal vs. external debate revisited," pp. 541–568 in A. W. Finifter, ed., *Political Science: The State of the Discipline*. Washington, D.C.: American Political Science Association.

Russett, Bruce and Harvey Starr. 1985. *World Politics: The Menu for Choice*, 2nd ed. San Francisco: W. H. Freeman.

Sabrosky, A. N., ed. 1985. *Polarity and War: The Changing Structure of International Conflict*. Boulder, Colo.: Westview Press.

Schelling, Thomas C. 1960. *The Strategy of Conflict*. Cambridge, Mass.: Harvard University Press.

———. 1966. *Arms and Influence*. New Haven: Yale University Press.

Schrodt, Philip A. 1976. "Richardson's model as a Markov process," pp. 156–175 in D. A. Zinnes and J. V. Gillespie, eds., *Mathematical Models in International Relations*. New York: Praeger.

Schroeder, Paul W. 1977. "Quantitative studies in the balance of power: an historian's reaction." *Journal of Conflict Resolution* 21: 3–22.

Shapiro, Michael and G. M. Bonham. 1973. "Cognitive processes and foreign policy decision making." *International Studies Quarterly* 17: 147–174.

Sherif, Muzafer. 1966. *In Common Predicament: The Social Psychology of Intergroup Conflict and Cooperation*. Boston: Houghton-Mifflin.

Singer, J. David. 1963. "Inter-nation influence: a formal model." *American Political Science Review* 57: 420–430.

———. 1969. "The level-of-analysis problem in international relations," pp. 20–29 in J. N. Rosenau, ed., *International Relations and Foreign Policy*, rev. ed. New York: Free Press.

———. 1970. "From A Study of War to peace research: some criteria and strategies." *Journal of Conflict Resolution* 14: 527–542.

———. 1972. "The 'Correlates of War' project: interim report and rationale." *World Politics* 24: 243–270.

———. 1976. "Rejoinder to the critique," pp. 128–145 in F. W. Hoole and D. A. Zinnes, eds., *Quantitative International Politics: An Appraisal*. New York: Praeger.

———. 1980. "Accounting for international war: the state of the discipline." *Annual Review of Sociology* 6: 349–367.

———. 1981. "Accounting for international war: the state of the discipline." *Journal of Peace Research* 18: 1–18.

Singer, J. David and Melvin Small. 1968. "Alliance aggregation and the onset of war, 1815–1945," pp. 247–286 in J. D. Singer, ed., *Quantitative International Politics*. New York: Free Press.

———. 1972. *The Wages of War, 1816–1965*. New York: Wiley.

Siverson, Randolph M. 1976. "Some suggestions for improving cumulation," pp. 198–203 in J. N. Rosenau, ed., *In Search of Global Patterns*. New York: Free Press.

Siverson, Randolph M. and Joel King. 1979. "Alliances and the expansion of war," pp. 37–49 in J. D. Singer and M. D. Wallace, eds., *To Augur Well: Early Warning Indicators in World Politics*. Beverly Hills: Sage.

——— . 1980. "Attributes of national alliance membership and war participation, 1815-1965." *American Journal of Political Science* 24: 1-15.

Siverson, Randolph M. and Harvey Starr. 1988. "Alliance and border effects on the war behavior of states: refining the interaction opportunity model of diffusion. " Paper presented at the Third World Congress of the Peace Science Society (International), College Park, Maryland.

Siverson, Randolph M. and Michael P. Sullivan. 1982. "War, power and the international elephant." Paper presented at the International Studies Association Annual Meeting, Cincinnati.

——— . 1983. "The distribution of power and the onset of war." *Journal of Conflict Resolution* 27: 473-494.

Small, Melvin. 1976. "The applicability of quantitative international politics to diplomatic history." *Historian* 38: 281-304.

——— . 1977. "Doing diplomatic history by the numbers: a rejoinder." *Journal of Conflict Resolution* 21: 23-34.

Small, Melvin and J. D. Singer. 1976. "The war proneness of democratic regimes." *Jerusalem Journal of International Relations* 1: 49-69.

——— . 1982. *Resort to Arms: International and Civil Wars, 1816-1980*. Beverly Hills: Sage.

Smoker, Paul. 1964. "Fear in the arms race: a mathematical study." *Journal of Peace Research* 1: 55-64.

Snyder, Glenn H. 1984. "The security dilemma in alliance politics." *World Politics* 36: 461-495.

Snyder, Glenn H. and P. Diesing. 1977. *Conflict Among Nations*. Princeton: Princeton University Press.

Snyder, Richard C., H. W. Bruck and B. Sapin. 1962. *Foreign Policy Decision Making*. New York: Free Press.

Snidal, Duncan. 1985. "The game *theory* of international politics." *World Politics* 38 (October): 25-57.

Sorokin, Pitirim A. 1937. *Social and Cultural Dynamics*. Vol. 3: *Fluctuation of Social Relationships, War, and Revolution*. New York: American.

Sprague, John. 1982. "Is there a micro theory consistent with contextual analysis?" pp. 99-121 in E. Ostrom, ed., *Strategies of Political Inquiry*. Beverly Hills: Sage.

Sprout, Harold and M. Sprout. 1956. *Man-Milieu Relationship Hypotheses in the Context of International Politics*. Princeton: Center of International Studies, Princeton University.

——— . 1965. *The Ecological Perspective on Human Affairs*. Princeton: Princeton University Press.

——— . 1968. *An Ecological Paradigm for the Study of International Politics*. Princeton: Center of International Studies, Princeton University.

——— . 1969. "Environmental factors in the study of international politics," pp. 41-56 in J. N. Rosenau, ed., *International Politics and Foreign Policy*. New York: Free Press.

Spykman, Nicholas J. 1944. *The Geography of Peace*. New York: Harcourt, Brace.

Stagner, Ross. 1967. *Psychological Aspects of International Conflict*. Belmont, Calif.: Brooks-Cole.

Starr, Harvey. 1972. *War Coalitions*. Lexington, Mass.: D.C. Heath.

——— . 1974. "The quantitative international relations scholar as surfer: riding the fourth wave." *Journal of Conflict Resolution* 18 (June): 336-368.

——. 1975. Coalitions and Future War: A Dyadic Study of Cooperation and Conflict. Beverly Hills: Sage.

——. 1976. "An appraisal of the substantive findings of the Correlates of War project," pp. 99–127 in F. W. Hoole and D. A. Zinnes, eds., *Quantitative International Politics: An Appraisal*. New York: Praeger.

——. 1978. " 'Opportunity' and 'willingness' as ordering concepts in the study of war." *International Interactions* 4: 363–387.

——. 1984. *Henry Kissinger: Perceptions of International Politics*. Lexington: University Press of Kentucky.

——. 1988. "Rosenau, pre-theories and the evolution of the comparative study of foreign policy." *International Interactions*.

Starr, Harvey and B. A. Most. 1976. "The substance and study of borders in international relations research." *International Studies Quarterly* 20: 581–620.

——. 1978. "A return journey: Richardson, 'frontiers', and wars in the 1946–1965 era." *Journal of Conflict Resolution* 22: 441–467.

——. 1983. "Contagion and border effects on contemporary African conflict." *Comparative Political Studies* 16: 92–117.

——. 1985a. "Patterns of conflict: quantitative analysis and the comparative lessons of Third World wars," pp. 33–52 in R. E. Harkavy and S. G. Neuman, eds., *The Lessons of Recent Wars in the Third World*. Lexington, Mass.: Lexington Books.

——. 1985b. "The forms and processes of war diffusion: research update on contagion in African conflict." *Comparative Political Studies* 18: 206–227.

Stein, Arthur A. 1976. "Conflict and cohesion: a review of the literature." *Journal of Conflict Resolution* 20: 143–172.

Steinbruner, John. 1974. *The Cybernetic Theory of Decision*. Princeton: Princeton University Press.

Stohl, Michael. 1980. "The nexus of civil and international conflict," pp. 297–330 in T. R. Gurr, ed., *Handbook of Political Conflict*. New York: Free Press.

Sullivan, Michael P. 1976. *International Relations: Theories and Evidence*. Englewood Cliffs, N.J.: Prentice-Hall.

Sullivan, Michael P. and R. M. Siverson. 1981. "Theories of war: problems and prospects," pp. 9–37 in P. T. Hopmann, D. A. Zinnes, J. D. Singer, eds., *Cumulation in International Relations Research*. Denver: University of Denver Monograph Series in World Affairs.

Thompson, William R., ed. 1983. *Contending Approaches to World System Analysis*. Beverly Hills: Sage.

——. 1986. "Polarity, the long cycle, and global power war." *Journal of Conflict Resolution* 30: 587–615.

Tinbergen, Nikko. 1968. "On war and peace in animals and man." *Science* 160: 1411–1418.

Toulmin, Stephen. 1953. *The Philosophy of Science: An Introduction*. New York: Harper.

Voevodsky, John. 1969. "Quantitative behavior of warring nations." *Journal of Psychology* 72: 269–272.

Von Bertalanffy, Ludwig. 1968. *General Systems Theory*. New York: Braziller.

Wagner, Harrison. 1983. "The theory of games and the problem of international cooperation." *American Political Science Review* 70: 330–346.

Wallace, Michael D. 1973. *War and Rank Among Nations.* Lexington, Mass.: Lexington Books.

——. 1979. "Arms races and escalation: some new evidence," pp. 240–252 in J.D. Singer and Associates, eds., *Explaining War.* Beverly Hills: Sage.

Waltz, Kenneth N. 1954. *Man, the State and War.* New York: Columbia University Press.

——. 1964. "The stability of a bipolar world." *Daedalus* 93: 881–909.

——. 1969. "International structure, national force, and the balance of world power," pp. 304–314 in J. N. Rosenau, ed., *International Politics and Foreign Policy,* rev. ed. New York: Free Press.

——. 1979. *Theory of International Politics.* Boston: Addison-Wesley.

Ward, Michael. 1982. *Research Gaps in Alliance Dynamics.* Denver: University of Denver Monograph Series in World Affairs.

——. 1987. "Things fall apart: or, logical analysis of the transition from peace to war." Paper presented at the International Studies Association, Midwest Annual Meeting, Lawrence, Kansas.

——. 1988. "Things fall apart: a logical analysis of crisis resolution dynamics." Paper presented at the American Political Science Association Annual Meeting, Washington, D.C.

Wayman, Frank W. 1984. "Bipolarity and war: the role of capability concentration and alliance patterns among major powers, 1816–1965." *Journal of Peace Research* 21: 25–42.

Weede, Erich. 1976. "Overwhelming preponderance as a pacifying condition among contiguous Asian dyads, 1950–1969." *Journal of Conflict Resolution* 20: 395–411.

——. 1984. "Democracy and war involvement." *Journal of Conflict Resolution* 28: 649–664.

White, Ralph K. 1970. *Nobody Wanted War: Misperceptions in Vietnam and Other Wars.* New York: Doubleday.

Wilkenfeld, Jonathan. 1968. "Domestic and foreign conflict behavior of nations." *Journal of Peace Research* 5: 56–69.

——. 1972. "Models for the analysis of foreign conflict behavior of states," pp. 275–298 in B. M. Russett, ed., *Peace, War, and Numbers.* Beverly Hills: Sage.

——, ed. 1973. *Conflict Behavior and Linkage Politics.* New York: McKay.

Wilkinson, David. 1980. *Deadly Quarrels.* Berkeley: University of California Press.

Woito, Robert. 1982. *To End War: A New Approach to International Conflict.* New York: Pilgrim Press.

Wright, Quincy. 1942 (second ed. 1964). *A Study of War.* Chicago: University of Chicago Press.

——. 1965. "The escalation of international conflicts." *Journal of Conflict Resolution* 9: 434–449.

Zetterberg, Hans L. 1966. *On Theory and Verification in Sociology,* 3rd ed. New York: Bedminster Press.

Zinnes, Dina A. 1976a. "The problem of cumulation," pp. 161–166 in J. N. Rosenau, ed., *In Search of Global Patterns.* New York: Free Press.

——. 1976b. *Contemporary Research in International Relations.* New York: Free Press.

————. 1980. "Three puzzles in search of a researcher." *International Studies Quarterly* 24 (September): 315-342.

Zinnes, Dina A., Barbara Hill, David Jones, and Stephen Majeski. 1982. "Modeling precrisis interactions," pp. 117-140 in J. A. Gillespie and D. A. Zinnes, eds., *Missing Elements in Political Inquiry.* Beverly Hills: Sage.

Zinnes, Dina A., Harvey Starr, Barbara Hill, and Stephen Portnoy. 1985. "From war to war: stochastic models of wartime alignment patterns," pp. 393-418 in Michael D. Ward, ed., *Theories, Models, and Simulations in International Relations.* Boulder, Colo.: Westview Press.

Zipf, G. K. 1949. *Human Behavior and the Principle of Least Effort.* Cambridge, Mass.: Addison-Wesley.

INDEX

ad hoc hypothesis testing, 8
Aggarawal, L. K., 192, 213
Alcock, Norman Z., 25, 192, 213
Alexandroff, Alan, 72, 195, 213
Alker, Hayward, 7, 8, 213
alliances, 60, 107–108, 208
Allison, Graham T., 29, 213
Altfeld, Michael F., 60, 213
analysis cube, 19
Ashley, Richard, 7, 32, 213
attackers and attacked, 85–87
Axelrod, Julius, 211, 212
Axelrod, Robert, 40, 43, 194, 210–211, 213
axioms, in analysis, 112, 116, 183
Azar, Edward, 72, 73, 93–94, 195, 197, 213, 216

Babst, Dean, 194, 213
Bachrach, Peter, 193, 213
balance of power, 85, 86–87
Baldwin, David A., 194, 205, 213
Baratz, Morton S., 193, 213
Barringer, Richard E., 42, 91, 197, 213
Barry, Brian, 18
Beer, Francis A., 72, 138, 193, 213
Ben-Dak, Joseph, 195, 213
Bernoulli trial analyses, 155, 158, 159, 162–167, 209
Blainey, Geoffrey, 43, 73, 214
Bloomfield, Lincoln P., 42, 91, 197, 214
Bonham, G. M., 194, 214, 223
Boolean logic, 177

borders, and war, 74, 198
Boulding, Elise, 192, 214
Boulding, Kenneth E., 31, 73, 94, 96, 137, 197, 198, 214
Boyd, James M., 37, 214
Boynton, G. Robert, 7, 11, 18–19, 26, 191, 201, 214
Brodie, Bernard, 184–185, 211
Brody, Richard C., 43, 195, 217, 221
Bronowski, Jacob, 201, 214
Bruck, Burton, 193, 224
Bueno de Mesquita, Bruce, 2–3, 5, 10, 36, 56–57, 60, 65, 91, 118, 122, 175, 188, 191, 193, 196, 199, 202, 205, 213, 214
Bulkeley, R. I. P., 192, 214
Burgess, Phillip, 195, 214
Busch, Peter A., 194, 214

Campbell, Donald T., 52, 214
capacity-to-risk (C-to-R) ratio, 108–109, 114–115, 122–123, 124–132, 187–188
Caporaso, James, 171, 214
case selection, 48–59
case study approach, 12–13, 18, 175, 182
Chan, Steven, 194, 215
Choucri, Nazli, 32, 195, 215, 221
Cioffi-Revilla, Claudio, 9, 72, 76, 78, 154, 170, 215
Claude, Inis, 36, 205, 215
closure, on research questions, 180–181, 184

cognitive behaviorism, 28, 33–34, 108, 122
Coleman, James S., 101, 202–203, 215
Comparative Research on the Behavior of Nations (CREON), 48, 200
"conceptual modeling" approach, 177–178
Conflict and Peace Data Bank (COP-DAB), 48, 138, 197, 200
contextual analysis, 17–18, 33; and "nice laws," 18–19, 21; and domain specific laws, 98, 113–114, 117, 118, 172, 174, 202–203
control groups, 52
Copson, Raymond W., 55, 215
Corning, Peter A., 194, 215
Correlates of War Project, 32, 48, 55, 72, 138, 195, 196
Coser, Lewis A., 37, 73, 82, 199, 215
critical tests, 116, 180–181, 183–184
cumulation, 2, 3, 6–10, 171; additive, 1, 7–8; integrative, 2, 7–8; and theory, 118–119, 171–173, 179–181

Dedring, Jurgen, 25, 192, 215
Denton, Frank, 193, 194, 215
deterrence, 39, 44–45, 85, 86–87, 150
Deutsch, Karl W., 34, 37, 191, 205, 215
Deutsch, Morton, 35, 215
diachronic study, 18
Diesing, Paul, 39, 73, 94, 200, 224
diffusion of war, study of, 3–4, 16, 30–31, 37, 43, 44, 60, 65, 91, 139, 178, 186, 191, 206
Dimensionality of Nations Project (DON), 55
Dougherty, James E., 205, 215
Dryzek, John, 7, 192, 215
Duvall, Raymond, 72, 195, 215
dyads, of states, 139, 141–144, 151

East, Maurice A., 200, 215–216
Eckhardt, William, 72, 73, 93–94, 195, 216
Eckstein, Harry, 172–174, 175, 182, 216
ecological triad, 26–29, 122, 186
"empty cell" problem, 110, 201–202
environmental possibilism, 27–28, 30–31, 38

environmental probabilism, 27–28, 32, 34
event data analysis, 174–175, 191, 195, 211
expected utility, 34, 56–57, 122, 188, 193
explanation, meaning of, 172–173

Falk, Richard A., 37, 216
Falkowski, Lawrence, 194, 216
Feraru, Anne T., 73, 216
form of relationships, 59–66
Forward, Nigel, 200, 216
Fox, Robin, 194, 216

Galtung, Johan, 32, 43, 73, 95, 101, 194, 197, 198, 216
Garnham, David, 56, 205, 216
George, Alexander, 175, 194, 216, 217–218
Gillespie, Judith A., 11, 216
Gilpin, Robert, 37, 187–188, 194, 212, 216
Gladstone, Arthur L., 39, 216
Gleditsch, Nils P., 193, 216
Gochman, Charles, 73, 216
Goldstein, Joshua S., 194, 216, 217
Goodsell, Robert, 197, 219
grand theory, use of, 99, 107–108, 118, 170, 185, 189
Gray, C. H., 192, 217
Greffenius, Steven, 152, 217
Guetzkow, Harold, 8, 200, 217
Gurr, Ted Robert, 14, 15, 25, 193, 194, 217

Haas, Ernst, 37, 217
Haas, Michael, 25, 192, 194, 217
Harrison, Robert, 40, 217
Hart, Jeffrey, 194, 205, 217
Hempel, Carl G., 181, 200, 217
Heradstveit, Daniel, 194, 217
Hermann, Charles F., 59, 191, 211, 217
Hermann, Margaret, 194, 217
Hill, Barbara, 197, 227
Hoggard, Gary, 37, 200, 219
Holsti, K. J., 90, 217
Holsti, Ole R., 43, 194, 195, 217–218, 221

Hoole, Francis W., 191, 195, 218
Hopmann, P. Terrence, 6, 218
Huth, Paul, 39, 218

incentive structures, 29, 38, 43, 169
interaction opportunity, 30–31, 140
interdependent outcomes, 4, 21, 68,
    76–78, 90, 97–98, 122, 169, 173
international system, 36, 134, 145,
    152–153, 155, 156, 160–161, 187–188
intervention, 73, 83–84
Intriligator, Michael, 193, 194, 218
islands of theory, 99, 100–101, 117, 118

Janis, Irving, 39, 218
Jervis, Robert, 35, 40, 43, 194, 201, 218
Job, Brian, 108, 181, 200, 218
Jones, David L., 197, 227

Kanigel, Robert, 184–185, 211, 218
Kaplan, Abraham, 171, 218
Kaplan, Morton, 36, 99, 135, 151, 205,
    218
Kaufman, M., 176, 218
Kegley, Charles W., 59, 191, 195, 211,
    217, 218
Kende, Istvan, 48, 72, 83, 93, 199, 218
Keohane, Robert O., 40, 43, 201, 210–
    211, 213, 218, 219
King, Joel, 36, 60, 223, 224
Krasner, Stephen, 40, 219
Kugler, Jacek, 194, 221
Kuhn, Thomas, 9, 219
Kurth, James R., 202, 219

Lakatos, Imre, 7, 8, 9, 175, 176, 219
Lalman, David, 193, 214
Lave, Charles A., 9, 140, 178, 182, 183,
    192, 219
Lawton, Raymond W., 195, 214
Leiss, Amelia, 42, 197, 214
Leng, Russell, 197, 219
levels of analysis, 25–26, 119, 186–189,
    199
Levy, Jack, 34, 36, 37, 194, 212, 219,
    220
Lipscomb, William N., 185
Lipson, Charles, 40, 219

Liska, George, 36, 219
logical analysis: and C/R ratio, 187–
    188; and case selection, 48–59; and
    case studies, 12–13; and diffusion,
    191; and form of relationship, 59–
    66; and formal languages, 11; and
    inquiry, 5–6; and research design,
    47–67, 189; and research triad, 2–3;
    and study of war, 69–71, 169; and
    substitutability, 103–104; and system
    structure, 147–149, 154–155; and
    theory evaluation, 173–179, 179–181,
    183
logical trees, 180–181, 183–184, 185, 189
long cycles, 187–188, 194
Luterbacher, Urs, 193, 219

Mack, Andrew, 194, 219
macro-level of analysis, 133–161
Majeski, Stephen, 197, 227
March, James G., 9, 140, 178, 182, 183,
    192, 219
McClelland, Charles A., 37, 219
McGaw, Dickinson, 186, 195, 219
McGinnis, Michael, 212, 219
McGowan, Patrick J., 199, 219
Meehan, Eugene, 173, 219
Mendlovitz, Saul, 37, 219
"menu," 28, 32, 34, 134
micro-macro linkages, 133–161, 187–
    189
Midlarsky, Manus, 43, 73, 193, 198,
    199, 219, 220
Milgram, Stanley, 35, 220
Mill, John Stuart, 18
Mills, C. Wright, 39
Modelski, George, 36–37, 187–188,
    194, 212, 220
Moody, Terry, 212
Morgan, Patrick, 37, 39, 212, 220
Morgan, T. Clifton, 36, 220
Morgenthau, Hans J., 210, 220
Most, Benjamin A., 3–4, 7, 9, 18, 30,
    37, 43, 44, 45, 46, 60, 72, 138, 141,
    177, 182, 184, 186, 187, 190, 191, 192,
    193, 195, 197, 200, 206, 207, 211,
    220, 225
Moul, W. B., 199, 220
Moyal, J. G., 194, 220

Nagel, Ernest, 173, 221
Naroll, Raoul, 44, 221
Narvesen, O., 194, 217
necessity, 5, 47, 50, 52–55, 62–63, 66,
   147–148, 170, 182, 196, 197
Nelson, Steven D., 194, 221
Newcombe, Alan and Hanna, 25, 192,
   197, 221
Newman, David, 175, 193, 214
nice laws, 97–132, 170, 172, 181, 183;
   and alternative triggers, 110–117
nonwars, study of, 89
North, Robert C., 26, 32, 43, 73, 91,
   193, 194, 195, 198, 215, 217, 221

O'Loughlin, John, 193, 221
Olson, Mancur, 13, 175, 221
opportunity and willingness framework, 4, 17–20, 23–46; and explanation, 172–173; and international
   systemic analysis, 121–123, 146, 150,
   150–160; and levels of analysis, 186–
   189; opportunity, 29–33; as organizing concepts, 23–26, 35–40;
   relationships between, 40–45; and
   study of war, 69–71; willingness, 33–
   35
organizational process, 29
Organski, A. F. K., 150, 194, 221
Ostrom, Charles W., 181, 218
Ostrom, Elinor, 18, 191, 201, 221
Oye, Kenneth, 40, 221

Papadakis, Maria, 7, 8, 46, 59, 171,
   174, 221
Passmore, J. R., 192, 214
Pasternak, Gavril, 212
Pasteur, Louis, 184
Pearson, Frederic, 73, 94–95, 221
Peleg, Ilan, 200, 221
Pert, Candance, 212
Pfaltzgraff, Robert, 205, 215
Phillips, Warren R., 2, 193, 194, 215,
   221
Pickus, Robert, 192, 221
Platt, John, 184, 221
polarity, 142, 144, 147 150, 159–160,
   187

political reliability, 76, 78, 154, 170
Popper, Karl, 175, 180–181, 200, 222
Portnoy, Stephen, 227
power, 75, 134, 135–136, 151, 152, 153
power parity-preponderance analyses,
   135–138, 139, 142, 144, 147, 152
Prigogine, Ilya, 178, 222
prisoner's dilemma, 39–40, 194
probability linkages between variables,
   147–148, 173
problem shift, 7
problemation stage, research design,
   14, 16–17, 170
process, study of, 4–5, 8, 42, 122, 168–
   170, 172, 173–175, 179, 183
Pruitt, Dean G., 192, 222
Przeworski, Adam, 174, 175, 198, 222
puzzles, 8, 170, 171, 185, 192

Rabushka, Alvin, 175, 193, 214
Rapoport, Anatol, 173, 194, 203, 222
Raymond, Gregory, 14, 15, 195, 200,
   218, 222
realism, 108, 169
reductionist approach (micro-
   analytic), 97–100, 119–123, 160
research design, 10–17; and case selection, 48–59
research triad, 2, 9–10, 10–17, 168, 191
Richardson, Lewis F., 33, 42, 48, 56,
   72, 73, 92–93, 95, 137, 138, 186, 193,
   194, 197, 212, 222
Riker, William, 205, 222
Rood, Robert, 195, 218
Rosecrance, Richard, 36, 195, 205,
   213, 222
Rosen, Steven, 94, 222
Rosenau, James N., 6, 7, 8, 9, 26, 36,
   59, 170, 191, 192, 200, 211, 217, 222
Ruggie, John G., 204, 212, 222
rulefulness, and theory, 172, 173
Rummel, R. J., 42, 72, 91, 193, 197,
   222
Russett, Bruce M., 6, 24, 26, 28, 32,
   39, 140, 180, 194, 218, 222, 223

Sabrosky, Alan N., 36, 223
Sapin, Burton, 193, 224

Schelling, Thomas C., 39, 73, 223
Schrodt, Philip A., 200, 220, 223
Schroeder, Paul W., 72, 223
security dilemma, 40, 43, 108, 110, 115, 131, 187
Shapiro, Howard, 199, 219
Shapiro, Michael, 194, 223
Sherif, Muzafer, 37, 223
Simon, Herbert, 211
Singer, J. David, 6, 25, 32–33, 39, 57, 72, 73, 83, 89, 93, 95–96, 119, 138, 193, 194, 195, 196, 199, 200, 202, 203, 205, 215, 218, 223, 224
Siverson, Randolph M., 8, 30, 36, 60, 147, 193, 199, 205, 220, 223, 224, 225
Skinner, Richard, 195, 218
Small, Melvin, 57, 72, 83, 93, 95–96, 138, 194, 195, 205, 223, 224
Smoker, Paul, 45, 224
Snidal, Duncan, 20, 40, 192, 224
Snyder, Glenn H., 39, 40, 73, 94, 200, 224
Snyder, Richard C., 192, 193, 222, 224
Snyder, Solomon H., 212
Sorokin, Pitirim, 72, 224
Sprague, John, 33, 224
Sprout, Harold and Margaret, 6, 26–28, 31, 75, 108, 122, 130, 169, 186, 193, 201, 224
Spykman, Nicholas J., 36, 224
Stagner, Ross, 35, 224
Stanley, Julian, 52, 214
Starr, Harvey, 3–4, 6, 7, 8, 18, 24, 26, 28, 30, 37, 43, 44, 45, 46, 56, 59, 60, 72, 130, 138, 141, 171, 174, 177, 186, 187, 191, 192, 193, 194, 195, 197, 200, 206, 207, 211, 220, 221, 223, 224, 225, 227
Stein, Arthur A., 37, 40, 195, 213, 225
Steinbruner, John, 194, 225
Stengers, I., 178, 222
Stohl, Michael, 177, 225
stylized facts, 136, 147, 171, 178, 181–183, 185, 189, 211
substitution: of policy choices, 21, 97–132, 160–161, 169, 172, 181, 183; and alternative triggers, 110–117

sufficiency, 5, 47, 50–52, 62–63, 66, 147–148, 170, 182, 196, 197
Sullivan, Michael P., 147, 193, 199, 205, 224, 225
synchronic study, 18

technology, 31, 40, 44
Teune Henry, 174, 175, 198, 222
theory: and cumulation, 118–119, 172; deadends, dealing with, 180–181; definitions of, 173, 192; evaluation of, 174–176, 179–181; fine and coarse, 119; and logic, 11, 71
theory-research feedback process, 9
Thomas, R., 176, 218
Thompson, William R., 187–188, 212, 225
Tinbergen, Nikko, 194, 225
Toulmin, Stephen, 203, 225

Urbain, J., 176, 218

Voevodsky, John, 197, 225
Von Beralanffy, Ludwig, 202, 225

Wagner, Harrison, 40, 226
Wallace, Michael D., 55, 200, 226
Waltz, Kenneth N., 25–26, 29, 35–36, 38, 44, 120–123, 134, 135, 150, 151, 188, 189, 200, 204, 205, 212, 226
war: conceptualization of, 57–58, 68–91; definitions of, 71–73, 92–96; general war, 187–188; and level of analysis problem, 89; and national attributes, 75–84; study of, 3–5; validity of, as an indicator, 87–89
Ward, Michael, 108, 169, 176–177, 195, 211, 226
Watson, George, 186, 195, 219
Wayman, Frank W., 36, 226
Weede, Erich, 194, 205, 226
Wert, James, 197, 221
Westphalian self-help system, 136–137
White, Ralph K., 35, 39, 226
Wilkenfeld, Jonathan, 194, 226
Wilkinson, David, 37, 193, 226
Willard, Matthew, 26, 193, 221
Woito, Robert, 192, 221, 226

World Event Interaction Survey
(WEIS), 48, 200
Wright, Quincy, 25, 42, 48, 72, 73, 92,
95, 138, 226

Zetterberg, Hans L., 52, 226
Zinnes, Dina A., 1–2, 6, 7, 8, 65, 74,
90–91, 107, 180, 191, 192, 194, 195,
197, 198, 199, 201, 218, 226, 227